WASHINGTON AND LINCOLN PORTRAYED

LINCOLN CROWNED BY WASHINGTON

Made by D.W. Butterfield
in 1864

Oct. 19, 1931

WASHINGTON AND LINCOLN PORTRAYED

National Icons in Popular Prints

by

HAROLD HOLZER

McFarland & Company, Inc., Publishers
Jefferson, North Carolina, and London

Frontispiece: *Lincoln Crowned by Washington,* a 20th century copy of an 1865 print by D. W. Butterfield, reissued in October 1931 for the Washington bicentennial (photograph: The Lincoln Museum).

British Library Cataloguing-in-Publication data are available

Library of Congress Cataloguing-in-Publication Data

Holzer, Harold.
    Washington and Lincoln portrayed : national icons in popular
prints / by Harold Holzer.
        p.   cm.
    Includes bibliographical references and index.
    ISBN 0-89950-825-1 (lib. bdg. : 70# gloss alk. paper) ∞
    1. Washington, George, 1732–1799—Portraits.   2. Lincoln, Abraham,
1809–1865—Portraits.   3. Portrait prints, American.   4. Symbolism
in art—United States.   I. Title.
N7628.W3H36   1993
769'.423'0973—dc20   92-50937
                                                                                        CIP

Manufactured in the United States of America

McFarland & Company, Inc., Publishers
  Box 611, Jefferson, North Carolina 28640

For my parents,
Rose and Charles Holzer

Acknowledgments

I have been writing about Lincoln iconography for almost 20 years, both alone and together with coauthors, but never without incurring substantial debts to the friends, colleagues, and family who supply invaluable help and inspiration. This project has proven no exception.

First, I owe special thanks to two friends with whom I have engaged in much research, and, I hope, useful work on the subject of Lincoln prints: Mark E. Neely, Jr., now John Francis Bannon Professor of History and American Studies at St. Louis University, and Gabor S. Boritt, Fluhrer Professor of Civil War Studies and director of the Civil War Institute at Gettysburg College. Our years of collaboration and shared enthusiasm have meant much to me. Additionally, Dr. Neely read and provided crucial advice that vastly improved the manuscript; and the Lincoln Museum in Fort Wayne, which he directed for two decades, generously provided many illustrations for this book.

I am also greatly indebted to Judith Blakely of the Old Print Gallery in Georgetown, who made available countless photographs from her superbly informative catalogues; to Donald Cresswell of the Philadelphia Print Shop, who generously provided fine photographs as well; to Kenneth Newman of the Old Print Shop in New York City, for access to his extraordinary photographic archives; and to Bernard Reilly and his staff at the Prints and Photographs Division of the Library of Congress, for their enormous help in photograph research.

Some of the themes explored on these pages were introduced in earlier published work, and I must acknowledge not only the collaborative work with professors Neely and Boritt, but also the enthusiasm of the many editors who, over the years, have welcomed my contributions on Lincoln graphics. Since this work constitutes a natural outgrowth of some of these earlier efforts, I thank them as well. They include Wendell Garrett of the *Magazine Antiques;* Mary Ellen McElligott, former editor of the *Illinois Historical Journal;* Catherine Hutchins at the *Winterthur Portfolio;* Kyle Husfloen at the *Antique Trader Weekly;* and the late R. Gerald McMurtry, who published my first article on Lincoln iconography in the *Lincoln Herald* in 1973.

I must not forget Thomas F. Schwartz of the Illinois State Historical Library in Springfield, who invited me to deliver a talk on Lincoln and

Washington in 1992 which formed the basis of the fourth chapter of this volume; or George Painter, historian of the Lincoln Home National Site, also in Springfield, who hosted me at a 1989 Lincoln Home Symposium, where I delivered a paper on images of the Lincoln family, many points from which have been incorporated into this text.

At my home base in New York, I am especially grateful to Amy Varney-Kiet, whose magic fingers and overheated keyboard helped turn a mangle of manuscript pages into a coherent book; and to Janice Banks and Vincent Lipani, who made my office, if not its principal resident, function seamlessly.

Finally, I am not unmindful that my home provides an ambiance that not only holds the graphic arts in high esteem, but encourages their study. My wife Edith not only tolerated an invasion of papers and books for *four* manuscripts that were, in effect, being prepared almost simultaneously, she provided her usual expert guidance as well, including a patient and most useful reading of the text. My daughters Remy and Meg, meanwhile, offered their customary inspiration and good humor (and 13-year-old Meg contributed her sure knowledge of mythology, which happily spotted several errors). I am painfully aware of the fact that this is the last book I wrote while Remy, now off to Harvard, lived at home. A wonderful writer herself, she now heads toward a writing career of her own, leaving me with little doubt that like the characters in this volume, the new generation will not only equal the old but outdistance it as well.

Harold Holzer
Rye, New York
November 1992

Table of Contents

Acknowledgments   vii

I.   Introduction: Washington and Lincoln Imagined   1

II.   George Washington: "Patience on a Monument"   7

III.   Abraham Lincoln: "A Good Head to Go Before
the People"   79

IV.   Washington and Lincoln: "Columbia's Noblest Sons"   173

Notes   237

Index   247

Away back in my childhood, the earliest days of my being able to read, I got hold of a small book ... Weems' Life of Washington. *I remember all the accounts there given of the battle fields and struggles for the liberties of the country ... and you know ... these early impressions last longer than any others. I recollect thinking then, boy even though I was, that there must have been something more than common that these men struggled for ... something that held out a great promise to all the people of the world to all time to come.*

— President-elect Abraham Lincoln, in a
speech to the New Jersey State Senate, the
day before Washington's Birthday, 1861.

George Washington made the Republic. Abraham Lincoln will save it.

— Telegram to Lincoln from a Philadelphia
supporter, November 9, 1864, the day
after his re-election to the presidency.

GEMS OF ART.

WASHINGTON.

LINCOLN.

I
Introduction: Washington and Lincoln Imagined

At first glance, the brittle old picture of George Washington *(Fig. 2)* appears familiar but unremarkable: an austere, rather lifeless adaptation of the most standard and emblematic of the first president's portraits, the ubiquitous "Athenaeum" painting by Gilbert Stuart. Its familiarity is easy to explain. It is the Washington that stares back at millions of modern Americans every day from the face of the one-dollar bill.

Here is the serious but somehow benign father of his country. His head may be girdled anachronistically in a white powdered wig, his neck swathed in frilly lace, but his thin lips are pursed sternly (only now can we guess why: those ill-fitting false teeth!) and his eyes radiate the resolve that we imagine saw their owner through the Valley Forge winter.

It is, in sum, the Washington of our childhood memories: the figure gazing down from the classroom wall; the remote national symbol who stood somehow apart, and almost always alone. And had this particular 19th century chromolithograph been displayed in a conventional picture frame, as were so many hundreds of similar images for generations before and after, it well might have appeared so forever.

But this Washington image proved unique. Printed directly on the reverse, on the same thick paper, was a portrait of another man—a beardless Abraham Lincoln—in a rather romanticized adaptation *(Fig. 1)* of a brutally harsh photograph that was widely copied during his 1860 campaign for president. This is neither the Great Emancipator

Opposite: J[oseph] E. Baker after Gilbert Stuart (Washington) and photograph by Anthony Berger (Lincoln), *Gems of Art./ Washington. Lincoln.* Lithograph, *ca.* 1865, published by J. H. Bufford & Sons, Boston. The weapons that won two revolutions—Washington's sword and Lincoln's pen—accessorize overlapping portraits of the first and sixteenth presidents in this print tribute to the Emancipation Proclamation, its author, and its historical inspiration. Because the images were copied slavishly from well-known models, the portraits of Washington and Lincoln do not face each other, but other printmakers would take sufficient liberties to unite the two—symbolically and figuratively—in dozens of similar prints issued the same year (photograph by Don Pollard).

startling new face to the people. "Yours truly," it says simply, "A. Lincoln."

The presidential Washington on one side, the pre–White House Lincoln on the other — at the very least an iconographical anomaly, and at a certain level a genuine pictorial mystery, and an insoluble one, since the two-sided portrait lacks a single clue in caption or label to document its creation or explain its purpose. Conceivably, it is nothing more than a surviving printer's experiment, designed merely to test, with a minimum of waste by using but a single piece of paper, whether each lithographic stone would yield true copies of its individual subject. How else to explain imprinting images on the front as well as the back of the same sheet, forever dooming

This is neither the Great Emancipator nor the Martyr of Liberty, but the rugged-looking westerner who came out of the wilderness to preserve the house divided. Clean-shaven, flap-eared, and lantern-jawed, his face deeply creased, his leathery neck emerging grotesquely from an absurdly oversized collar, he seems to sniff the air with his great nose with a mixture of bemused curiosity and perfect confidence. And yet it is the face of a new man, an as yet unknown man, looking as if he is making his very first appearance in important company (or for that matter in the graphic arts). As if to punctuate that impression, at the bottom of the portrait is a facsimile autograph, suggesting that the picture was indeed designed specifically to introduce the

Fig. 1 (top). **Printmaker unknown after photograph by Roderick M. Cole,** Yours truly/ A. Lincoln **[facsimile signature]. Lithograph with tintstone,** ca. 1860. Fig. 2 (bottom). **Printmaker unknown after Gilbert Stuart,** [George Washington]. **Chromolithograph,** ca. 1860.

dooming one or the other portrait to be hidden against a wall or buried in the recesses of a picture frame? And how else to explain the fact that only one copy has ever been located?

But what is far more intriguing than the fact that this sheet was created at all is the fact that someone—some early, anonymous, prescient admirer unwilling to discard the picture—preserved it. Did he or she sense that the reputation of the frontier Republican would eventually approach that of the already deified *patriae pater?* Whatever the motivations, this unknown collector surely deserves the title of the first to preserve an image of Washington and Lincoln together, since this indeed may be the first such image ever created.

Five years later, America would be flooded with images of the two presidents, now united on single sides of these rude, gaudy, romanticized, and sometimes wildly imaginary graphics. Such portraits not only celebrated the nation's father and savior, but the durability of a government that in the Civil War had survived its worst crisis.

Innovative, resonant popular prints showing Washington and Lincoln sharing a unique pantheon of national glory would by 1865 firmly etch the notion of their almost mystical association onto the popular mind, reinforcing the power of each picture with suggestive titles: typically "founder and defender of the Union," "founder and preserver," or in the most spiritual, examples, "father and savior." Any doubt as to the message of joint deification was resolved by the titles. Their display was more than decorative; it was devotional.

For several generations, until the fashion waned for hanging portraits of political heroes at home, these images held honored places in family parlors, on display precisely where—and how—

earlier generations had displayed religious icons. In the words of one caption, the subjects were deified through these prints as "Columbia's Noblest Sons," household gods whose display testified not only to love for the great men themselves, but to national indomitability as well. Prints showing Washington alone retained astonishing popularity, and those of Lincoln alone remained cherished keepsakes as well. But images of the two together—showing Washington at first inspiring Lincoln, then ultimately sharing with him a rarefied pantheon of national glory—symbolized faith in democracy, respect for the past, and confidence in the future. Washington and Lincoln became nothing less than secular national saints.

But surprisingly, despite the recent appearance of a virtual shelf of literature on both Washington and Lincoln print portraiture, no study has yet focused comprehensively on the almost cultish reverence for images of the two in tandem. This is the first.[1]

The first Lincoln eulogists and postassassination biographers certainly took note of his connection with Washington, and historians have long quoted their canny observations. The early visual tributes, however, have been recalled separately, or not at all. Yet the same spirit that inspired the writers and churchmen also energized the printmakers, and fascinated the public that patronized their art. It is time to examine together the cultural forces that motivated many such tributes, and equally important, how the pictures were regarded and displayed at the time. The answers may finally help produce for prints a status beyond the minimal recognition generally afforded them today—as mere illustrations. In their own time, they meant far more, as this study will attempt to show.

Still, it remains difficult to explain why the Washington-Lincoln phenomenon in the graphic arts has been so persistently ignored. As early as 1886, an all-but-forgotten author named Francis F. Browne came closest to recognizing it — closer, certainly, than his contemporaries ever did, but not quite close enough to appreciate the graphics themselves for the influence they might be exerting on presidential reputations. That year, Browne published a collection of "pen pictures . . . by those who knew him" under the title *The Every-Day Life of Abraham Lincoln.*

To Browne, it was clear that America's first century had produced two incomparable native giants — and two only. "The list is not long of our veritable heroes," he wrote, "but at its head stands, without question, the Father of Our Country, who led the hope of our American colonies throughout the desperate struggle of Revolution; and next to him comes our martyred President, who held the helm of State during the more awful warfare of the Great Rebellion, who saved our glorious Republic from the ruin of a dissevered Union, and restored to a race of bondmen their God-given right of freedom."

Browne went on to draw parallels about lives which, to most of his fellow countrymen at the dawn of the Gilded Age, seemed wholly different yet inexorably connected:

Both men were patriots, sages, statesmen, and heroes. Both in their separate ways went through the hard school of adversity. Both were tried by the severest tests, and both came out victorious. The noblest virtues of humanity formed the basis of their characters: honesty, fidelity, courage, determination, fortitude, and sublime capacity for self-sacrifice. And both had, in remarkable degree, judgement, foresight, purity of purpose, lofty ambition, love of country, and consideration for the feelings of the rights of their fellow-men.

The dignity of Washington was balanced by the tenderness of Lincoln; the polished manners and courtly bearing of the high-born Virginian, by the stainless life, in private and public, of the homely and lowly pioneer of the West. From his childhood, Lincoln revered the memory of Washington, keeping his image ever before him as a pattern to be imitated in his own life and conduct.[2]

Of course for some twenty years, Americans had literally kept such images before *themselves* as well. Now, as if to acknowledge their impact, Browne illustrated his panegyric with a modest little engraving. Here were profile portraits of the two presidents made to stare directly at each other, as if to reduce the chasm of generations and events that separated them. The caption below the dual images neatly summarized the peerless reputation the two leaders now shared: "Washington and Lincoln — the two great figures of American history."

For years, popular prints — lovingly displayed on walls once dominated by religious icons — had been vividly making precisely the same point. More than any other medium, popular prints documented — and perhaps even inspired — the metamorphosis of Washington and Lincoln from products of our history to products of our imagination. They offered Americans a mirror in which was reflected the best of our leaders — the best of what the democracy could produce — and thus the best in ourselves as well. In good and bad times alike, these coveted pictures may well have come to illumine what Lincoln himself had said of America's future even as he confronted the dark clouds of disunion and war: "a great promise . . . to all time to come."[3]

II

George Washington: "Patience on a Monument"

The year was 1811. The American presidency had survived its first full generation. Now, James Madison was at the midway point of his first term as chief executive. His predecessors, Jefferson and Adams, were living in retirement, their bitter feud at last thawed by a correspondence between Monticello and Braintree that would thrive until their nearly simultaneous deaths on Independence Day 15 years later.

Meanwhile William Henry Harrison was about to defeat the Indians at Tippecanoe, earning a reputation as a military hero that would eventually propel him toward the White House, too. And on the Kentucky frontier, a two-year-old child of illiterate parents was growing up in hardscrabble obscurity in a dirt-floor, prairie log cabin. Years later, when he learned his letters, he would read about the life of the first of the presidents, George Washington, already dead for a dozen years, but still a vivid memory to untold thousands of living American who could recall seeing him in the flesh. The little boy's name was Abraham Lincoln.

The new nation was also spawning new industries. In New York State,

Robert Fulton had introduced steamboat travel only three years before. In Maryland, workers were just now beginning to cut down thick forest to clear a path for the Cumberland Road, the first important route to the west, and the still-distant Louisiana territories.

One of the oldest domestic industries — slavery — had been dealt a supposedly devasting blow just three years earlier, when slave importation was banned by law. Over the next two generations, some would later estimate, a quarter of a million new slaves would nevertheless be brought here illegally in defiance of that statute. And while the South continued to trade in slaves, the North began flexing its manufacturing muscle in a host of new and promising industries. In cities like Boston, New York, and Philadelphia, for example, publishing had emerged as a major trade. The new nation needed newspapers, almanacs, broadsides, books, and pamphlets. And it needed pictures.

The printmaking industry was struggling for a commercial foothold here — its products still competing against better-made foreign pictures, while battling lingering indifference

5

from a public only beginning to learn to celebrate its own institutions and heroes pictorially. In other words, printmaking was still in its infancy, its market penetration small and its impact minimal. Or so we have thought.

Yet in that very same year, 1811, a Russian diplomat, author, and artist named Pavel Petrovich Svinin began three years of travel in the country he aptly called the "Picturesque United States of America." And here he was astonished to find the nation all but "glutted with bust portraits of Washington." As he observed in a memoir of his trip:

> Every American considers it his sacred duty to have a likeness of Washington in his home, just as we have images of God's saints. Washington's portrait is the finest and sometimes the sole decoration of American homes.[1]

Not everyone was pleased to see Washington's face in every home or to hear Washington's name on every tongue. Cantankerous John Adams, for one, objected strenuously to the idolatry afforded his successor. Encomia like "'our Saviour,' 'our Redeemer,' 'our cloud by day and our pillar of fire by night,' 'our star in the east' . . . and 'our guide on earth, our advocate in heaven,'" he complained, properly belonged only to the Holy Trinity. His warning went unheeded.[2]

Future generations only confirmed the growing ubiquity—and apparent permanence—of the Washington image in America. Gustave de Beaumont, who accompanied Tocqueville to this country, advised travelers to America

in the 1830s: "Do not look . . . for monuments raised to the memory of illustrious men. I know that this people has its heroes; but nowhere have I seen their statues. To Washington alone are there busts, inscriptions, columns. This is because Washington in America *is not a man but a God.*" As the *American Magazine of Useful and Entertaining Knowledge* observed around the same time, "prints of Washington dark with smoke" had long been firmly "pasted over the hearths of . . . many American homes." Smoke-blackened or not, the image of George Washington, the magazine declared, "in some of its innumerable representations must have met every eye." They continued doing so for the better part of the century.[3]

For the next two generations, even as engravers and lithographers began winning more enthusiasm and patronage for a widening variety of graphic products, and despite rapid changes in decorative tastes, the Washington image—to paraphrase the famous tribute by "Light Horse" Harry Lee—remained first in war, first in peace, and first on the walls of his countrymen. And the results of the attention were transfiguring.

The American graphic arts, in their infancy when Washington ascended to undisputed prominence, first military, then political, were still a relatively new medium when the first president's death in 1799 elevated him to a national sainthood to which he had staked a firm claim in life. The image-makers' response helped Washington secure and tenaciously cling to

Opposite: **Original invitation to a *National Birth-Night Ball* at Jackson Hall in Washington, D.C. on February 22, 1848. The invitation is crowned by an Endicott portrait of Washington, and listed below among the list of managers for the event is Congressman A. Lincoln of Illinois. This is the first time the two men—one a dead president, the other a future president—were connected in a popular print (photograph: The Lincoln Museum).**

NATIONAL BIRTH-NIGHT BALL.

UNDER THE SPECIAL PATRONAGE OF

MRS. POLK, MRS. MADISON, MRS. ADAMS, MRS. HAMILTON.

G. Washington

The honor of *Mr. & Dr. Fowler* company is requested at Jackson Hall, in the evening of the 22d February, 1848.

Managers.

Hon. GEORGE M. DALLAS,

Hon. JAMES BUCHANAN,	Hon. ROBERT J. WALKER,	Hon. WILLIAM L. MARCY,
Hon. JOHN Y. MASON,	Hon. CAVE JOHNSON,	Hon. NATHAN CLIFFORD.

Hon. J. W. BRADBURY } Me.	Hon. A. P. BUTLER } S.C.	Hon. SAM HOUSTON } Texas	JAMES M. CARLISLE
" HIRAM BELCHER	" I. E. HOLMES	" D. S. KAUFMAN	JOHN POTTS
" C. J. ATHERTON } N. H.	" T. BUTLER KING } Ga.	" DAVID S. YULEE } Fla.	SAMUEL HUMES PORTER
" JAMES WILSON	" HOWELL COBB	" E. C. CABELL	WILLIAM MAY
" S. S. PHELPS } Vt.	" DIXON H. LEWIS } Ala.	" WM. THOMPSON } Iowa	CLEMENT MARCH
" L. B. PECK	" JOHN GAYLE	" SHEP. LEFFLER	J. KNOX WALKER
" DANIEL WEBSTER } Mass.	" JEFFERSON DAVIS } Miss.	" JOHN W. TWEEDY } Wis.	JOHN P. WOLF
" GEORGE ASHMUN	" P. W. TOMPKINS		P. BARTON KEY
" JOHN M. NILES } Conn.	" HENRY JOHNSON } La.		JOHN A. LINTON
" J. A. ROCKWELL	" ISAAC E. MORSE	Gen. G. GIBSON	
" A. C. GREEN } R. I.	" THOMAS CORWIN } Ohio	Gen. R. JONES } U.S.A.	**Board of Managers of**
" B. B. THURSTON	" J. D. CUMMINS	Col. J. G. TOTTEN	**the Monument Society.**
" J. A. DIX } N. Y.	" J. J. CRITTENDEN } Ky.	Maj. W. G. FREEMAN	WILLIAM BRENT
" F. A. TALLMADGE	" LINN BOYD		W. W. SEATON
" JACOB W. MILLER } N. J.	" H. L. TURNEY } Tenn.	Com. L. WARRINGTON } U.S.N.	Gen. A. HENDERSON
" JOSEPH E. EDSALL	" WASH. BARROW	Com. C. S. SKINNER	WALTER JONES
" SIMON CAMERON } Pa.	" E. A. HANNEGAN } Ind.	Com'dr. L. M. POWELL	Col. J. J. ABERT
" J. R. INGERSOLL	" R. W. THOMPSON	Lt. J. R. GOLDSBOROUGH	J. B. H. SMITH
" JOHN M. CLAYTON } Del.	" S. A. DOUGLASS } Ill.		GEO. WATTERSTON
" JOHN W. HOUSTON	" A. LINCOLN	JOSEPH GALES	THOMAS CARBERY
" JAMES A. PEARCE } Md.	" D. R. ATCHISON } Mo.	THOMAS RITCHIE	PETER FORCE
" ROBERT McLANE	" WILLARD P. HALL	BENJAMIN OGLE TAYLOR	WILLIAM A. BRADLEY
" R. M. T. HUNTER } Va.	" LEWIS CASS } Mich.	JOSEPH H. BRADLEY	P. R. FENDALL
" JOHN M. BOTTS	" R. McCLELLAN	JOHN W. MAURY	THOMAS MUNROE
" W. P. MANGUM } N. C.	" CHESTER ASHLEY } Ark.	W. W. CORCORAN	MATHEW F. MAURY
" A. W. VENABLE	" R. W. JOHNSON	McCLINTOCK YOUNG	WALTER LENOX.
		S. L. GOUVERNEUR	

undisputed preeminence, a mythic
figure whose image became a secular
icon that replaced those earlier idols,
both religious and royal, that had decorated American homes from the era of
the early colonists. There he became,
in the words of historian Barry
Schwartz, "a new republican effigy." He
was the great Rebel leader who somehow seemed almost monarchical; unquestionably authoritative, and yet
reassuringly benevolent; prudent in his
use of power, modest in his disdain for
its trappings. In short, a wholly
American king among men.[4]

So it is no surprise that even as
late as the dawn of the Civil War—
perhaps particularly as Washington's
union began to crumble—the poet Walt
Whitman would still observe of Washington: "His portrait hangs on every
wall, and he is almost canonized in the
affections of our people." No figure
before or since has ever won such universal acclaim, or widespread display.
His dominance remained unap-
proached, not to mention unchallenged,
until the martyrdom of Abraham Lincoln in 1865.[5]

The story of Washington's preeminence in American iconography is not
only a tribute to his spotless reputation
as both founding father and emblematic
character, but a tribute, too, to the extraordinary work of painters, engravers, and lithographers who overcame
the challenges posed by painfully
limited access to their illustrious
subject—whipsawed by growing public
demand for his portraits—to focus their
attention sharply and effectively on
Washington, and with remarkable success. The printmakers transformed the
revered but remote figure into something more intimate and adored than
he had ever seemed before. They made
him a household god.

Washington himself observed, with
surprising candor even for him: "The
miraculous care of Providence . . . pro-
tected me from beyond all human ex-
pectation." The image-makers at the
very least illustrated, perhaps influenced the forging of that all but impervious reputation. Historian Noble
E. Cunningham, Jr., has astutely reminded us that in his own lifetime
President Washington did come in for
his share of criticism ("thou'rt a man—
although, perhaps the first," went the
words to an anti–Federalist poem in the
National Gazette in 1793. "But man, at
best, is but a being frail;/ And since
with error human nature's curst,/ I
marvel not that thou should'st sometimes fail"). But for the most part,
Washington was not judged as other
men, and surely not portrayed as other
men, either. The father of his country
seemed as aware of this incomparable
status as his many admirers.[6]

If Washington would not accept
royal robes for himself, then the printmakers were prepared to create for him
the metaphorical equivalent in the
graphic arts. They portrayed him with
horses, alongside the ancient cluster of
rods known as a fasces, or before impressive pillars and columns (all
classical symbols of authority). They
draped him in togas and armor, however incongruous or laughable the
results. They showed him marching up
emblematic steps toward immortality,
and ascending into the billowing clouds
of heaven in death. They literally gave
him both pedestals on which to stand,
and historical pantheons to bestride.
The reputation created, or at least
affirmed and illustrated for Washington
in the popular arts—as well as in the
popular mind—elevated him high
above his fellow Americans even while
he lived (and was presumably subject

to the same sorts of criticism as ordinary men). In prints, Washington
knew no peers.

Surely this status owed as much to
something distinguishing and ennobling
in Washington personally as it did
merely to the individual chapters of his
evolving public biography. His image
in military prints, for example, bore little resemblance to the man whose true
Revolutionary War record boasted
more narrow escapes than great victories. Author Lillian Miller has noted
the early comparisons to Jason and
Ulysses, pointing out that a more apt
parallel might have been found in the
career of the Roman General Fabius,
who won his fame by eluding Hannibal
during the Punic Wars, ultimately defeating him, much the way Washington
bested the British, through evasion and
pluck.[7]

Of course, there were additional,
intriguing elements that meshed dis-
tinctively to make the Washington image particularly appealing, as well as
more august than scrupulous analysis
might have justified. Not least among
them was the General-President's legendary, and apparently genuine, reluctance to serve. He seemed a modern-
day Cincinnatus — the early Roman
hero who became dictator, defeated the
Aequians on Mount Algidus, and then
quickly renounced his office to return
to his farm. Like the hero of 458 B.C.,
Washington, too, was called forth from
the land to the battlefield to serve his
people in time of need. In Washington's case, it seemed unimportant that
this particular Cincinnatus' land was
tilled by slave labor. Such details did
not much matter, even to 19th century
antislavery men like Abraham Lincoln,
who admired Washington uncondition-
ally. As for power, command, much
like slavery, was to Washington "a

heavy burden," and in reluctantly ac-
cepting both, he counted himself fortunate to survive, reputation intact,
"the quicksands and mires which lay" in
his way. He was perpetually eager to
retire to Mount Vernon, and after the
war looked forward to the prospect of
there living out what he predicted
would be a short life, in peace among
trees "which my hands have planted."
His poignant lack of ambition only
endeared him to his public more — as
did his honesty, virtue, and poise — and
made his admirers clamor for him to
lead the government once it created the
office no one else but Washington
seemed suited to fill.[8]

In a sense, the image-makers were
able to make each triumph of Washington's life shine the brighter for the lack
of ambition that accompanied it. And
his Virginia roots and slaveholding
history notwithstanding, he remained
universal, not sectional. Finally, the
Washington image benefited enormously from the hero's early death.
Unlike nearly all his fellow founders,
he did not live to welcome the new century. Predictably, his death unleashed a
torrent of public demand for likenesses
of the much mourned national father.
He was now "in Glory," announced an
inscription on one typical mourning
likeness, leaving "The World in
Tears."[9]

Yet there was much more to the
Washington image than the sum of its
sober and unassailable parts; more
even to the face than the painfully taut
jaw and the rather frigid blue eyes captured by painters and copied by innumerable printmakers. Indeed there
had to be something more, because
no two life portraits of Washington
look quite alike. As indelible as the
Gilbert Stuart image seems to modern
Americans, Washington was in truth

portrayed not only in different contexts, but with wholly different physiognomies in the popular prints that began coming off the presses even before American independence was formally declared, much less won. It was not for several generations more that an observer joked that if Washington himself were to return from the dead and fail to resemble the emblematic Stuart portrait, he would undoubtedly be labeled an imposter. In his own time, and for a while thereafter, there was a Washington for every taste. And in an era in which graphics were precious and rare, not the commonplace, easily discarded pictures that bombard us every day of our modern lives, each image, no matter how like or unlike the original, probably found a special place in American homes—there to earn the singular honor of being aged and time-toned by smoke from the family hearth.[10]

It is useful to recall that while Washington lived—and for a generation after he died—the medium of lithography (the cheaper and easier to produce form of printmaking) did not yet even exist. Painter Bass Otis first produced a landscape lithograph in 1819. The Pendleton Brothers did not launch their lithographic enterprise in Boston until 1825; the Kelloggs did not begin in Hartford until 1833; and Nathaniel Currier did not open shop in New York City until 1834. It was left to engravers to produce the first portraits of the first legendary American, and they could do so only by laboriously carving their designs into delicate copper plates. Their painstaking work was made even more difficult by the lack of easily available models to copy.[11]

No printmaker had access to a photographic model of any American hero until at least 1840, when the daguerreotype process arrived from France. Before then, print artists were compelled to rely exclusively on the results of painters' life sittings (or rival engravers' original works, which could be copied with little fear of notice, much less prosecution). In one way or another, printmakers were all dependent on the results of the precious (but sufficiently frequent) occasions on which Washington posed for artists in the flesh. That printmakers managed to produce any images at all under such circumstances is remarkable. That they did so with such a wide variety of offerings is truly astonishing. It is no wonder that their products became so popular. By the Civil War era, it is worth remembering, the beloved man's beloved home, Mount Vernon, had been allowed to decay into a near ruin, in desperate need of a national subscription campaign to save it. Even as late as the centennial of the American Revolution, Washington devotees had yet to muster the necessary resolve or financing to complete the Washington Monument, still an unfinished stone stump lingering in suspension since the 1840s, and by the 80s, much more a national embarrassment than a national tribute. Yet even as *public* Washington contributions lagged, *private* Washington images continued to proliferate—as if there was a separate, more intimate ethic involved in honoring the first president in the family home.[12]

In his lifetime, Washington made the process somewhat easier by making himself available to a number of painters for life sittings. Even this he did with completely convincing reluctance. As early as 1785, he complained: "I am so hackneyed to the touches of the Painters [sic] pencil, that I am altogether at their beck, and sit like

Patience on a Monument whilst they are delineating the lines of my face." Printmakers would use the results of these sittings to attach Washington so firmly to the "monument" he had so patiently scaled that he would never thenceforward descend it.[13]

Patrons of the fine arts, too, saw in him a useful representation of genuine immortality. Typically, when the city of Charleston, South Carolina, commissioned John Trumbull (1756–1843) to paint Washington, city fathers wanted no ordinary portrait, but rather "the best in existence of Washington's military character, depicting him at the most sublime moment of its exertion." Trumbull's first work was rejected, perhaps only because it showed the general in New Jersey, rather than South Carolina. The artist nonetheless insisted that it reflected "the best, in my estimation, which exists, in his heroic military character." Predictably, it would later be engraved for a popular print, in which form it undoubtedly reached audiences even in the state whose leaders had rebuffed the original.[14]

A few years earlier, a similar project had been undertaken in Pennsylvania, launching the most intimate and fruitful relationship Washington ever enjoyed with an artist or printmaker. It began when Charles Wilson Peale (1741–1827) was commissioned to paint a Washington portrait for the state capitol. The Pennsylvanians clearly had more in mind for the result than mere decoration, and their expectations provide a valuable clue to the inspiration such images were expected to generate. It was anticipated that merely gazing at Peale's likeness would "excite others to tread in the same glorious and disinterested steps" as Washington, a path that invariably led to "public happiness

and private honor." Unfortunately, the display of Peale's portrait was not destined to be happy at all. In fact, it proved a disaster. For soon after it was placed an exhibit, a vandal disfigured it—to the horror of one journalist, who spoke for a shocked nation in a published tirade that reflected not only disdain for the criminal but reverence for the icon which he had violated:

> Last night, a fit time for the sons of Lucifer to perpetuate the deeds of darkness, one or more volunteers in the service of hell, broke into the State House in Philadelphia, and totally defaced the picture of his Excellency George Washington.... Every generous bosom must swell with indignation at such atrocious proceedings. It is a matter of grief and sorrowful reflections that any of the human race can be so abandoned.... A being who carries such malice in his breast must be miserable beyond conception. We need wish him no other punishment than his own feelings.[15]

Pennsylvania's shame—and artist Peale's likely chagrin—may have by then been assuaged by the increasing availability of individual images of the great man for secure display at home. No one would do more to make available such portraits than Peale himself.

The face and figure he ultimately captured for posterity were classically heroic. Nothing less could be expected. Few court painters had ever shown a great king in less than the grand manner, and few of the early painters of Washington or the engravers and lithographers who first copied their work would deviate from this Enlightenment tradition. If contemporary descriptions are to be believed, Washington was one great hero who looked to all the world the very part history expected him to play.

As early as 1785, a fellow army officer described him as "padded with well-developed muscles, indicating great strength." A "gracefully poised" head and a "benevolent though . . . commanding countenance" completed and striking picture. Concluded the admirer in a sentence that could as easily have been penned after the Revolution: "His demeanor at all times [is] composed and dignified. His movements and gestures are graceful, his walk majestic." Later observers merely validated this early description. To an eyewitness who saw him arrive to take over the Continental army, Washington seemed incomparably impressive. "The expression 'born to command' is peculiarly applicable to him," the observer gushed. "I could not but feel that he was reserved for some great destiny." And the artist Benjamin Rush gushed to a friend after seeing Washington: "Perhaps you will be pleased to hear, that he has so much martial dignity in his deportment, that you would distinguish him to be a General and a Soldier, from among ten thousand people: there is not a king in Europe but would look like a valet de chambre by his side." So he would be portrayed by the artists who placed Washington "at their beck," as well as the printmakers who were dependent on their monumentalized interpretations as models.[16]

It is difficult to know precisely which Washington image was the very first provided to satisfy public curiosity in the late 18th century. Paul Revere, among others, provided early cuts for primitive "almanacks," but the resulting daubs not only failed to illuminate Washington but bore little resemblance to any living person anywhere. They may have succeeded in piquing more interest than they satisfied. Some of the lingering curiosity—at least for those who could afford them—was satisfied by the first imported engrav-

ings for home display in the colonies.[17]

London's printmakers may have been geographically remote from the evolving independence struggle in America, and unsympathetic to it in the bargain, but English-made prints had long been visible in the homes of wealthy colonists. Apparently their publishers grew as reluctant to lose their American faithful as King George himself. Revolution or no, printmakers appeared perfectly willing to portray "traitors" like Washington as long as they could earn profits from the results exported across the ocean. Washington iconography pioneer Wendy Wick Reaves has described these earliest European print portraits as "completely fictitious," yet "immensely influential." More than likely, the fanciful pictures were also the first detailed print likenesses from any hand to be made available here for Washington's growing audience of admirers. A London engraver named C. Shepherd contributed one such wholly imaginary Washington *(Fig. 3)* as part of a series of prints produced in the mother country to sell to the upstart revolutionaries in the colonies. Washington was depicted respectfully, impressively uniformed and pointing meaningfully to a generic battle scene unfolding in the background. And although the print, attributed to a so-called life portrait by one "Alexander Campbell of Williamsburg," bore scant resemblance to the wartime Washington, it probably did not much matter. The image-starved public did not yet know what the general looked like, anyway. Hence Shepherd could safely employ what the Boston Library's longtime "keeper of prints," Sinclair Hitchings, aptly called "an all-purpose human face" to portray him. Not surprisingly, a portrait of Charles Lee for the same Shepherd print series of famous Americans would in form, feature, and gesture, look all but indistinguishable from that of Washington. These first prints, however inaccurate, were easily marketable. And they were timely. Shepherd's milestone Washington print portrait was available for sale here by September 1775 — ten months before Independence Day.[18]

It was left to Charles Wilson Peale to contribute the quintessential image of Washington as commander, his hand resting nobly on a cannon, a Revolutionary War battle raging in the background. The artist painted this Washington from life in the watershed year of 1779 *(Fig. 4)* — not the first time he had posed the great man, but certainly the most successful and important of his sittings. Commissioned by John Hancock on behalf of the Continental Congress, the result was promptly engraved for popular prints, going on to remain the principal model for Washington graphics for nearly a decade. Painter Peale was also a trained mezzotint engraver, having learned the craft in London in the 1760s. And in 1778, dissatisfied with the first adaptations by other printmakers, he determined to engrave his Washington painting himself. The laborious process would occupy some two years of his life, an indication of the primitive status of the infant industry, as well as the arduous labor required for the essential work of engraving on the plates.

It was in October 1778 that he recorded in his diary: "Began a drawing in order to make a medzo-tinto [sic] of Gen. Washington. Got a plate of Mr. Brookes and in pay I am to give him 20 of the prints in the first 100 struck off." Not until August 26, 1780, did the artist take an advertisement in the *Pennsylvania Packet* to announce at last the arrival of the first impressions *(Fig. 5)*, which now emerged on paper as a mirror-image of the original, a fault later generations of printmakers would overcome by learning to engrave in reverse so prints pulled from their plates would come out precisely like the originals after which they were modeled. There were other, more subtle differences to be found in the print as well. The sash adorning Washington's chest in the painting, for example, no longer part of the Continental Army uniform, was omitted. And the flag visible in the canvas was updated to reflect its latest configuration of stars and stripes. Prints, unlike paintings, could keep pace with such small but crucial changes. Declared Peale's notice in the *Packet:*

> The subscriber takes this method of informing the Public, that he has just finished a Mezzotinto PRINT, in poster size of his Excellency GENERAL WASHINGTON, from the original picture belonging to the state of Pennsylvania. Shopkeepers and persons going to the West Indies may be supplied at such a price as will afford a considerable profit to them, by applying at the South-west corner of Lombard and Third-streets, Philadelphia.
>
> N.B. As the first impressions of this sort of prints are the most valuable, those who are anxious to possess a likeness of our worthy General are desired to apply immediately.[19]

Peale offered the engravings of $2 each, "or Six Pounds per Dozen to Shop Keepers, or any persons going abroad," he announced in a subsequent newspaper notice. But there is some evidence to suggest that, at least initially, Peale's effort was not generously received by the public. For one thing, the painter did not again focus personally on the art of engraving until 1785; he contented himself with sending

Done from an Original, Drawn from the Life by Alex.ᵗ Campbell, of Williamsburgh in Virginia.   Joh: Martin Will excud. Aug.Vind.

GEORGE WASHINGTON, Esqr.

GENERAL and COMMANDER in CHIEF of the CONTINENTAL ARMY in AMERICA.

Published as the Act directs 9.ᵗ Sept 1775 by C. Shepherd London.

Fig. 3. John. Martin Will after "Alexander Campbell," *George Washington, Esqr./ GENERAL and COMMANDER in CHIEF of the CONTINENTAL ARMY in AMERICA.* Published by C. Shepherd, London, 1775 (Library of Congress).

Fig. 4. Charles Wilson Peale, *Washington at the Battle of Princeton*. Oil on canvas, 1779 (Library of Congress).

Cha.ʳ Willſon Peale Pinx.ʳ et fecil

His Excellency George Washington Esquire Commander in
Chief of the Fœderal Army.——
This Plate is humbly Inscribed to the Honorable the Congreſs of the United States of America
By their Obedient Servant Cha.ʳ Willſon Peale

his subsequent portraits off to England to be engraved overseas. Printmaking was something to practice, he confided, only when he had "no other business to do, for the sale is not such as to induce me to pursue it otherwise." Yet mea-

sured in terms of influence, Peale created a remarkably successful Washington image. His distinguished portrait of a majestic warrior — the trappings of war in the foreground, and the memory of his beloved Mount Vernon

His Ex.cy George Washington Esq.r

Captain General of all the American Forces

Fig. 6. John Norman, *His Excy. George Washington Esqr./ Captain General of all the American Forces.* Engraving, Boston, 1781 (Library of Congress).

Opposite: Fig. 5. Charles Wilson Peale, *George Washington Esquire, Commander in/ Chief of the Federal Army.* Mezzotint engraving, Philadelphia, 1780 (Library of Congress).

represented in the distance — seemed to suggest that here was a general who understood perfectly what he was fighting for. Peale had confided that "By this business of Prints I hope I shall get something in return for my great Expense of time in making my collection of Portraits." But it is possible that his great expense went unrewarded. What he got instead was the honor of influencing and inspiring his fellow printmakers for years.[20]

If Peale failed to profit from his inspirations, it was not for lack of trying. By late 1779 he had determined to "etch a Set of Heads of the Principal Characters who have distinguished themselves during this Contest." Then, in 1787, when Washington came out of retirement to preside at the Constitutional Convention "with the utmost reluctance" (and doubtless an eye on renewed audience demand), Peale petitioned Washington for another life sitting. "It gives me pain to make the request," he apologized, "but [for] the great desire I have to make a good mezzotinto print that your numerous friends may be gratified with a faithful likeness (several of whom I find is [sic] not satisfied with any portraits they have seen)." Washington consented again. For three successive July mornings, he posed for Peale, and by September, the artist published a jowly but ingratiating engraved adaptation that was quickly lauded in the Pennsylvania *Gazette* as "the best that has been executed in print." A notice in a rival Philadelphia newspaper agreed: "Mr. Peale has by his practice overcome difficulty in the execution of Mezzotinto Prints." The results would be sold at "two thirds of a dollar each, which is at or below the London prices."[21]

So often would Peale's prints be reissued, and so progressively poor did the copies of copies become, that when the Swiss poet and self-proclaimed "physiognomer" Johann Kaspar Lavater saw one example, he had trouble reconciling it with what he had heard of the American's majestic appearance. "If Washington is the author of the revolution," he wrote, ". . . it is positive that the designer must have lost some of the most striking features of the original." Ubiquity could obviously breed mediocrity. It would be up to the more ambitious artists to try for more originality.[22]

John Norman (*ca.* 1748–1817) of Boston was one such artist. As early as 1779, he engraved a Peale-inspired portrait for the *Philadelphia Almanack for 1780,* and now he contributed works as original and unusual as a full-length study (also based on a Peale model) of this Enlightenment hero clad in classical ancient armor. Yet Norman also contributed a hopelessly rudimentary standing Washington (*Fig. 6*) for the 1781 book, *An Impartial History of the War in America.* Left to his own devices, Norman could do little more than caricature Peale's subtler skills. In the absence of much competition, however, the history book was nonetheless particularly praised in its time for its "beautiful Copper Plates."[23]

The military Washington remained a favorite subject for popular engravings through the 1780s. Richard Brunton produced a crude adaptation of a painting by John Trumbull, and John Trenchard, John Norman, and Charles Wilson Peale himself all produced variations on Peale's likeness from life. And then, the American Cincinnatus was summoned back from the land to renewed public service — now in the highest civil office. Washington's second coming created yet another outpouring of interest, but now military

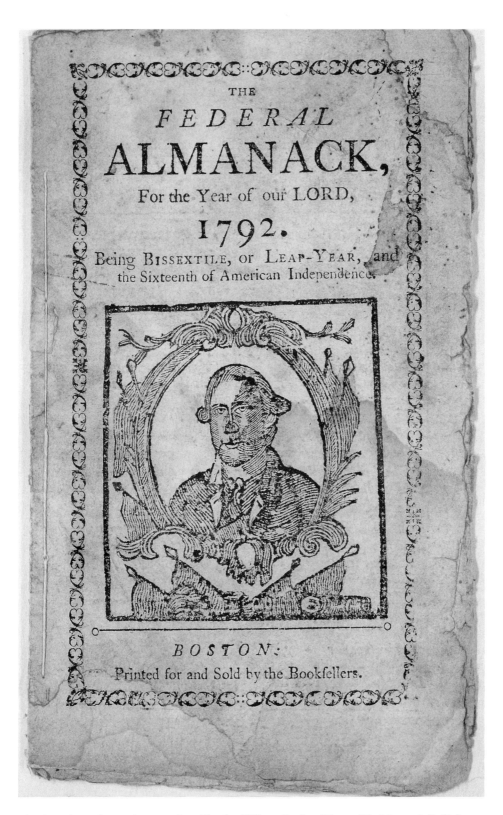

THE

FEDERAL

ALMANACK,

For the Year of our LORD,

1792.

Being BISSEXTILE, or LEAP-YEAR, and
the Sixteenth of American Independence.

BOSTON:

Printed for and Sold by the Bookfellers.

Fig. 7. Printmaker unknown after Charles Wilson Peale, *[George Washington].* Relief cut engraving, published for Bumstead, 1790 (Library of Congress).

Fig. 8. Edward Savage, *George Washington Esqr./ President of the United States of America/ From the Original Portrait Painted at the request of the Corporation of the University of Cambridge in Massachusetts.* Mezzotint engraving, London, 1793 (National Portrait Gallery).

portraits were quickly supplanted by civilian likenesses. Washington graphics remained commemorative, not political, and never approached the partisan. Washington was elected without opposition and in the absence of the kind of hulabaloo that would characterize future presidential contests and in turn inspire printmakers to supply pictures for parades and party headquarters. Alone among political leaders, George Washington began his career as a subject for graphics precisely as he ended it: an icon. Thus when *The Federal Almanack for 1792* commemorated "the Sixteenth [year] of American Independence" with a cover portrait *(Fig. 7)* of Washington, it did not even require a caption to identify its illustrious subject. Here was America's first, and thus far only president — barely recognizable in the primitive woodcut whose fancy scrollwork and flag motif did little to disguise its lack of artistic polish.

The following year, Edward Savage (1761–1817) contributed a presidential image *(Fig. 8)* that boasted as much resonance as Peale's military portrait of the decade before. Based on his own painting too, it portrayed a somber and dignified Washington clutching a plan for the new national capital that was destined to be named in his honor. On October 6, 1793, Savage sent copies of this and a companion mezzotint to the President, remarking:

> I have taken the liberty to send two prints. The one done from the portrait I first sketched in black velvet, labors under some disadvantages as the likeness never was quite finished. I hope it will meet with the approbation of yourself and Mrs. Washington as it is the first I ever published in that method of Engraving.

Washington by this time was building his own formidable collection of engravings. He particularly liked American scenery, but his walls were now boasting a number of his own portraits as well, Savage's included. Others admired it, too. It may have been the Washington portrait and other Savage engravings on display in a shop window in Philadelphia that inspired another artist, John Wesley Jarvis, to become a professional engraver.[24]

But Edward Savage's greatest — and most enduringly influential — work was yet to come: the invention and idealization of the image of the American first family. Savage had not only painted the President, but earlier had captured likenesses from the flesh of Martha and her two grandchildren. Now he devised the idea of an ingenious composite that would bring the entire family together.

The print *(Fig. 9)* took no liberties with Washington's own strong belief in the sustaining diversions of domestic life. Returning home to Mount Vernon after the war, he felt "eased of a load of public care." He hoped to spend the remainder of his days "in the practice of the domestic Virtues." His dream of quiet retirement was, of course, realized only briefly. By 1789 he had assumed the presidency, and when he returned to his beloved home for good, he had only two years left to live. This was the Washington that Savage determined to depict at home.[25]

Savage's subsequent triumph, however, was attributable not merely to the way he showcased Washington's beloved home, but the ingenious manner in which he confronted the ironic truth that the Father of His Country was himself childless. Since his wife had children from her previous marriage, it was clear to most Americans that the "fault" was evidently his, a fact of which, several biographers have suggested, he was painfully aware.

The WASHINGTON FAMILY. — La FAMILLE de WASHINGTON.

George Washington, his Lady, and her two Grandchildren by the name of Custis.

George Washington, Son Épouse et les deux petits Enfants du Nom de Custis.

But there is evidence, also, that Washington was a devoted stepfather to Martha's son, John Parke (Jackie) Custis, and her daughter, Martha Parke (Patsy) Custis. What was not generally known by the public was that Washington's stepson was both spoiled and woefully resistant to education; and that his stepdaughter died tragically of an epileptic seizure in 1773.

Jackie died young, too, in 1781, soon after belatedly entering the war as an aide to his stepfather. That same year, Jackie's wife bore a son, George Washington Parke Custis, and the baby and his older sister, Eleanor (Nellie) Custis were brought to Mount Vernon, where they became nothing less than replacement children in the Washington household. This is the way Savage presented them, too, in the group he depicted surrounding the family table in his painting and popular print. What was somehow—perhaps intentionally—sacrificed in the composition was any identifiable sense of time. Here was a postpresidential, 1798 engraving that not only presented Washington incongruously attired in his old Revolutionary War uniform (even if only to symbolize his military glory), but also alongside small grandchildren who were, in fact, much older than they were made to appear here. By the time Savage's engraving was offered for sale, Jackie was already 17 years old; but the print presents him as a child. All the characters thus seem frozen in a reality-defying time warp—all but immune to chronology, which was perhaps the only way to fashion a convincing portrayal of the ultimate public man as a believable private man.

Importantly, artist Savage did not attempt to domesticate Washington unrealistically in his painting, and that perhaps was its genius. Washington is shown dressed in full uniform; it is possible he is enjoying only a brief respite between public commitments. As it to emphasize this crucial point, his sword and a war map are seen on the sanctified family table before him. His wife Martha, living symbol of Washington's private side, seems almost to yield to her husband's extraordinary public obligations by holding a corner of the map open, going so far as to cross the line between the domestic and military spheres by pointing to a detail of the map with her fan. Typically for the day, the painter took nearly two years to produce a handsome stipple engraving of his canvas (although some contemporaries insisted that Savage had done very little of the work himself). The final print boasted captions in both English and French, suggesting that Washington's considerable reputation had by then found a willing audience for graphic testimonials on the European side of the ocean as well.

By February 1798—around the time of Washington's 66th birthday, an occasion its publishers may have used to market the picture—the engraving could be found on view for prospective subscribers at M'Elwee's Looking Glass Store in Philadelphia. There the new print was described to customers as "representing General Washington and his family, all whole lengths in one group." Then, barely a week after the finished print was first advertised in the Philadelphia

Opposite: Fig. 9. **[Edward] Savage and [David] Edwin,** *The Washington Family./ George Washington his Lady, and her two Grandchildren by the name of Custis.* **Stipple engraving, Philadelphia and London,** *ca.* **1798 (National Portrait Gallery, Smithsonian Institution).**

newspapers, George Washington himself was moved to order four copies for his own home. Writing to leading local citizen Clement Biddle on March 19, he declared: "In consequence of the opinion given by you of Mr. Savages [sic] Print (presuming it is his you allude to), I pray you to request him to chose [sic] four for me." Three he would keep; one was for Mrs. Washington to present as a gift. He asked only that the prints be placed in "handsome, but not costly, gilt frames with glasses." Here was an image that the usually self-effacing subject seemed particularly eager to possess—in quantity. Savage happily obliged his famous customer, and then wrote him to explain proudly the genesis of his undertaking, as well as the early evidence of its commercial success.

> I delivered four of the best impressions of your Family Print. They are choose [sic] out of the first that was printed. Perhaps you may think that they are two [sic] dark, but they will change lighter after hanging two or three months. The frames are good sound work.... The likenesses of the young people are not much like what they are at present. The Copper-plate was begun and half-finished from the likenesses which I painted in New York in the year 1789. I could not make the alterations in the copper to make it like the painting which I finished in Philadelphia in 1796. The portraits of yourself and Mrs. Washington were generally thought to be likenesses. As soon as I got one of the prints ready to be seen I advertised in two of the papers that a subscription would be open for about twenty days. Within that time there were 331 subscribers to the print and about 100 had subscribed previously, all of them the most respectable people in the city. In consequence of its success and being generally approved of I have continued the Subscription. There is every probability at present of its producing me at least $10,000 in one twelve month. As soon as I have one printed in

colours I shall take the liberty to send it to Mrs. Washington for her acceptance. I think she will like it better than a plain print.

Washington gratefully acknowledged receipt of the prints.[26]

The Savage engraving proved a critical triumph as well. The *Pennsylvania Gazette* called it "an elegant Engraving," complimenting its "capital likenesses" of George and Martha, and adding: "The whole is executed in a style evincive of the rapid progress of an elegant art, which has hitherto been in a very crude state in this country." Further proof of its impact could be detected in the number of copies it inspired—not to mention the later examples of the presidential family genre, which it all but introduced.[27]

One such effort, a 19th century lithograph by M. E. D. Brown of Philadelphia *(Fig. 10)*, not only testified to the enduring appeal of Savage's picture, but the severe limitations of the lithographic art, then barely 20 years old. The process unavoidably blurred the sharp details of the original stipple engraving, but perhaps intentionally changed the face of Washington, now basing it on the universally popular portrait by Gilbert Stuart *(see Fig. 13)*. And perhaps as a concession to an increasingly racist marketplace, Brown took the respectful portrait of the family servant, Billy Lee, and converted it into a near stereotype.[28]

The sustained popularity of Washington family images was apparent even after the Civil War had split, and then reunited, the Union Washington had founded. In 1866, another Philadelphia printmaker, William Sartain, offered his own *Washington and His Family,* describing it in an advertising brochure as a "great national engraving" based on an original painting by Christian Schussele.[29]

But the image the brochure went on to describe—featuring "the faithful house servant in the background," "a map" (now of the grounds of the U.S. Capitol) spread out on a table before the family—sounds suspiciously as if it was pirated from the old Savage & Edwin original—this time, unlike Brown's effort, without attribution in its caption credits. Inexplicably, painter Schussele maintained instead that his inspirations were the Gilbert Stuart Athenaeum portrait and Trumbull's full-length oil at New York's City Hall. "A mere glance will satisfy any one that its superiority over all similar works partakes of a striking contrast," the advertisement concluded. "It will ever stand among the highest productions of art worthy of a place in every American home, speaking volumes to every loyal heart."[30]

Newspapers seemed to agree, the Providence *Journal* calling it "a beautiful picture" whose "exquisite light and shade" would earn it "a Cherished place in many a patriotic home." Echoing these sentiments, the Rochester *Evening News* prophesied that the engraving would win "a broad place in the hearts of the American people." And a Maine paper declared "Sartain's group" nothing less than "the best ever executed by any artist." Yet the triumph clearly owed a huge, if unpaid debt to the pace-setting work of Edward Savage. Whether that artist ever secured more than the 400 subscribers he proudly boasted to Washington had signed up to receive copies in 1796, whether he indeed earned the $10,000 he hoped the print would yield him within a year, he certainly inspired enough imitators to secure his place as one of the great Washington image-makers.[31]

As Washington prints increased in popularity and ubiquity during his second term as president, the range of offerings appeared to broaden further. An engraver known only as Bols produced a small, delicate engraving *(Fig. 11)* in 1796, featuring an oval portrait that bore scant resemblance to the emerging consensus likeness of the perplexing subject, suggesting that audiences were familiar enough with the subject by then to crave variety. In London, Thomas Cheesman engraved John Trumbull's heroic canvas of *General Washington at Trenton,* the same likeness that had been rejected earlier by the city fathers of Charleston. Now it returned to favor as a popular print *(Fig. 12)*, inspiring the New York *Commercial Advertiser* to comment favorably on its "considerable merit." The Cheesman adaptation of Trumbull's painting represented yet another image watershed for Washington: the arrival of the historical graphic portrait. So long had Washington dominated the national landscape that audiences were apparently now prepared to accept retrospective representations of their president in scenes attesting to his reputation-building military glory. Cheesman's was one of the first such retrospective popular prints, but it would by no means be the last.[32]

It is not difficult to understand the burgeoning interest in pictorial evocations of Washington's early triumphs. And it is easy to comprehend why the genre grew in popularity on into the new century. What remains perplexing is that, despite the bounty of well-known paintings available by then to adapt for print portraits, and despite the resulting harvest of original 18th century prints that frankly invited further copying, much of Washington iconography became firmly fixed within

WASHINGTON FAMILY.

G. WASHINGTON.
1796

Fig. 11. **Bols,** *G. Washington./ 1796.* **Engraving, 1796.**

the controversial vision of one artist: Gilbert Stuart (1755–1828).

The great Washington biographer James Thomas Flexner, for one, hated Stuart's standard, so-called "Athenaeum" portrait *(Fig. 13)*. Because it so emphasized Washington's pained expression, he felt it produced an "effigy" to a "deformity"—Washington's cumbersome false teeth—instead of a true portrait. It did win almost universal acceptance during succeeding generations, so it is ironic to learn that Flexner also suggested that it might have been more a product of its artist's revenge than his perception. According to Flexner, Stuart

tried to relax his famous subject during their sittings: "Now, sir, you must let me forget that you are General Washington and I am Stuart the painter." To which Washington replied icily: "Mr. Stuart need never feel the need for forgetting who he is and who General Washington is." If the painter determined to punish Washington for his riposte, the result seems neither cruel nor unusual. Stuart's Washington even outlived the fashion for the popular prints it eventually dominated as a model.[33]

In fact, "Stuart the painter" seemed to understand his subject perfectly. He recalled of their first encounter:

> There were features in his face totally different from what I had observed in any other human being: the sockets of his eyes were larger than whatever I met with before, and the upper part of his nose broader. All his features were indicative of the strongest passions; yet like Socrates his judgement and self-command made him appear a man of different cast in the eyes of the world.[34]

Stuart's style proved ideally suited to the task of portraying Washington: he specialized in "authentic hints rather than exquisitely-wrought details," in the assessment of pioneer 19th century art historian Henry T. Tuckerman. Tuckerman added some insights of his own that served almost as an extended caption for Stuart's irresistibly pure likeness. To Tuckerman, Washington's

> appearance ... left an impression harmonious rather than original; like all that is truly grand in nature, in life, and in humanity, it was the balance of all and

Opposite: Fig. 10. **M. E. D. Brown after Edward Savage,** *Washington Family./ George Washington, his Lady & her two Grandchildren by the name of Custis. From an Engraving by E. Savage.* **Lithograph, published by William F. Geddes and I. S. Earle, Philadelphia, 1839 (Library of Congress).**

not the predominance of a few qualities that rendered him illustrious. In vain the observer sought to carry from his presence a single extraordinary feature whereby to identify the man; in vain the painter watched for effective attitudes, melodramatic situations, or a characteristic phase of dress, manner, or look; Washington was too complete, too accordant, too humanly representative, too evenly as well as largely gifted with the elements of our commoner nature, to serve a theatrical purpose . . . for the limner.

Tuckerman thought Stuart's "majestic, benignant, and serene" likeness nothing short of a "masterpiece." It came closest, he believed, to capturing Washington's "tranquility of self-approval," blended with "wisdom and truth, so as to form a moral ideal in portraiture. It is lamentable," he added, "that such inadequate copies of this head have gone abroad owing, in some instances, to the inability of engravers."[35]

Still, Washington remained, even within the republican simplicity that required no allegorical acoutrements, a figure of compelling strength and dignity, the very clenched expression captured by Stuart appearing to exude both determination and virtue. It is no wonder that some writers responded to the Stuart as if resenting the fact that an artist of the brush had seized the initiative for forging the Washington image from artists of the pen. William Makepeace Thackeray, the English novelist, reportedly joked when he first saw a print of the "Athenaeum" Washington: "Look at him. Does he not look as if he had just said a good, stupid thing?" And his American contemporary, Nathaniel Hawthorne, was moved to ask irreverently: "Did anybody ever see Washington nude? It is inconceivable. He had no nakedness, but I imagine he was born with his clothes on, and his hair powdered, and

made a stately bow on his first appearance in the world." If, in fact, Stuart's interpretation seemed cold and pompous, it is no wonder that one historian condemned it as a "bloodless icon." But it is equally unsurprising that it remained a dominant icon, for it was universal without being ordinary, and formal without being forbidding. And to some, like Ralph Waldo Emerson, it had "Appalachian strength, as if it were truly the first-fruits of America and expressed the country." By 1932, the year of Washington's 200th birthday, the picture had attained such legendary status that J. L. G. Ferris created an illustration called *Painter and President,* showing Washington contentedly posing for Stuart. And that picture, too, became a popular print in the only variation of the old genre still popular: the wall calendar.[36]

In the end, no other portrait ever won the universal acceptance of Stuart's attempt—whether in a conscious rage or a discriminating inspiration—to tone down the baroque Washington image that had dominated art and commerce until then; to strip away the uniform, epaulets, and sword; to exclude battle detritus and the symbolic acoutrements of statecraft. Here was a Washington of the people and for the people, less grand than before, but perhaps slightly more accessible as a result. In short, here was the ideal model for popular prints. It would be instantly embraced as such, and it would know no iconographic competition from that point forth. As the New York *Commercial Advertiser* commented on one early adaptation in 1800: "Much as we have heard of Gen. Washington, there has not until very lately, been any Portrait of him that deserved much notice . . . but the leading portrait is one copied from Stuart . . . which in point of

Fig. 12. Thomas Cheesman after John Trumbull, *George Washington*. Stipple engraving, London, 1796 (National Portrait Gallery, Smithsonian Institution).

resemblance, is said by those who have seen the General, to be uncommonly faithful." It comes as no surprise that the "bust portraits" whose ubiquity Russian traveler Pavel Svinin attested to in his memoirs had all been adapted "from the brush of this master."[37]

One of the earliest and most resonant of its subsequent print adaptations—although it was not immediately or easily identifiable as such—perhaps more firmly than any other Washington print planted its subject upon the figurative pedestal he was by then so firmly occupying in the culture as a whole. In fact, this particular pedestal had a deep and literal historical importance of its own.

In 1776, as the French engraving, *La Destruction de la Statue Royale à Nouvelle New York,* had stylishly recorded, a statue of George III on Bowling Green in New York had been hauled down by an angry band of colonists. Not until 1792 did another statue supposedly rise on the very same pedestal (although historians disagree over whether this wooden statue actually took the place of the King's). Those who claimed it did, contended it was an image of George Washington.[38]

The alleged arrival of the new Washington statue—or maybe just the hope that it should soon be commissioned—inspired gifted amateur artist Dr. Charles Buxton to craft a symbol-laden view designed to make the point that Washington was nothing less now than "sacred to patriotism," a sentiment voiced in caption on the image.

Engraved by Cornelius Tiebout in 1798 *(Fig. 14)*, two proof copies were sent by Dr. Buxton to the former president on April 27, 1799, eight months before Washington's death. It may have been the last print portrait of himself he saw. It was one of his favorites.

The artist explained that the adaptation had not been "originally intended," noting in a letter to Washington that "the flattering encomiums of a Bookseller, after repeated application, obtained the temporary use of the Drawing for that purpose, and by whom I was presented a small number of the first Impressions; Your acceptance of those forwarded will prove an ample gratification To, Sir, One who feels all the gratitude which ought to warm the hearts of every American, & ardently inspire him with the most lively wishes for the continuation of your life & happiness."[39]

A month later, Washington wrote back to Buxton to acknowledge receipt in the "last Post" of "two proof Prints elegantly executed ... engraved from your emblematic Picture, designed to perpetuate the idea of the American Revolution." Admitted Washington appreciatively of the image which remains to this day in Mount Vernon:

> Were not the late President of the United States a conspicuous character in the Piece I might say more than would now become me of the fruitfulness of the design.[40]

It may have struck Washington that for all its carefully arranged symbolic touches—obelisks labeled "Independence" and "Liberty," pillars of state, background scenes of the evacuation of the British, and in the near distance, the empty pedestal where the George III statue previously stood—it was Washington's face, modeled after Stuart's "Athenaeum" portrait, that seemed particularly suited to the majestic vista it now dominated. The stacked arms and overflowing cornucopia at Washington's feet in the foreground only reinforced the fatherly image and its potent message: Wash-

Fig. 13. Gilbert Stuart, *George Washington* [Athenaeum Portrait]. Oil on canvas, 1796 (National Portrait Gallery, Smithsonian Institution).

ington had secured for his people the blessings of liberty.

Even earlier, as a second — and final — retirement neared invitingly, President Washington perhaps found solace in the fact that his portraits had taken intractable hold in American domestic culture. Artists remained inspired by him as by no other subject. (Peale recalled in 1798 that he doggedly

Fig. 14. **Cornelius Tiebout after Charles Buxton and Gilbert Stuart, *Geo. Wa[sh]ington/ Sacred to Patriotism*. Engraving with etching published by C. Smith, New York, 1798 (National Museum of American History, Smithsonian Institution).**

"sharpened my tools and worked on the plate of Genl. Washington to make it stronger.") And even after he left office, printmakers paid him the ultimate commercial tribute: selling portraits of his far less revered successor, Adams, as a pair with portraits of Washington (if not merely to honor the first president, then to trigger sales of the second). In 1798 the *Federal Gazette* would advertise "striking likenesses" of both presidents, "elegantly framed in the best burnish gold frames with enamel glasses." The prints could only be had as a pair: $6 for both, $8 for prints on satin instead of paper. In all these formats, Washington reigned supreme as the nation's household God, moving one native poet known only as "Mr. L" to observe with perhaps unwitting double meaning

Far be the din of arms,
Henceforth the olive's charm
  Shall war preclude;
These shores a HEAD shall own,
Unsully'd by a throne
Our much lov'd WASHINGTON,
  The great, the good.[41]

It is thus easy to understand that George Washington's death at age 67 in December 1799 — only a few months after receiving and lauding the Tiebout engraving of his statue at Bowling Green — inspired the most intense and universal period of national mourning before or since. Tributes and accolades poured from the mouths of great orators. Citizens lined up in long processions to pay silent tribute to the dead hero. It did not escape notice, as historian Barry Schwartz has pointed out, that Washington had died near the birthday of an earlier saviour, Jesus, and only days from the start of a new century. Now a newspaper understandably felt justified in reporting the sad event in a worshipful dirge. No mere announcement would do:

Oh Washington! Though Hero, Patriot,
  Sage
Friend of all climates, pride of every age,
Were thine the laurels which the world
  could raise,
The mighty harvest were penurious
  praise.[42]

In an impressive display of sensitivity to the marketplace, America's

printmakers likewise responded to Washington's sudden passing, quickly, inventively, and reverentially. In print-after print, as one caption declared, the "genius of liberty" was made to weep symbolically "over the urn of her Hero." In much the same way, print makers now literally depicted ordinary Americans in lamentation graphics: mourning beneath metaphorical weeping willows before the symbolic urn itself *(Fig. 15)*.

These pictures were designed to be timely — and in some cases timeless. In the former category, Philadelphia publisher Benjamin Carr managed to produce sheet music for a funeral dirge entitled *Dead March and Monody* in time for a memorial tribute in that city's Lutheran Church on December 26, 1799, only days after Washington's death. Like so many of his contemporaries, Carr modeled his small decorative cameo likeness of Washington on the "Athenaeum" portrait by Stuart. But Carr's illustration was something of an innovation, too: he was one of the first publishers to include portraiture for sheet music, a device that became common by the mid–19th century.[43]

Now firmly enshrined in the historical afterworld, Washington also emerged in an engraving by David Edwin *(Fig. 16)*, possibly based on a Rembrandt Peale (1778–1860) transparency, which in turn owed an obvious debt to the Benjamin West painting (and its 1786 engraved adaptation), *Apotheosis of Princes Octavius and Alfred.* It showed Washington rising to heaven above the clouds encircling Mount Vernon, there to be crowned with a hero's laurel as he is reunited with two martyrs of the Revolution, generals Joseph Warren and Richard Montgomery. In late 1800, the New York *Mercantile Advertiser* carried a notice announcing

IN MEMORY OF GENL. GEORGE WASHINGTON AND HIS LADY.

FROM THE ORIGINAL PICTURE PAINTED BY TRUMBULL, 1804, IN POSSESSION OF THE WASHINGTON FAMILY.

Published by S. Kennedy, N? 179. Chesnut Street, corner of 4.th Philadelphia

Printed by R. Peale

Engrav'd by E.

APOTHEOSIS of WASHINGTON

Fig. 16. David Edwin after Rembrandt Peale, *Apotheosis of Washington.* Stipple engraving, published by S. Kennedy, Philadelphia, 1800 (National Portrait Gallery, Smithsonian Institution.)

Opposite: Fig. 15. [John H.] Bingham & [William Henry] Dodd, *In Memory of Genl. George Washington and his Lady./ From the original picture painted by Trumbull in 1804, in possession of the Washington Family.* Chromolithograph, published by M. H. Campbell and J. R. Johnson, Hartford, 1859 (The Old Print Gallery, Washington, D.C.).

the publication of the "elegant Engraving of the apotheosis of Washington wherein there is at one view descried all that can be said of the Soldier, the Statesman, the Husband and the Friend." Continued the advertisement:

> We hear the composition of the plate represents a whole length portrait of Washington, rising gently in a graceful attitude on light clouds, from Mount Vernon, which appears underneath: On one side are the portraits of Warren and Montgomery, among clouds, descending in an inviting attitude toward our principal Hero: on the other side, a figure of Cupid, suspended in the air, attentively admiring Washington, and holding a wreath of Immortality over his head.[44]

Other printmakers suggested immortality not symbolically but in crude deathbed scenes (needless to say there were no artists on hand at Mount Vernon to record accurately Washington's final hours, though they were widely reported to have been characteristically dignified). But apotheosis scenes appear to have exerted a special tug at native audiences: depictions not of Washington's last moments on earth, but his first in the secular heaven he seemed destined to dominate. It seems difficult to imagine that the market could have supported two such otherworldly prints, but a few years after Edwin's engraving made its appearance, John James Barralet followed with an even more ambitious variation on the same theme *(see Fig. 119)*.

Barralet was no newcomer to Washington image-making, having produced in 1799 a symbol-rich print of *General Washington's Resignation,* and four years earlier, an accomplished portrait after Walter Robertson (*ca.* 1750–1802). Barralet's striking version of Washington's apotheosis was, in the words of art historian Phoebe Lloyd Jacobs, nothing less than "a re-enactment of the

antique rite of deification upon a Christian Scaffolding." Here the mythical hero rises to be greeted by representations of faith, hope, and charity, while leaving behind on earth such manifestations of his mortal life as a Mason's symbol. Jacobs points out that Barralet relied heavily on Cesare Ripa's *Iconology* for his metaphorical symbols, which, if unknown to most members of the engraver's audience, could still inspire figures with which many print buyers could identify: Barralet's so-called "spiritual and temporal genius," for example, was clearly distinguishable to Americans of the day as Father Time.[45]

For those who needed help with interpretations, there was also an explanatory advertisement for the print in the Philadelphia *Gazette* on December 19, 1800. It described

> The subject General Washington raised from the tomb, by the spiritual and temporal Genius—assisted by Immortality. At his feet America weeping over his Armour, holding the staff surmounted by the Cap of Liberty, emblematical of his mild administration, on the opposite side, an Indian crouched in surly sorrow. In the third ground the mental virtues, Faith, Hope, and Charity. To be seen at Messrs. Shaudron's No. 12, Third Street, at J. J. Barralet's corner of 11th and Filbert-streets, where the books lie for subscriptions.

Prints like Edwin's and Barralet's helped Americans preserve an eternal image of George Washington—though risen above them, before them still. John Adams had told the press after Washington's death, "For his fellow-citizens, if their prayers could have been answered, he would have been immortal." Prints helped Washington remain precisely that.[46]

Now a likeness of Washington by Rembrandt Peale *(Fig. 17)*, Charles' talented and ambitious son,

Fig. 17. Rembrandt Peale, *[George Washington]*. Oil on canvas, *ca.* 1824 (National Portrait Gallery, Smithsonian Institution).

would be labeled *Patriae Pater*—father of his country—in its print adaptation *(Fig. 18)*, not only a "National Portrait and standard likeness," but in the words of its artist, a "grand and imposing" image "calculated for public buildings." Peale fashioned what appeared to be a portrait of a sculpture—framed in the manner of a bas relief. This image, in turn, inspired piracies and copies like P. S. Duval's *(Fig. 19)*. In the words of the caption to an illustrated tribute to Washington's suddenly revived first inaugural address:

Fig. 18. [William S.] Pendleton & Co., *Portriae Pater/ Washington/ From the Original Portrait Painted by Rembrandt Peale.* **Lithograph, Boston, 1827 (National Portrait Gallery, Smithsonian Institution).**

Tho' shrined in dust, great Washington now lies,
The memory of his deeds shall ever bloom:

Twin'd with proud Laurels shall the Olive rise,
And wave unfading o'er his honoured Tomb.[47]

But while some historians have attributed Washington's unique hold on the American public to the Colonial revival that peaked with the 1876 celebration of the centennial of Independence, the evidence to be found on the copyright dates of earlier 19th century popular prints suggests that the fashion for displaying Washington icons at home hardly faded even temporarily with the memory of the living man. If anything, the public appetite for such tributes increased.

Surely General Lafayette's farewell tour to America in 1824 provided inspiration to perpetuate Washington's appeal. His reverent visit to his old comrade's grave was lithographed by Nathaniel Currier *(Fig. 20)* in 1845. It reduced the French hero to a mere silhouette, emphasizing instead the massive weeping willow above Washington's vault—in effect, a symbol used graphically to mourn another symbol. Audiences might have recalled that Lafayette, like Washington, had been compared to Cincinnatus, the man of the land responding to the call to war—and that Washington may well have inspired Lafayette to this role. No less inspired was printmaker Nathaniel Currier. Over the next generation, Currier, and the succeeding partnership of Currier & Ives, would issue no fewer than 123 separate lithographs of George Washington, including portraits, family and official groups, and a staggering array of historical scenes. In all these and other prints, in the words of the caption to one undated N. Currier portrait, the first president remained "first in valor, wisdom, and virtue." And first in sales appeal as well.[48]

Among the other 19th century tributes was Asher Durand's attempt in 1833 to capitalize on the public affection for Houdon's neoclassical bust of Washington *(Fig. 21)*, one of the few likenesses from life that could compete with Gilbert Stuart's painting for mass appeal. Houdon and the elder Peale had besieged Washington for sittings around the same time, prompting the exasperated subject to proclaim: "No dray moves more readily to the thill than I to the painter's chair" ("thill" was a period word for "wagon"). If Washington felt himself pulled inexorably in a direction he did not choose, he would be able to console himself while he still lived that his final destination was immortality. As for Durand's engraving, it not only celebrated Washington, it acknowledged a rival medium's effort to enshrine his likeness from the flesh. By the time Houdon's full-length work was unveiled in the U.S. Capitol, it surely was lost on those who remembered Washington's petulance about posing that the sculptor had placed a plow not in front, but behind his subject. The thill was no longer following the dray. And the national secular cathedral, the domed Capitol Building, now featured not only the Houdon statue, but Trumbull's painting *The Declaration of Independence,* which featured Washington and which, coincidentally, Asher Durand had received $3,000 to engrave in 1820. The effort took him three years.[49]

Inevitably, it was Gilbert Stuart's Washington that lived the longest iconographical life, enduring long enough to grace the 1932 two-cent stamp and in turn inspire one Sam Walter Foss to write:

> I'm the little red stamp with George
>   Washington's picture;
>   And I go wherever I may.
> To any spot in George Washington's
>   land;
>   And I go by the shortest way.

There could be no doubt that it was a

Fig. 19. P[eter]. S. Duval & Co., *Washington./ Drawn by Rembrandt Peale from His Original Portrait.* Lithograph with tintstone, Philadelphia, 1856 (National Portrait Gallery, Smithsonian Institution).

tribute not only to the Post Office, not only to Washington, but to the Stuart Washington image that now decorated envelopes as well as currency, and was never far from any American's sight.[50]

The 19th century print manifesta-tions that had kept the Stuart likeness before the public—and, to Henry Tuckerman, revealed the painful inade-quacies of their creators—included adaptations by Currier & Ives and En-dicott; Jean Nicolas Laugier's 1839

THE TOMB OF WASHINGTON.
MOUNT VERNON VA

Fig. 20. N[athaniel]. Currier, *Lafayette at/ The Tomb of Washington./ Mount Vernon.* Lithograph, New York, 1845.

engraving *(Fig. 22)* of a Leon Cogniet original that was little more than a Trumbull body topped by a Stuart head; S. Topham's mid-century engraving *(Fig. 23)*, which almost made Washington smile in spite of himself and Stuart both; Charles Fenderich's mirror image reversal *(Fig. 24)*, probably designed to delude audiences into thinking it was a new and original image, but undoubtedly unsuccessful in disguising its indebtedness to Stuart; and Sarony & Major's 1846 lithograph *(Fig. 25)*, which imposed the familiar Stuart head onto a rather narrow-chested, short-limbed body, and placed the resulting seated figure in an ornate setting that resembled neither

Fig. 21. A[sher]. B. Durand, *Washington./ From Houdon's Bust.* Engraving, New York, 1833 (Library of Congress).

19th century history books, and also reigned supreme over Thomas Gimbrede's separate-sheet engraving of *The First Four Presidents,* a display piece (with Washington shown in uniform), published in 1812. In 1825, the Boston *Columbian Centennial* would acknowledge the sustained popularity of the genre:

> *Portraits of Presidents.* Messrs. Doggetts of this city have received from France *Lithographic Plates* of the fine Portraits of the five Presidents of the United States from the pencil of Stuart.... We learn that the plates are most excellent samples of the skill of the first of the French artists.

Printmaker Doggett aptly nicknamed the set his "American Kings."[51]

The "kings" continued to reign — Doggett would eventually report importing 70 boxes of his presidential engravings — until Jackson arrived at the White House in 1828. Like no event before it, Old Hickory's elevation seemed to usher in an iconographic revolution in Washington portraiture.[52]

Suddenly the select group of leaders — in the words of a caption to one celebratory print, a "national galaxy" (whose stars had thus far included only founding fathers except for the second Adams, who was at least connected to the Revolution by blood) — was thrown out of kilter by the ascendancy of a western populist. Jackson, after all, even threw open the doors of the White House for a public inaugural reception (and saw the president's house suffer thousands of dollars in damage). He was no Washington, and harbored no ambition to emulate him.

At first his election may have seemed a natural historical progression,

Washington's official presidential residence nor Mount Vernon so much as it did the kind of Victorian parlor whose decorative style did not come into vogue until long after his death.

Washington's image did not take on significantly new dimensions until the election of a second general-president, Andrew Jackson, in 1828. Until then, Washington's image had typically been employed to add luster, as well as a sense of continuity, to the institution of the presidency. The Washingtonian likeness typically adorned group portraits featuring the first four, and then the first five chief executives in early

WASHINGTON.

Fig. 22. Jean Nicolas Laugier after Leon Cogniet and Gilbert Stuart, *Washington.* Engraving, published by James Herring, New York, 1839 (The Old Print Gallery, Washington, D.C.).

at least to Europe, where A. Blanchard engraved a portrait of Washington in uniform *(Fig. 26)* that was not only "dedicated to General Jackson," but bore more resemblance to the sixth president than the first. It was not only Jacksonian but Napoleonic—and decidedly in the Romantic style, leaving neoclassical traditions behind.

Soon, Washington's image was being used not as a tribute to presidential continuity, but as a warning against

Painted by G Stuart.   Engraved by S. Topham

Fig. 23. S. Topham after Gilbert Stuart, [George Washington]. Engraving, published by Davis & Booth, Leeds, 1820 (Library of Congress).

Fig. 24. Charles Fenderich after Gilbert Stuart, *G. Washington.* Lithograph, Philadelphia, *ca.* 1834 (Library of Congress).

WASHINGTON.

THE PATRIOT, THE STATESMAN, AND THE WARRIOR.

Fig. 25. [Napoleon] Sarony & [Henry B.] Major after Gilbert Stuart, *Washington./ The Patriot, the Statesman, and the Warrior.* Lithograph, Philadelphia, 1846 (Library of Congress).

DESSINE PAR COUDER.　　　　　　　　　　GRAVÉ PAR A. BLANCHARD.

WASHINGTON.

Dédié à S. E. le Général Jakson, Président des Etats-Unis d'Amérique.

*Par son très-respectueux admirateur
le Typographe N. Bettoni.*

Fig. 26. A. Blanchard after Louis Charles Couder, *Washington./ Dédié à L. E. le Général
Jakson, Président des Etats-Unis d'Amérique.* "Typograph," published by N. Bettoni,
[Paris], *ca.* 1829 (Library of Congress).

HIGH PLACES IN GOVERNMENT LIKE STEEP ROCKS ONLY ACCESSIBLE TO EAGLES AND REPTILES

Published April 1836, by the proprietor H. R. Robinson, 48 Courtland St. New York

Fig. 28. Thomas Moore, *Independence Declared 1776. The Union Must Be Preserved.*
Lithograph, designed and published by Joseph A. Arnold, Boston, 1839
(Library of Congress).

Opposite: Fig. 27. H[enry]. R. Robinson, *High Places in Government Like Steep Rocks Only
Accessible to Eagles and Reptiles* —. Lithograph, New York, 1836 (Library of Congress).

Jacksonian excesses. H. R. Robinson suggested in his caricature, *High Places in Government Like Steep Rocks Only Accessible to Eagles and Reptiles (Fig. 27)*, that Jackson's hand-picked successor, Martin Van Buren, was little better than a snake, and old Jackson a snapping turtle, the former ascending from and the latter descending to a fetid "pool of corruption." The print was designed as a tribute to yet another general, William Henry Harrison, shown here as a soaring eagle, but destined despite the pictorial accolade to go down to defeat at Van Buren's hands. The one device that required no explanation or caption in the print was the presence of an image on the hilltop — not a bird or beast, but a variation on the old Tiebout monument-on-a-pedestal image of Washington, identified only as *"Pater Patriae,"* and appearing, by comparison to his squabbling successors, more a giant among men than ever.

The Jacksonian point of view had its own Washington icons. Again borrowing considerably from Tiebout's old Bowling Green scene, printmaker Joseph A. Arnold used Washington's resplendent uniformed image for an 1839 print, *The Union Must Be Preserved (Fig. 28)*, showing President Van Buren and his predecessor, Jackson, joining hands above the words of Jackson's celebrated toast to the Union, offered in the face of the Nullification crisis and the threat to the Union which Washington symbolized. But despite the presence in the scene of all seven presidents looming above in coarse vignettes, the focus is on a full-figure Washington below. He occupies

the foreground, displaying a copy of the Declaration of Independence to representatives "from each of the thirteen states" (though, oddly enough, there are only 11 such figures in the scene). Symbolic columns celebrating Warren and Lafayette frame the composition, while in the background, a tableau attesting to domestic beauty and commerce celebrates national progress since Washington. With a strong Whig White House challenge looming from William Henry Harrison, this print may have been designed to suggest that the Jacksonian Democrats were best equipped to hold the country together — in the Washington tradition. Whatever its precise political intentions, this caricature, too, managed above all to celebrate Washington as still without peer in the "national galaxy."

But print patrons who preferred that their Washington images present their principal subject more generically, far beyond petty politics, still enjoyed a huge number of graphics from which to choose, during and beyond the Jacksonian era. Through mid-century, for example, history prints of Washington abounded — illustrating not only his public life, but offering new glimpses, however fanciful, into his private life as well.

In the early 1850s, for example, the giant French lithography firm of Goupil issued a famous series of prints entitled *Life of Washington*, engraved by Regnier after original paintings by Junius Brutus Stearns (1810–1885), a leading American portraitist. Printed in Paris by Lemercier and distributed by the firm of M. Knoedler in New York,

Opposite: Fig. 29. **Regnier after Junius Brutus Stearns,** *Life of George Washington/ The Citizen.* **Lithograph, printed by Lemercier, Paris, and published by M. Knoedler, New York, and Goupil et Cie, Paris, 1854 (Library of Congress).**

the prints revealed their biographical episodes in formal and rather lifeless tableaus, often accompanied by reverential caption material attesting to Washington's nobility. *The Farmer (see Fig. 110)*, for example, a print celebrating Washington as the American Cincinnatus, contained an excerpt from a John Marshall testimonial about the first president: "Having effected the great object for which he was placed at the head of our armies, we have seen him convert the sword into the ploughshare and sink the soldier in the citizen."[53]

Its shortcomings notwithstanding, the series offered something entirely new: romantic historical genre scenes, the likes of which would have been unimaginable in the classical-bound 18th century graphic arts. Another entry in the Regnier series, *Life of George Washington / The Citizen (Fig. 29)*, showed his marriage to Martha Custis as a panorama reminiscent of a royal wedding, erring graciously, too, in its flattering depiction of the bride. In truth, Martha had been far plumper than the print showed at the time of her marriage at age 27 (nearly a year older than George). What was more, at five feet in height, she barely reached her husband's chest when she stood beside him. But Stearns portrayed her as both thinner and far taller than she was in reality, perhaps to present her as a wife befitting her great husband (whether or not she really looked the part in life). Moreover, judging by her portrait — from the back, for some reason — in the series' deathbed scene, inexplicably subtitled *The Christian (Fig. 30)*, (for there was nothing particularly religious about the scene), Martha gained not a pound in the ensuing forty years of her marriage. Of course, such was hardly the case, but the print was more interested in symbolism than reality. Overall, it suggested a rite of passage far more convincingly than it did a human death. But it seemed realistic compared to N. Currier's 1846 lithograph *(Fig. 31)*, which suggested that the former president had donned a powdered wig for his final breaths in an effort to emulate as closely as possible the Gilbert Stuart likeness to which his admirers had become so accustomed.[54]

The Currier print did share with the more polished, but equally unrealistic, Stearns-Regnier depiction, a slavish reliance on the conventions of 19th century heroic death. Great men were supposed to die peacefully, and in rather public settings graced by family, friends, physicians, and servants. What both prints failed to report truthfully was that Washington had in fact died a painful death. Suffering from an inflamed throat that impaired his breathing, weakened by repeated efforts to bleed him, Washington tossed and turned in an anguished effort to find comfort. At one point his secretary, Tobias Lear, actually got into bed beside him, Lear would recall, so he might "raise him, and turn him with as much ease as possible." Of course, such details could hardly be recorded in prints for the family parlor. Suffering was not to be emphasized. Pain was to be avoided at all costs. Americans wanted to see their heroes die placid deaths. And they wanted their death pictures to show, as Goethe had put it, that the victim "had accomplished his

Opposite: Fig. 30. **Regnier after Stearns, *Life of George Washington/ The Christian.* Lithograph, printed by Lemercier, published by M. Knoedler, New York, and Goupil et Cie, Paris, 1854 (Library of Congress).**

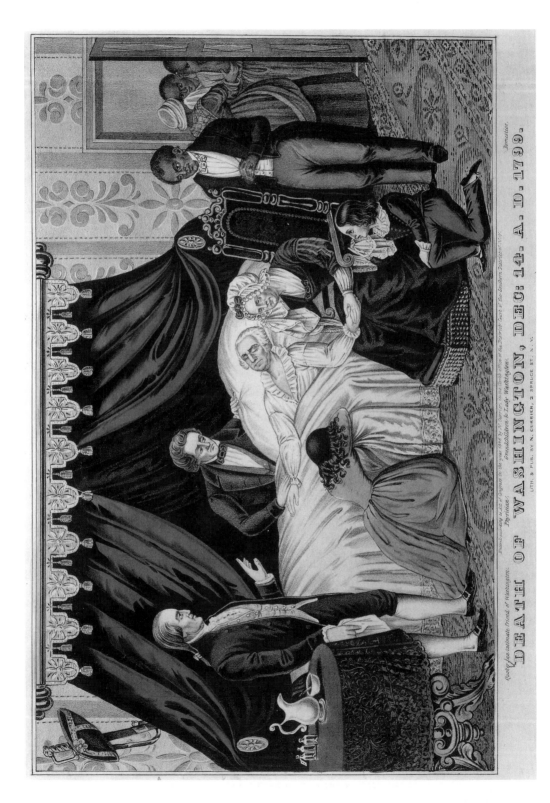

Entered according to the Act of Congress in the year 1844 by N. Currier in the Clerks office of the District Court of the Southern District of N.Y.

Cushis an intimate Friend of Washington.   Physician.   Domestics.

Grandchildren & Lady Washington.

DEATH OF WASHINGTON, DEC: 14th A. D. 1799.

Fig. 32. John Landis, *George Washington*. Lithograph, probably Lancaster, Pa., *ca.* 1840 (The Old Print Gallery, Washington, D.C.).

Opposite: Fig. 31. N. Currier, *Death of Washington, Dec: 14. A.D. 1799*. Lithograph, New York, 1846 (Library of Congress).

mission perfectly, and it was time . . . to go so that others might still have something left to do in a world created to last a long while." After all, it was, in the words of a French woman writing in 1825, an "age of beautiful deaths." Where Washington was concerned, that is precisely the kind of scene that was provided. He might have admitted on his deathbed, "I die hard." But Americans who continued purchasing his deathbed scenes well into the next century (in defiance of standard expectations that such portrayals were only popular as newsworthy items immediately after such tragedies occurred) could forever see their hero going gently—if unrealistically—into his good night.[55]

American audiences had been well prepared for such simplistic depictions by the flurry of prints that poured off the presses once perfection of the lithography process brought America out of the dark ages of the graphic arts. The results were cruder, but they were also easier and far quicker to produce, and priced so that more patrons could afford them. Lithography made it possible, too, for the work of a new generation of portraitists to be adapted for the graphic arts. Eighteenth century engravers had predictably produced prints only of the finest works by the greatest painters; now that lithography increased the need for source portraits, printmakers turned increasingly to the work of less talented artists. The object was speed, not perfection, and the ethic commercial, not artistic. The results, at best, varied wildly. There was apparently no vision of Washington, however primitive, lifeless, or uncharacteristically regal that did not find both enthusiastic publishers and gullible buyers.

When, for example, one publisher issued an 1846 collection of presidential messages, each volume boasting a frontispiece portrait of a chief executive, a critic was moved to describe the "utterly wretched . . . engraved heads," including Washington's, as "worthy of censure." The observer claimed to "have never seen anything more abominable," adding: "They look as if they had been etched on clay and moulded of cast iron; and even in that case, they must have been badly done. By the way they look, the cares of State must have made terrible inroads upon them." Yet, when portrait, historical and religious painter John Landis (b. *ca.* 1805), produced an equally wretched portrait of Washington in prayer it, too, was quickly fashioned into a popular print. Landis, an avid lithographer, may have produced the scene himself *(Fig. 32)*. The composition attempted to dovetail the images of the public and private Washingtons before God. A globe and state chair in the foreground reminded viewers of Washington's role as national leader and world symbol, and a discarded sword on the floor (so awkwardly placed that anyone entering this fictional room would likely have tripped over it and stumbled into the kneeling Washington) testified to the subject's military greatness. In truth, Washington, in religion a Deist, displayed before those who saw him in church a much talked-about reluctance to kneel—precisely the unlikely posture in which Landis showed him. The domestic setting here suggests that Landis saw Washington not as secular, but as religious saint. His Stuart-inspired portrait was tilted upward to peer out the window, toward the heavens, and God. His hands were clasped in prayer. And his white collar and long black coat were drawn to make them look like a minister's vestments. To punctuate the impression, a print within the print—hanging on the wall in the background—depicted the resurrection of Christ. To reinforce the message, Landis included a long poetical tribute to his man-of-God Washington: As the last verse suggested, this was "Washington! America's Friend," as he

> Implores Jehuvah! to extend
> His protecting Power and Grace
> That America's sons may many days
> Prosper under High Heaven's smile
> To be a people free from guile
> To be a people Holy! Happy!!
> Here and throughout Eternity.[56]

Other printmakers, too, experimented with the religious genre, and the results proved decorative staples for an Evangelical age. The Kelloggs, for example, presented a uniformed, kneeling *Washington at Prayer* in a print that seemed no more convincing than the Landis image. It, too, carried the inescapable scent of incongruity. Gods, after all, do not pray.

Besides, there was enough that was godlike about Washington in more conventional, impersonal postures to inspire sufficient ardor among Americans in the new century, as they faced the tug of seemingly irreconcilable sectional differences, perhaps longing for the serenity and nationalism represented by Washington.

Emanuel Leutze (1816–1868) probably came closest to capturing the emblematic image of Washington as ultimate leader of men in his painting of *Washington Crossing the Delaware,* a work that achieved such widespread and enduring fame that when New York celebrated the centennial of Washington's presidential inauguration in 1889, one of the most admired floats in a massive parade there successfully recreated the Leutze canvas. Americans had infinite patience for hearing and rehearing— and also seeing—depictions of the fa-

mous event on Christmas night, 1776, when, according to a script for a 19th century *tableau vivant,* "the patriot troops are conveyed across the river, and amid the packed ice, and in the bitter cold, the future Father of his Country ... CROSSES THE DELAWARE."[57]

Other artists would copy it, printmakers would adapt it with and without official sanction, and tens of thousands of people would see the original on exhibition. From the 1850s on, no image of George Washington could rival the popularity, ubiquity, and impact of Leutze's masterpiece of patriotic art. Born in Germany and initially trained in his adopted home of Philadelphia, Leutze later became a student of the famous Düsseldorf school of history painting. There he learned, as he recalled years later, to "first form the clear thought" of an idea, and only then "adopt or create some anecdote from history or life, since painting can be but partially narrative and is essentially a contemplative art."[58]

It has been speculated that in this particular case, Leutze's "clear thought" may have been to provide in his Washington painting an artistic metaphor for the 1848 revolutions in Germany, where it was painted. If such was his intention, however, it was all but ignored in America, where the canvas was celebrated at face value: a dramatically composed tribute to the decisive event that had proven the ability of Washington's army to overcome adversity and win victories (the daring river crossing enabled the troops to surprise the Hessians in Trenton).

Leutze began sketching his friezelike interpretation of the famous crossing in 1849. Soon thereafter a visitor to his Düsseldorf studio witnessed the painter's very first attempt to lay out his composition in charcoal on the

monumental canvas he had ordered for the project. "All the figures were carefully corrected from models when he came [later] to paint them," the visitor noted, adding that Leutze did have "difficulty in finding American types for the heads and figures, all the German models being either too small or too closely set in their limbs." In a desperate search for the right physiques, Leutze "caught every American that came along and pressed him into service" as a model. The visitor who had witnessed the first application of charcoal to canvas was himself talked into posing as Washington, spending two full hours "without moving, in order that the cloak of Washington be painted at a single sitting." Clad "in Washington's full uniform, heavy chapeau and all, spy-glass in one hand and the other on my knee," the sitter recalled: "I was nearly dead when the operation was over. They poured champagne down my throat and I lived through it."

For the head of Washington, Leutze relied on a more precise model: the Houdon bust in profile, a choice that inspired the man who had posed for the general's torso to marvel at Leutze's passion for accuracy, as he made his subject gaze "intently but calmly through the cold mist to the opposite shore vaguely visible over fields of broken ice."

In fact, the canvas was riddled with inaccuracies, although few observers of the time took note of them. For one thing, as art historian Natalie Spassky has pointed out, no horses crossed with the men, an error clearly visible in the boat crowded with both soldiers and mounts in the background; the horses were brought across only after all 2,500 men had reached shore safely. In addition, the flag shown in Washington's boat was not in use until the following year; the huge chunks of ice bobbing in the river look nothing like the thin ice floes described by Washington in his own official reports; it is doubtful whether any man, even Washington, could have stood erect in his boat during a winter river crossing; and most crucial of all, the wooden boats depicted in the canvas would surely have capsized under the weight of so many occupants. In reality, Washington and his men had crossed the Delaware in decidedly stronger, if less picturesque, flat-bottomed iron-ore boats.

But Leutze's misconceptions were so artfully rendered, his portrait of Washington—as unyielding as a ship's prow—so irresistibly monumental, that it is doubtful that many viewers would have cared even had they known about such errors. What seemed undeniable was that here was an idealized rendering perfectly suited for adaption into a popular print. Inevitably, by early 1851, even as the final touches were being added to the huge canvas, another visitor to Leutze's studio, artist Eastman Johnson, was asked to make a copy "on a reduced scale from which an engraving is to be made." The commission was evidently arranged even before the final painting was completed. Johnson went on to work alongside Leutze while the latter finished his 20 by 16 foot original.

After the original canvas was finally done, Leutze brought it to the

Opposite: Fig. 33. Emanuel G. Leutze, *Washington Crossing the Delaware.* Oil on canvas, 149 × 255 inches. This is the original canvas that inspired the popular print (The Metropolitan Museum of Art, New York; gift of John S. Kennedy, 1897).

United States. Here, the president of the influential American Art Union instantly declared it "one of the greatest productions of the age, and eminently worthy to commemorate the grandest event in the military life of the illustrious man whom all nations delight to honor." When it was first placed on public view in New York City in October 1851, the *Evening Mirror* agreed, declaring that it was nothing less than "the grandest, most majestic, and most effective painting ever exhibited in America." Even Henry James regarded it as an "epoch-making masterpiece," though he saw it as an eight-year-old child. Viewing it when it was dramatically illuminated by gaslight, the dazzled future novelist found the painting an indelible marvel, brilliantly conveying "the profiled national hero's purpose" merely by showing him "standing *up*" under impossible conditions. "Mr. Leutze's drama," James recalled, "left behind any paler proscenium." By the time its New York exhibition closed down in February 1852, some 50,000 spectators had paid to gaze at the canvas, and the picture had been sold for a staggering $10,000. But first it was taken to Washington, and placed on temporary exhibit in the Capitol Rotunda, where rival artist John Vanderlyn huffed that not only was it blocking the view of one of his own compositions, but worse, that no one seemed to mind. The exhibit was so successful that Senator John P. Hale was moved to suggest that the canvas be purchased for the White House. The painting had become, in the words of the *New York Times*, the "chief ostensible attraction" in American art.

Earlier, in the fall of 1851, Goupil & Co., the same company that would publish the landmark "Life of Washington" series, paid $6,000 for a copy of the painting (undoubtedly Eastman Johnson's), and commissioned Paul Girardet of Paris to engrave it for a popular print. Two years later, in 1853, the Goupil effort was published *(Fig. 34)* to instant acclaim in America. It became so widely popular for so long that Mark Twain would note thirty years later in his book *Life on the Mississippi* that the print was still, in the 1880s, a staple in "the home of the principal citizen" in every town "all the way from the suburbs of New Orleans to the edge of St. Louis."

Rival printmakers proceeded to copy it (Currier & Ives alone issued no fewer than five thinly disguised adaptations, the last in the centennial year of 1876). George Caleb Bingham attempted without comparable success to reinterpret the event on canvas, and modern artists from Grant Wood to Larry Rivers have included it in works of their own. Edward Sorel even substituted Richard Nixon for George Washington in an unforgettable 20th century lampoon. Its impact was unrivalled.

If George Washington is the preeminent American icon, there can be little doubt that the Luetze image is the preeminent *Washington* icon—the quintessential portrait of the indomitable commander, standing inspiringly, if unbelievably firm, even as ordinary men all around him struggle against natural forces to which he appears impervious. Braving wind and wave, standing like a rock, Washington

Opposite: Fig. 34. **Paul Girardet after Emanuel Leutze,** *Washington Crossing the Delaware.* **Engraving, published by M. Knoedler, New York, and Goupil et Cie, Paris, 1854 (The Philadelphia Print Shop, Ltd.)**

WASHINGTON CROSSING THE DELAWARE.

EVENING PREVIOUS TO THE BATTLE OF TRENTON, DEC. 1ST 1776.

Published by James Baillie, 87 th St near 3 d Avenue N.Y.

256

emerged from the image as an inde-structible symbol of his nation's fight for independence — America's towering totem at full mast.

What the success of the painting also confirmed was how easily Washington's image had suited the artistic conventions of both the age in which he lived and the generations that followed. Neoclassicism, its art emphasizing tradition, virtue, and proportion, fit neatly with the Enlightenment virtues of reason and morality that prevailed while the Father of his Country reigned over the national family. He looked natural amidst symbolic pillars and other classical acoutrements. But he could as easily be a hero in the art of the Romantic age, depicted touring his farms or holding center stage at a splendid wedding ceremony. He could personify the evangelical movement in America in scenes that showed him, however unrealistically, kneeling in prayer. And now, as Leutze proved, he could emerge into the post–Romantic era as potent a symbol as ever. For in the native American culture, George Washington was above all a unifying, reassuring, and timeless symbol of valor and virtue. Washington transcended cultural movements because in America, his was not only our representative image, not only our ideal image, but also our defining image. When the Boston daguerreotypists Southworth & Hawes took a memorable photograph of a young woman gazing intently at a Gilbert Stuart–inspired portrait of the first president, it was clear that the image had successfully embraced new technologies and new generations alike. The countenance of

George Washington had become more even than a national icon. It was a national landmark.

With Leutze's indelible interpretation so well known so quickly, and for so long, it is difficult to imagine that James Baillie's version of the scene *(Fig. 35)* aroused nearly as much sympathy, affection, or patronage. Yet his history print may in fact be the more realistic. Baillie assigned Washington his most natural role, not merely a passenger in a boat, but a commander, seeing to the safety of his soldiers as *they* cross the river first. It is a significant difference. Washington's attention here is focused not on the men who move away from the icy shores, but on the troops who are lining up for the next boats — the ones for whom he has yet to provide a safe crossing. It is, in its way, an altogether more sympathetic image than the Leutze view of the general being rowed across by his battered men. But judging by its rarity today, it likely did not find a very large audience anyway.

Washington did regain his familiar place, standing up in a rowboat, in *Washington's Adieu to His Generals (Fig. 36)*, an engraving by New York printmaker George R. Hall based in part on a drawing by William Pate, whose own greatest fame was earned as an engraver as well. Depictions of the Cincinnatus giving up the sword had long been a staple of Washington iconography when this print was published. They were crucial to the image of a commander who appeared to desire nothing more than relinquishing command. They were also image-ameliorating complements to more grandly

Opposite: Fig. 35. **James Baillie,** *Washington Crossing the Delaware./ Evening Previous to the Battle of Trenton,* **Decr. 26, 1776. Lithograph, New York,** *ca.* **1848 (The Old Print Gallery, Washington, D.C.).**

WASHINGTON'S ADIEU TO HIS GENERALS

heroic works like P. S. Duval's 1860 chromolithograph, *Washington's Triumphal Entry into New York,* a mammoth, 3 by 4 foot print advertised as "the largest specimen of Chromolithograph ever executed."[59]

Hall's Cincinnatus print was less triumphal, to be sure, but it did point to the continuing appeal of the Washington who not only memorably entered, but unforgettably exited great scenes, eager, as always, to return to the embrace of land and family. That proclivity would also be stressed in an influential mid-century biography by novelist (and namesake) Washington Irving. Appropriately, the print of *Washington's Adieu* would now be used to promote the new book.

According to the caption to Hall's print, Pate's drawing of the scene had in fact come from Irving's own personal collection. Moreover, now it could be found illustrated in volume four of his five volume biographical work, his last great effort before his death. Even the specific page number was referenced on the print, which more than likely was issued specifically as an advertisement for the books.

But as portraiture, this Washington was sadly deficient. The wisest thing Pate did in composing it was face the general away from the viewer, so as little of his profile showed as possible— the better to conceal the limitations of the likeness. It was almost as if, in preparing an illustration for the Irving book, Pate had experienced the same problems in creating a portrait in art as did the author in creating a portrait in words. For as Irving confessed:

I had a great deal of trouble to keep the different parts together, giving a little touch here and a little touch there, so that one part should not lag behind the other nor one part to be more conspicuous than the other. I felt like old Lablache when he was performing in a rehearsal of his orchestra . . . bringing out a violin here, a clarinet there, now suppressing a trombone, now calling upon the flutes, and every now and then bringing out the big bass drum.

But Pate's illustration, if designed to be the "big bass drum" of mid-century Washington prints, barely made a sound.[60]

While he lived, Washington had pointedly if sometimes unsuccessfully eschewed the grand gesture (although his departure from New York harbor, as portrayed by Pate, had in truth proven a significant exception). The Cincinnatus preferred returning as quickly and quietly as possible to Mount Vernon, even if his public would allow him only a brief postwar retirement before summoning him back to its service.

During this interregnum he did welcome back to America Lafayette, the man who called himself Washington's "adoptive son," during his first visit since the Revolution. Whether or not his subsequent departure from Mount Vernon was quite as formal as one anonymous history print *(Fig. 37)* suggested is impossible to know for certain. But it seems highly unlikely that the Washington who, as Marshall wrote, had converted "the sword into the ploughshare," would have hosted his old comrade long after the Revolution wearing a full uniform of the Continental army, complete with epaulets.

Opposite: Fig. 36. **George R. Hall after Felix Octavius Carr Darley,** *Washington's Adieu to His Generals. . . .* **Engraving, printed by William Pate, New York, 1860 (The Old Print Gallery, Washington, D.C.).**

GEN.L LAFAYETTE'S DEPARTURE FROM MOUNT VERNON 1784.

PUBLISHED BY E. FARRELL 167 HESTER ST. N.Y.

Mount Vernon was Washington's escape. For all its crudity, an 1852 N. Currier lithograph *(Fig. 38)* probably better captured the image of the Cincinnatus in final retirement: personally supervising his field hands, riding his plantation, wearing a farmer's hat instead of a wig, looking for all the world like a country squire, not a national emblem. The rarity of this particular depiction, however, suggests that Americans did not want such realities intruding on their celestial image of Washington. Soldier, statesman, and demigod he would be in America's family parlor. Anything less seemed unacceptably mundane.[61]

He was, and he would remain, even as the Union he helped create began crumbling, the "emblem of the free," in the apt words from the caption of an 1862 lithograph by Samuel Canty *(Fig. 39)*, which showed Confederate President Jefferson Davis falling under the treasonous temptation of Satan despite the formidable presence of Washington's ghost in the background.

Here was a tribute not just to Washington, but to the *image* of Washington, for as the "original music" accompanying the print warned Davis ominously:

> The shade of WASHINGTON
> 　　Condemns you from above;
> His calm, majestic brow
> 　　Denotes his country's love.
> E'en Royalty could not,
> 　　With all its tinsel glare,
> Induce him to betray
> 　　Our Nation's banner fair.

That Davis would not only betray his country, but also the image of its first president, were sins of equal gravity. (Ironically, in the South, Confederate

printmakers were meanwhile portraying Davis as the second coming of Washington in portraits defiantly labeled, "Our First President."[62])

But as the Civil War continued, Washington became much more than the forbidding specter warning new generations of leaders against disunion. He became more even than the majestic if remote hero on the parlor wall. Another sea change occurred with the introduction in 1861 of *cartes-de-visite:* small, visiting card–size photographs that could be reproduced in great quantities. Their invention liberated photography from the constraints of earlier, one copy only processes, and quickly inspired, in turn, the development of both specially designed leather albums to display the pictures, and widely available celebrity photographs for sale to the public to fill their pages alongside pictures of family and friends. Though he had lived and died long before the invention of even the most primitive forms of photography, Washington now became one of the most popular subjects for *carte-de-visite* cameras. The proprietors of photo galleries simply purchased readily available Washington engravings or lithographs, photographed them, and issued the results as "new" pictures for the family album.[63]

Thus prints like *Washington's last interview with his mother* *(Fig. 40)* and *Washington and Family* *(Fig. 41)*, the latter a truncated, rearranged version of the famous Savage and Edwin engraving, now made their reappearance as intimate collectibles for parlor table instead of the parlor wall. And what better portraits could there be to begin a patriotic citizen's family album than a

Opposite: Fig. 37. **E. Farrell, *Genl. Lafayette's Departure from Mount Vernon 1784.* Lithograph, New York, *ca.* 1867 (Library of Congress).**

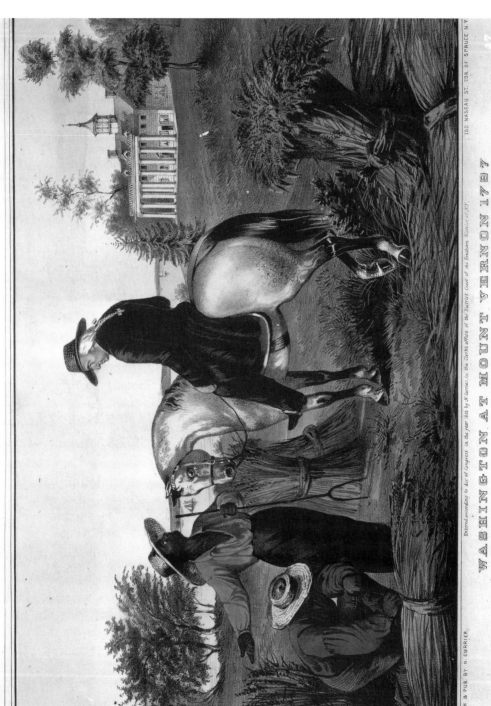

LITH & PUB. BY N. CURRIER.

Entered according to Act of Congress in the year 1852 by N.Currier in the Clerks office of the District Court of the Southern District of N.Y.

152 NASSAU ST. COR. OF SPRUCE N.Y.

WASHINGTON AT MOUNT VERNON 1797

Agriculture is the most healthy, the most useful, and the most noble employment of man. WASHINGTON.

pose of the first president greeting his old mother (with the family dog sniffing nearby), or a portrait of Washington in *his* own family parlor, the ironically childless Father of His Country surrounded by the comforting presence of his wife and her grandchildren?[64]

Judging from the abundance of surviving Civil War era *cartes,* there was apparently room in the family album, too, for more formal representations of the great man, and perhaps no image was more widely photographed and disseminated in *cartes-de-visite* than the so-called "Lansdowne" Washington (so named because it was painted for Lord Lansdowne, the British statesman who had shown considerable sympathy toward the American colonies before the Revolution). It was another of Gilbert Stuart's creations, this time a full-figure pose showing Washington as president, clutching a sword in his left hand and offering a majestic gesture of welcome with his right. It came as close as any portrait ever did to capturing the characteristic Washingtonian posture Jefferson had once described as "easy, erect, and noble"—a bearing which the French minister Chevalier de Luzerne perceptively summed up in two words: "military grace." In February 1800, London printmaker James Heath (1757–1834) had issued an engraving of the Lansdowne original that quickly won critical and popular acceptance in America. That June, the New York *Commercial Advertiser* said of it:

Much as we have heard of Gen. Washington, there had not until very lately, been any Portrait of him that deserved much notice. One, sometime since pub-lished by Cheesman, from a picture by Trumbull, has considerable merit, but the leading Portrait is one copied from Stuart by Heath, and which in point of resemblance, is said by those have seen the General, to be uncommonly faithful.

Ironically, the person who may have been least pleased by the good notice was artist Gilbert Stuart. Apparently he had not been consulted about the project to engrave the Landsdowne portrait, and to add insult to injury, the plate identified him as "Gabriel" Stuart. He thereupon declared himself "mortified to observe, that without any regard to his property, or feelings, as an artist, an engraving has been recently published in England; and is now offered for sale in America." To the painter, the print should never have been consigned by "his Lordship" to "the graver," and would not possibly "satisfy or supercede the public claim, for a correct representation of the American Patriot." Stuart might have been far less angry had he been sharing in the profits. For "handsomely framed" prints were being sold for the staggering price of $15, and "elegantly framed" proofs for $20. Even plain, unframed prints were dear: a wealthy $8 apiece.[65]

Not surprisingly, the print inspired innumerable copies over the years, ranging from outright piracies of the Heath original for reissue as *cartes-de-visite* **(Fig. 42)**, to ludicrous lithographed adaptations like James Baillie's print **(Fig. 43)**, the latter of which so clumsily rearranged Washington's feet that he now resembled a ballet dancer in third position . . . and a portly one in the bargain. Rembrandt Peale, an artist who as a young man had observed

Opposite: Fig. 38. **N. Currier,** *Washington at Mount Vernon 1797/ Agriculture is the most healthy, the most useful, and the most noble employment of man. — WASHINGTON.* **Lithograph, New York, 1852 (Library of Congress).**

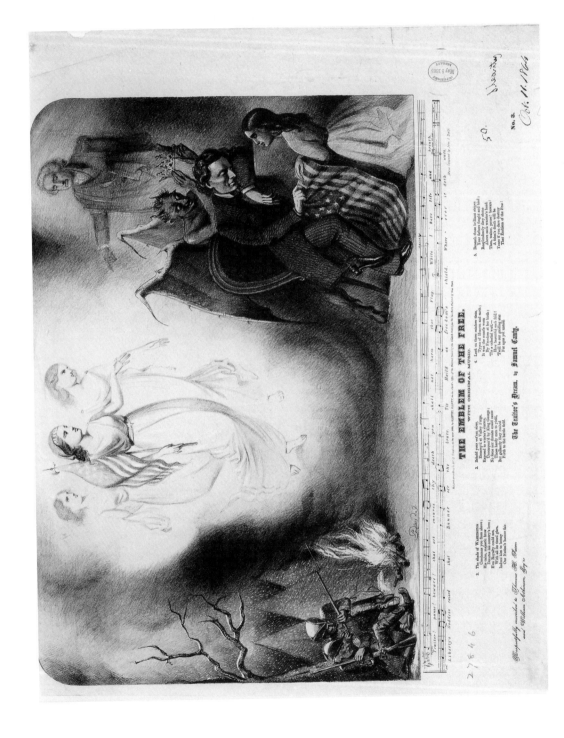

THE EMBLEM OF THE FREE.

WITH ORIGINAL MUSIC.

The Traitor's Dream, by Samuel Canty.

Respectfully inscribed to Thomas W. Reese
and William Johnson, Esqr.

Fig. 40. Photographer unknown, *Washington's last interview with his mother.*
Carte-de-visite photograph of a lithograph, *ca.* 1861.

Opposite: Fig. 39. B[enjamin H.]. Day [Jr.], *The Emblem of the Free.* Lithographed song
sheet, published by Samuel Canty, New York, 1862 (Library of Congress).

Washington from the flesh, and more important, had his own paintings and prints to sell, thought the flood of Landsdowne-inspired pictures nothing less than revolting. These "coarsely engraved" prints, he complained jealously, "were framed and *wonderfully praised* by their fortunate owners, as literally *striking* likenesses." "They were tolerably good in the upper part of the head," he admitted, "but shockingly disgusting in the lower part."[66]

Nor did Washington's extraordinary physique quite reveal itself in the Lansdowne portrait. George Washington Parke Custis, the first president's adopted son, wrote a memoir in 1860, in which he asserted: "His manliness has been misrepresented by bulkiness, while his vigorous, elastic frame, in which so many graces were combined, has been modeled upon Ajax instead of Achilles. With all its development of muscular parts, the form of Washington had no appearance of bulkiness, and so harmonious were its proportions that he did not appear so passing tall as his portraits represented him." To Custis:

> In his prime, Washington stood 6 feet, 2 inches, and measured precisely 6 feet when attired for his grave. To a majestic height was added corresponding breadth and firmness, and his whole person was so cast in Nature's finest mould as to resemble the classic remains of an ancient piece of statuary, where all the parts contribute to the beauty and perfection of the whole. His limbs were long, large and sinewy. His chest broad and expansive. His frame of equal breadth from the shoulders to the hip, and showed an extraordinary development of bone and muscles. His joints were large, as were his feet, and could a cast have been preserved of his hand, to be exhibited in these degenerate days, it would be said to have belonged to a being of a fabulous age.[67]

The Gilbert Stuart "Lansdowne" portrait — in adaptations by Heath, Savage, Nutter, Ritchie, Baillie, and others — may have deserved "notoriety," in the eyes of an eyewitness who knew Washington personally, but it did succeed unquestionably in personifying yet another aspect of Washington: the ultimate republican. Besides, even Peale would acknowledge that the purpose of portraiture was to communicate "the *best* of true likeness." And what could be more desirable, he admitted, than for "Americans to possess the likeness of Washington, whose knowledge & *control* of *Character,* and whose influential energy were devoted to *perpetuate,* more than language, our liberties & our Union?" Besides, as Peale conceded, when he himself tried to paint Washington, he was painfully aware of his own "deficiency." Yet Peale insisted that Washington had died with his "family & friends grieved" not just over losing him, but because "there was no Portrait of him which conveyed an adequate idea of his mild, thoughtful & dignified, yet firm and energetic Countenance." In truth, had they looked carefully, his family and friends surely would have seen most of their criteria illuminated in the Lansdowne adaptations.[68]

However crude its many incarnations, the power and popularity of the "Lansdowne" Washington should not be underestimated. Garry Wills has suggested that the print succeeded because it vivified not only Washington's authority over the state, but its laws' authority over him. True, Washington stands before a chair of state emblazoned with an emblematic stars-and-stripes shield, and alongside a table whose legs are fashioned from a fasces, the classical symbol of state power.

WASHINGTON AND FAMILY.

Fig. 41. Photographer unknown after Edward Savage, *Washington and Family. Carte-de-visite* photograph of a lithograph, *ca.* 1861.

Too, all is set before symbolic pillars also inserted to represent the state. But nearby as well are crucial props of a different sort — books: a history of the Revolution, *The Federalist,* the *Journal of Congress.* They testified with equal vividness to the legal foundations of the new republic. Here, complete with his "gesture of greeting," argues Wills, was "*citizen* Washington, the founder giving men laws by giving up power."[69]

All but forgotten during the Lansdowne image's long reign as an icon was the fact that, even in its earliest engraved form (direct from the original, and presumably faithful to it), the unnaturally short body Stuart provided Washington constituted little more than a new pedestal for his old Athenaeum portrait, with almost every inch of space in the new composition cluttered with un–Stuartlike symbols. It did not much matter. This, perhaps, came closest of all Washington images to the way his fellow countrymen wanted to recall him — in their albums, on their walls, and in their hearts: as close to the regal-republican ideal figure as America ever produced.

So popular did the Lansdowne image become and remain that an English visitor named Mrs. Basil Hall found herself face to face with it almost everywhere she traveled in the America of 1827 and 1828. Finally, she took pen in hand and wrote acerbically after one such experience — attesting perhaps unwittingly to its incomparable ubiquity:

> In this room hangs one of the only two prints to be seen at every inn, great and small . . . George Washington holding in one hand a roll of paper and in the other, extended in a position which indicates . . . what the Americans would call a very lengthy speech, at least this is my feeling of the matter, but perhaps this arises from my being thoroughly sickened of the eternal picture.[70]

Obviously, the eternal picture did not "sicken" American audiences. Quite the contrary. It — and the countless other portraits that decorated the nation for more than a century after George Washington's death — nourished and inspired them. His image became all but holy. He was a revered icon — the king of the pantheon of the American parlor wall.

It was possible, of course, in later years when "advertising mania" predominated, to observe, as the *New York Times* did in 1886, Bowery shopkeepers manifesting "a little patriotism" by displaying "a huge portrait of Washington" that informed onlookers "that the Father of His Country never had an opportunity to purchase six linen shirts for $7, nor did his patriotic eyes ever behold such bargains in neckware as might be found inside the particular store displaying the picture." But it was also possible, even as late as 1932, for officials planning the Washington bicentennial to pledge to distribute a million portraits to decorate the nation's schools. The pledge was kept. And in the ceremonies that officially marked the 200th birthday, President Herbert Hoover, about to yield power to a new chief executive in the best Washington tradition (albeit under highly different circumstances), summed up the timeless appeal of the man and monument. Speaking specifically of the granite obelisk whose construction had over the years finally caught up with its subject's unflagging appeal in popular prints, Hoover offered words that might as easily have characterized the engravings and lithographs instead.[71]

In a very real sense, as Hoover expressed it, the formal yet avuncular popular prints of George Washington represented, like the monument itself,

Fig. 42. **Photographer unknown after Gilbert Stuart and James Heath, [*George Washington;* Lansdowne Portrait].** *Carte-de-visite* **photograph of an engraving,** *ca.* **1861.**

"a pledge in the sight of all mankind, given by Washington to his countrymen, to carry forward the continuing fulfillment of his vision of America."

It was no accident that when a prototypical Civil War veteran was portrayed—in an 1866 Dominique Fabronius print of a Trevor McClurg painting—returning to hearth and home, the reassuring picture visible above that hearth was of George

Washington, symbol of the union he had fought to preserve.[72]

Such prints also represented no small commercial triumph by generations of engravers and lithographers who had succeeded in satisfying the public's unquenchable thirst for Washington's emblematic likenesses. Mason Locke Weems, that canny shaper of Washington legends whose biography influenced the young Lincoln and thousands of others, printmakers doubtless included, spoke both for himself and generations of engravers and lithographers when he confided: "You have a great deal of money lying in the bones of old George if you will but exert yourself to extract it." That is precisely what the picture publishers went on to do: they exerted themselves to extract Washington pictorially and preserve him for the ages.[73]

Whatever motives were behind the production of their pictures—a desire to illuminate, ennoble, inspire, celebrate the best of what Americans and America could be, or simply earn profits for themselves—most engraved and lithographed portraits of George Washington had one thing in common. As William S. Barker put it in 1880, all "these copies and pictures" were alike "calculated to please the popular taste." Judging by the sheer number and variety of the images produced, by the depth and duration of their popularity, and by their influence on the observers of several generations, that is precisely what they did.[74]

Speaking for himself, but surely reflecting what all the Washington image-makers felt as they created their haunting likenesses, Rembrandt Peale summed up the unforgettable experience of observing—and portraying—America's *patriae pater:* "There never was a Portrait painted with feelings of higher excitement," he remembered. "No human being could have felt more devoted admiration of the character of Washington, and no Artist ever found his pride more strongly excited than mine to rescue from oblivion the aspect of a Man who would forever be venerated as the 'Father of his Country.'"[75]

So many graphic artists were so "strongly excited" for so many years, and did so much themselves to rescue his "aspect" from "oblivion," that the words written to honor President Washington on one of his national tours could as easily, and as accurately, have been used to describe the state of his country's parlor walls—then, and for a century to come:

> There view Columbia's favourite Son,
>   Her Father, Saviour, Friend and
>   Guide!
> There see th'immortal WASHINGTON!
>   His Country's Glory, Boast and Pride![76]

Visiting the United States for one of his own celebrated tours in 1842, Charles Dickens would find "Columbia's favourite son" on perpetual view here. Stopping at a "little inn" in Pennsylvania, he saw Washington portraits adorning the parlor. And even on "the bar-room walls" of a sordid tavern in New York's notorious Five Points slum, Dickens observed "colored prints of Washington" hanging in a place of honor amidst the squalor. "There is, in some sort," he concluded almost reluctantly of the United States, "a taste for decoration even here. Enough so that writer Henry Tuckerman would acknowledge on the eve of Abraham Lincoln's election to the presidency 61 years after Washington's death that by then "every object in the economy of trade and domestic life, was decorated . . . with that endeared and hallowed countenance."[77]

WASHINGTON,

FIRST IN WAR, FIRST IN PEACE, AND FIRST IN THE HEARTS OF HIS COUNTRYMEN!

Fig. 43. J. Baillie after Gilbert Stuart, *Washington,/ First in War, First in Peace, and First in the Hearts of his Countrymen.* Lithograph, New York, n.d. (Library of Congress).

III

Abraham Lincoln: "A Good Head to Go Before the People"

There is considerable irony in the fact that Abraham Lincoln, whose appearance was first a source of embarrassment to him, and later a source of humor, came eventually to benefit from the proliferation and palatability of his printed image to help him both politically and historically. Lincoln's rugged, rustic looks were routinely mocked by foes, excused by admirers, and wittily denigrated by Lincoln himself. Yet virtually from the moment of his emergence as a presidential candidate, through his career in the White House, and on to his ultimate deification as an apotheosized martyr, America's engravers and lithographers recognized, fulfilled, and exploited the public's desire to see Lincoln—albeit a Lincoln largely unlike the original. They provided a national audience with colorful, romantic, inexpensive—and sometimes exaggerated and fanciful—pictures of the man who confessed once that realistic portraiture was "exactly what I would like to avoid." In Abraham Lin-

coln, art, commerce, and subject all found a common focus from which each could benefit.[1]

In Lincoln's case, artistic attention could not have been lavished on a more physically impoverished subject. No historical figure of his time stood to benefit more from the cosmetic traditions of romantic portraiture than Abraham Lincoln.

So the press noticed. The hostile Charleston *Mercury,* for example, dismissed Lincoln as "a horrid looking wretch . . . sooty and scoundrely [sic] in aspect, a cross between a nutmeg dealer, the horse-swapper, and the night man." And to the Houston *Telegraph,* he was "the leanest, lankest, most ungainly mass of legs, arms, and hatchet face ever strung upon a single frame."[2]

Even his supporters acknowledged his shortcomings. His law partner conceded that his skin was "coarse, pimply, dry hard, no blood seemingly in it." The best that a sympathetic Ohio journalist could say after seeing Lincoln for

Opposite: **Early heroes of the Civil War are portrayed in this premium for the United States Insurance Company. Washington continues to hold the central place in the grouping, as a hero of both the military and political spheres; Lincoln is at top in this J. C. Buttre engraving (photograph: The Lincoln Museum).**

the first time was that he was "exceedingly 'well-preserved.'" Noting that "his head sits well on his shoulders, but beyond that . . . defies description," a Chicago newspaper pointed out that while "never fashionable," Lincoln was, at least, "always clean"; while "careless," he was "not slovenly." And this came in the context of a favorable report from a pro–Lincoln journal.[3]

Lincoln may well have known that he suffered from what today's political strategists and media consultants would call "an image problem." Perhaps he even heard reports that during the convention which nominated him for president, his backers had hauled out a painting of the new nominee that was so "hideous" it shocked the delegates — many of whom had never seen Lincoln in person. Thus it comes as no surprise that to artists who encountered him in the years to come, he would profess with mock seriousness his wonder that anyone should want his picture, unless, as he supposedly joked to a photographer, "it is because I am the ugliest man in the State of Illinois." On another occasion he declared himself "a very indifferent judge" of his own likenesses, insisting, "my judgement is worth nothing in these matters." And yet, perhaps he sensed, too, that something could be done by image-makers to mask his deficiencies, and make the most of the weatherbeaten face, the gnarled hands, and the towering height that, in the words of a modern art historian, "set him apart from the sleek conventionality of rival politicians."[4]

Lincoln himself entertained no real illusions about his appearance. Accused publicly once of being two-faced, he turned the insult to self-deprecating advantage by replying: "If I had another face, do you think I'd wear this one?" So when he claimed to know "nothing"

about such "matters" as art, and professed indifference about his own likenesses, the protestations sound suspiciously like studied, down-home variations on the prevailing niceties of Victorian modesty. In all likelihood, Lincoln knew better. He surely sensed that flattering depictions could be his cosmetic salvation, for he usually did what he could to make sure good portraits were produced — even when it was less than convenient for him to do so.[5]

Throughout the relatively brief period of his prominence in national politics, Lincoln was a cooperative subject for artists in all media, who besieged him with requests for sittings. During the last five years of his life alone he posed for more than a hundred photographs. He consented to sit for painters and sculptors, and even patiently endured the application of wet plaster directly to his face — at best a disagreeable process, at worst, a rather painful one. And he did so not once, but twice. Lincoln likely suffered through these inconveniences and assaults, at least at the outset of his national fame, not because he felt his face should be recorded for posterity, but because he sensed that, sympathetically portrayed and aggressively marketed, the sittings might help him win elections and retain popular support.[6]

Curiously, perhaps the most effective artistic medium in achieving such results, quickly and ubiquitously, actually required the least cooperation from him: the popular print. Ambitious lithographers and engravers obliged with myriad portraits, most of which were either intentionally modeled after or shamelessly stolen from existing paintings, photographs, or other prints; they required neither active cooperation nor personal approval from the subject. And the results could spread — and ameliorate—the Lincoln image on a scale impossible, certainly in the watershed year of Lincoln's rise, in any other art medium. For in 1860, the age of the *carte-de-visite* (multi-copy paper photographic prints for the family album) had not yet dawned; and paintings and sculpture were then still firmly planted in the realms of private patronage and small exhibition halls. The public art museum movement was still a dream, and the little that was on display remained centered in urban America, inaccessible and all but invisible to a still largely rural country most of whose people lived in scattered communities far from metropolitan culture. What both paintings and photographs *could* do for the Lincoln image as early as the 1860 presidential campaign, however, was inspire popular print adaptations. And they did.[7]

Photographs were routinely copied by engravers and lithographers, both with and without official consent in this age of lax copyright protection. Those print publishers with the funds and ambition to dispatch artists to Illinois to make original models for print portraits would become the first patrons to order pictures of Lincoln from life. Audiences would embrace all the results. As a 19th century advertisement for one such print would point out, it was not necessary to adorn homes with "paintings that . . . cost hundreds or thousands of dollars. . . . Engravings and other pictures of their class . . . bring them within reach of people of average means having good taste, and wisdom enough to buy them for themselves or others."[8]

True, in recording the highlights of the last five years of Lincoln's life—from winning the presidential nomination in the spring of 1860 to his assassination in the spring of 1865—America's engravers and lithographers were seldom demanding or discerning portraitists. Determined to produce pictures that appealed specifically to Lincoln's admirers, the printmakers glamorized their subject—a circumstance Lincoln would probably have been the first to admit worked to his distinct advantage. Unconstrained by the boundaries of reality, engravings and lithographs could soften the perception of the camera eye—take the "poor subject" and bestow physiognomical riches. Such riches were, of course, undeserved, and in endowing them on Lincoln, the printmakers did more than justice to his image by doing kindly injustice to his true appearance.

Print portraits more often than not flattered the homely Lincoln. They skillfully brought color to his sallow complexion, added glamour to his drab wardrobe, padded flesh onto his cadaverous face and frame, shortened his elongated neck, flattened his ears, modified the wild arrangement of his hair, and ironed out his moles, warts, and wrinkles. One result was so ridiculously flattering it was reportedly nicknamed by Lincoln's Illinois neighbors the "Greek God." But it did not much matter to the printmakers that, occasionally, Lincoln bore only slight resemblance to the image on their prints. Evidently they rationalized that an idealized Lincoln was what their customers wanted. And that is what they usually got.[9]

Despite the flaw of idealization, Lincoln print portraits enjoyed distinct advantages over photographs and paintings. And however primitive, prints were nonetheless far more refined than the crude woodcuts of Lincoln that at first decorated contemporary newspapers. For one thing, it was obvious enough that prints were more colorful than the stark images captured by the cameramen of Lincoln's day. While photographs were "painfully truthful," as Lincoln himself once observed, prints offered a romanticized vision of their subject, tinted in flesh tones to create a lifelike hue that photography, then in its infancy, could not duplicate. The talented engraver or lithographer could also strip away the mask which Lincoln admitted overcame his face every time he froze for the unnaturally long exposure required by 19th-century camera techniques.[10]

What was more, the printmaker could also place Lincoln in scenes in which he was unlikely to be posed by the photographers. Although Lincoln was photographed more often than all but a handful of his contemporaries, the overwhelming majority of his sittings took place in studios, and with rare exceptions, he posed alone. On the other hand, print portraitists could depict Lincoln in the foreground of a host of dramatic, if unlikely, outdoor and heroic scenes, some symbolic, others fanciful.[11]

Although Lincoln never posed with his wife for photographers (it is believed that Mrs. Lincoln, much shorter than her husband and sensitive about the difference, rejected all proposals for such sittings), printmakers manufactured domestic scenes anyway. Although Lincoln did not pose with his cabinet or with his generals, the printmakers created these groupings as well. And although the 16th president was not photographed on horseback or outdoors at the White House, printmakers created equestrian scenes and panoramas in which he was made to dominate skylines from Springfield to Washington to Richmond.[12]

Formal paintings of Lincoln could

be equally colorful, heroic, allegorical, and flattering. They were also more original in conception and certainly more often than not created by far more talented artists than those who created prints. But as noted, paintings were priced prohibitively. Their audience was restricted to those patrons who commissioned original canvases and the relatively few Americans who saw the finished works on display at political clubs or art galleries, although exhibitions in cities like New York drew large crowds. Prints enjoyed far wider distribution. Not surprisingly, only those paintings of Lincoln that were engraved or lithographed for mass distribution achieved national acclaim quickly. In contrast, inexpensive and well-distributed print portraits were available everywhere and priced so that nearly everyone could afford them.[13]

Without question, print portraits combined the advantages of both the life painting—color and dramatic license—and the photograph—mass distribution at low cost—while minimizing the disadvantages of each: for photography, its lifelessness; for painting, its limited availability. For all these reasons print portraiture successfully filled—in quantity if not always in quality—the otherwise unsated national appetite for exciting, inexpensive images of Abraham Lincoln. Commercially, their success was indisputable, a fact reinforced by the huge number and variety of Lincoln print portraits that survive to this day.[14]

While a generally naïve and eager public made printmakers' works on the subject of Lincoln highly profitable, the ensuing competition among publishers inevitably produced a flawed artistic archive. Too much of what poured off the presses bore the unmistakable evidence of retouching, contrivance, and heavy-handed mythification. Yet it is crucial to an understanding of the importance of these images in the Civil War–era American home that modern observers separate the huge popularity of the prints from their success or failure as art. Measured only in terms of breadth of circulation, the prints were undeniably successful. Judged in terms of artistry and honesty, they were far less so. But calculated in terms of impact, they were inarguably potent.

True, at various periods of peak interest in the 16th president between 1860 and 1865, when print portraitists could not keep pace with the public demand for new and original Lincolns, they resorted to obvious fakery, thinly disguised restrikes, deceitful revisions, and even outright piracy to sell their pictures. And even the most outlandish of these efforts appears to have been accepted on the market. But in fairness to the printmakers, it should be noted that Lincoln was a highly unstable subject. Four major and unexpected developments in his physical appearance and in the image of him held by the American people surfaced at odd intervals between 1860 and 1865. To printmakers, they were crises of unpreparedness. Each posed a distinct challenge to the image-makers, testing their skills, spontaneity, artistic integrity, and publishing efficiency. On a certain level, they did not always pass such tests. Honesty was not always the principle objective of craftsmen working under severe deadline pressure in races with competing firms for the honor, and considerable commercial advantage, of first publication.

Had Lincoln prints been in constant, rather than sporadic, demand, the print portraitists might have enjoyed the leisure to create more imaginative scenes and more faithful likenesses. But for most of 1861 and nearly all of 1862, then again in 1864 and the early part of 1865, Lincoln was not an especially popular subject.

The vast majority of Lincoln print images was inspired by the unexpected developments in his life and career, and, in turn, limited by the printmakers' understandable difficulty in responding. These factors explain in part why so much of Lincoln print portraiture, rushed to market under adverse conditions, was inaccurate, fabricated, or derivative. Many printmakers inevitably responded to public demand by rushing barely suitable works to market without the care one imagines they would have taken had Lincoln been a consistently popular pictorial subject throughout his career.

But whatever the degree of quality reflected in the output during each of these peak periods of demand, the degree of quantity was extraordinary. The speed and volume in which the printmakers sold their images indicated industriousness and ingenuity.

Of course, the first Lincoln image-makers benefited from technological and cultural transformations that made swift graphic response possible. Partisan politics, for example, required portrayals of candidates—not just those who had secured national fame. And photography made models readily available to printmakers. Unpreparedness could easily be overcome.

Where Lincoln was concerned, the first rush for Lincoln portraits coincided with his nomination for president. He unexpectedly emerged victorious from the 1860 Republican convention at the "Wigwam" in Chicago, defeating better-known rivals. Printmakers across the North frantically scrambled to create and supply images of the newly anointed nominee.[15]

ABRAHAM LINCOLN.

FROM A PHOTOGRAPH BY HESLER.

Fig. 44. F[ranklin]. H. Brown, *Abraham Lincoln/ From a Photograph by Hesler.* Woodcut engraving, Chicago, 1860 (The Lincoln Museum, Fort Wayne, Indiana).

Lincoln's subsequent victory in the November election might not in itself have triggered a second wave of demand for his pictures. But he again surprised the printmakers. Without warning, he began letting his whiskers grow, forcing printmakers to quickly revise now-obsolete plates and stones.[16]

Later, printmakers proved unprepared yet again for President Lincoln's momentous decision to issue the Emancipation Proclamation in September 1862. Had there been ample warning, printmakers might have assembled a more impressive body of commemorative work, and produced it more quickly. But, as before, Lincoln's decision came as a surprise and compelled the engravers and lithographers speedily to concoct their pictorial responses, while in this case reflecting some timidity about political, especially racial controversy. Many postponed their commemorative works until Lincoln's death transformed all of his acts into sacraments.

Finally, the shocking assassination of Lincoln in 1865 created the largest demand yet for his prints, now in poses suitable for a martyr and a myth.

These four events dictated the difficult conditions under which American printmakers were forced to see Lincoln and then quickly transfer their perceptions into pictures for the people. A detailed, sequential examination of each of these events and the prints published in response reveals little artistic integrity. Most were hastily modeled after existing, occasionally outdated, sources; many were clumsily reworked to disguise their antecedents. But to audiences with simple taste in art and uncomplicated reverence for the subject, such pictures reflected both a newsworthy sense of immediacy and a glory that gave many of the images icon status in the American home.

The mutually rewarding relationship between the printmakers and Abraham Lincoln began in 1860. Appropriately, the very first known Lincoln print was circulated at the precise moment Lincoln went over the top in the balloting for the Republican presidential nomination in Chicago in May 1860. As the decisive votes were announced for Lincoln in dramatic last-minute shifts of allegiance on the convention floor, Lincoln supporters in the galleries literally "showered" the hall with engravings of the new standard bearer *(Fig. 44)*. The prints, rudely colored wood engravings captioned only with Lincoln's name and the motto of his home state of Illinois, gave no specific indication that he was a presidential aspirant. Possibly, Lincoln supporters had commissioned the simple prints as delegate-swayers, but not necessarily for the spot at the head of the ticket (he had been a vice presidential aspirant four years earlier). The print's omissions have led some modern observers to suspect that, even as the convention neared, his boosters remained unsure of his strength and were willing to accept second place on the ticket. Had Lincoln been nominated for vice president and not president, the same print would undoubtedly have been distributed to delegates.[17]

The image itself was quite unremarkable. Based on an outdated, three-year-old photograph by Alexander Hesler *(Fig. 45)*, the crudely drawn image lacked detail save for a rather elaborate patriotic border. There had certainly been time, but perhaps not yet the motivation, to create a more sophisticated print. From then on, printmakers seldom again had the luxury of contemplation with

Fig. 45. Alexander Hesler, *[Abraham Lincoln]*. Photograph, Chicago, February 28, 1857 (The Lincoln Museum).

which to prepare their portraits of Lincoln.[18]

Lincoln had once admitted that the Hesler photographic model found little favor in his own home. His wife apparently disliked it, he explained, because of the "disordered condition of the hair." Lincoln had sat subsequently for several other, far more distinguished-looking photographs, especially once he began traveling about the state campaigning against Stephen A. Douglas for the United States Senate in 1858. It is tempting to speculate that the engraver of the so-called "Wigwam Print" showered on the 1860 convention delegates considered, but then rejected, these sleek alternatives. Perhaps he consciously chose the older, more rustic pose precisely because Lincoln's "wild Republican hair," in the descriptive words of one of its admirers, seemed especially suitable for illustrating the log-cabin-to–White House image his supporters were cleverly crafting in the candidate's behalf.[19]

For all its potential charm, the theory is bogus—and based on the wrong criterion: political. Printmakers were driven by convenience and commerce, not politics, and their choice of models was usually haphazard, not careful. Besides, accustomed as modern Lincoln students may be to viewing his photographs equally, it is unlikely that many of his early pictures found their way into the public domain until at least 1860, perhaps until 1861 with the invention of the widely available, multiple-copy *cartes-de-visite*. Early poses were almost always taken at the request of local Lincoln supporters or friends, in whose hands they sometimes remained until the pioneer Lincoln picture historians of the late 19th and early 20th centuries unearthed them and published them in their compilations,

without analyzing their relative prominence or obscurity in their own age.

In the case of the "Wigwam Print," whose source photo, too, had been commissioned by Lincoln's friends, it happened to be taken in Chicago, site of the 1860 presidential nominating convention and its attending flurry of excitement, and headquarters, also, of F. H. Brown, the engraver who adapted it. It is easy—and logical—to imagine Brown, hired at the time to quickly produce a Lincoln print, rushing to the studios of Alexander Hesler, the city's most prominent photographer, in search of a suitable model, current or not, which he could transform into a popular print. That is no doubt exactly how it happened—and why Hesler himself received the benefit, only occasionally provided photographers thereafter, of a credit ("From a Photograph by Hesler") within the caption of this print.

However the Hesler image came to be adapted for the graphic arts before any others, it certainly went on—either through Hesler's own initiatives or the immediate impact of the Brown woodcut—to inspire a number of additional adaptations by rival printmakers throughout the country. It seemed particularly appropriate as the model for a daub-like portrait of the very young Lincoln which the same F. H. Brown now depicted piloting a flatboat *(Fig. 46)*. This biographical image was used as the central scene in a crude, but information-laden broadside issued for the election campaign. Hesler's "tousled hair" photo inspired several additional campaign prints as well, from the grotesque campaign poster *(Fig. 47)* that showed Lincoln alongside his vice presidential running mate, Hannibal Hamlin (and much the worse for the comparison), to a

LINCOLN AS A FLATBOATMAN ON THE MISSISSIPPI RIVER.

QUINCY IN THE DISTANCE.

Peter the Great, to whose genius Russia owes her fame, served an apprenticeship to ship building. Abraham Lincoln has served an apprenticeship to flatboat-ing, and may he yet guide the Ship of State with his own inherent honesty of purpose.

Fig. 47. J. D. Lovett after photograph by Alexander Hesler, *Free Territory for a Free People./ A. Lincoln. H. Hamlin.* Woodcut engraving, New York, 1860 (Brown University Library).

Opposite: Fig. 46. F. H. Brown after E. Whitefield, *Lincoln as a Flatboatman on the Mississippi River./ Quincy in the Distance.* Woodcut engraving, published by Rufus Blanchard, Chicago, 1860 (Brown University Library).

surpassingly elegant rendition by New York engraver Thomas Doney *(Fig. 48)*, the last-named of which the printmaker proudly sent directly to the candidate, no doubt hoping for the potentially valuable personal endorsement it deserved.

He was surely disappointed by the response. "The picture (I know not the artistic designation) was duly and thankfully received," Lincoln wrote tersely to Doney. "I consider it a very excellent one," he added in his most expansive surviving comment on the printmaking genre, but going on to caution: "Truth to say, I am a very indifferent judge."[20]

Perhaps the most thought-provoking—even if not the most beautiful—adaptation of the irresistible Hesler photographic model was a symbol-laden engraving by Baker & Godwin of New York *(Fig. 49)*. A copy was registered at the Library of Congress in Washington on May 29, 1860, a scant 11 days after Lincoln's nomination as President—seemingly speedy work for image-makers of the day. But all the engravers did to create the print is dust off an old woodcut from Millard Fillmore's third-party White House run four years earlier *(Fig. 50)*, and insert Lincoln's image into the identical design. The anachronistic Fillmore symbolism—he had run on the anti–Catholic, anti-immigration "American Party" ticket—included scales of justice, a document labeled "Union," a statue of Liberty, a copy of the Constitution, and a hooded liberty pole, symbol of the manumission of slaves. Happily for the printmaker, all these ornaments seemed even more appropriate for Lincoln than they had been for his predecessor. It was the first—but not the last—time the head of a former head of state would be sup-

planted by Lincoln in the graphic arts.

However successful in conveying such rich messages visually, or even in merely portraying him with reasonable accuracy, all these pictures of the little-known nominee served in a sense to represent the candidate in the presidential race. True to tradition, Lincoln did no personal campaigning in the ensuing months (his rival Douglas, did: a rarity). Lincoln, on the other hand, depended solely on the proliferation of printed copies of his speeches, photographs, and engraved and lithographed portraits to campaign *for* him throughout the nation, just as he had depended upon a print to represent him at the Republican national convention he had chosen not to attend. He limited his campaign activity to greeting occasional visitors to Springfield, and writing letters pointedly declining to be drawn into partisan discourses. But voters wanted to see the new and controversial candidate, and it was left to the portraitists to prepare and distribute quantities of his prints for mass viewing—and reap the promising financial harvest in the bargain. Selling Lincoln pictorially proved to be politically necessary for the Republicans and commercially rewarding for the print-makers.[21]

In Lincoln, the engravers and lithographers found a subject who would be especially good for a business reaching the zenith of its potential, coincidentally, at precisely the same time Lincoln was doing the same. Lincoln's homeliness had been so widely reported and mocked that people now wanted these rumors confirmed or disproved pictorially. Nor did Lincoln's own supporters fail themselves to calculate the potential value of flattering print portraits. They sensed that idealized prints, especially those manufactured under the supervision of Lincoln's own election team, could dispel damaging stories about his appearance and help him build a more impressive majority in the fall elections. For the most part, however, the campaign images of Lincoln were marketplace phenomena, not campaign propaganda — independently conceived and sold by commercial publishers to meet public demand; quite different in this respect from today's headquarters-commissioned political posters, buttons, and bumper stickers.

In the rush to produce the first eagerly awaited Lincoln print portraits some engravers and lithographers commendably attempted to prepare altogether new and original work. Never again during the subsequent periods of demand for Lincoln prints was so much ambitious pictorial material published. Unfortunately, the majority of printmakers preferred to copy existing, readily available, inexpensive sources, and to rush the unimaginative results to the markets, setting the precedent for speed, not style, that dictated the manner in which most print portraitists would portray Lincoln in the future.

In the initial period of demand for Lincoln pictures, though, several printmakers commissioned artists to travel to Springfield to paint life portraits from which engravings and lithographs could be modeled. W. H. Schaus and Company, a New York print publisher and distributor, sent a Boston-born artist, Thomas Hicks (1823–1890), to travel west to produce one such effort. Inspired by the enthusiasm of publisher Horace Greeley, who said of Lincoln, "There . . . is a good head to go before the people," and armed with a letter of introduction from Greeley's assistant Charles A. Dana, Hicks convinced the candidate to sit for him and thereupon

produced the very first painting of Lincoln from life. One of the best lithographers of the period, Parisian-born Leopold Grozelier, drew the painting on stone, and his print became an immediate best-seller.[22]

Not long after this experience, John Meredith Read, a wealthy Pennsylvania jurist and leader of the state's Republican party, fearing that the "horrible caricatures" of Lincoln would cause the Republicans to lose his state unless misconceptions about the candidate's appearance were corrected, offered the princely sum of $175 plus expenses to send Philadelphia artist John Henry Brown (1818–1891) to Springfield to paint a model for a print. Brown, who was best known as a miniaturist, arrived in August, immediately arranged to have special photographs of Lincoln made for his use as models, and painted a precise miniature on ivory. Lincoln's personal secretary, John G. Nicolay, helped supervise the production of Samuel Sartain's mezzotint engraving of the Brown painting *(Fig. 51)*. Nicolay knew that Read wanted a "good looking" likeness on the print "whether the original would justify it or not." Lincoln himself thought the highly romanticized result "without fault" — or so he wrote the artist. Whether the publication of the equally flattering Sartain print adaptation had an ameliorating effect on voters remains unproved; however, Lincoln received a decisive 56 percent of the votes cast in Pennsylvania and thus secured its 27 electorial votes.[23]

Yet another print publisher who sent an artist to Springfield was C. H. Brainard of Boston. He dispatched a young local painter, Thomas Johnston (1834–1869), predicting that "everyone will be clamorous for the picture" he planned to create from life sittings. But

Fig. 48. Thomas Doney after photograph by Alexander Hesler, *Yours truly/ A. Lincoln* (facsimile signature]. Mezzotint engraving, published by William Pate, New York, 1860 (Library of Congress).

the print adaptations that Brainard ultimately published *(Fig. 52)* remained obscure, possibly because it looked so informal. Far better known was an effort by the same artist-publisher team to offer a lithograph of a standard but outdated photograph.[24]

Sadly, many of the finer life portraits made during this period of Lincoln's career were never adapted into print portraits. G. P. A. Healy's magnificent 1860 profile, for example, and George Frederick Wright's full-face portrait (which Lincoln himself liked well enough to buy), were neither engraved nor lithographed. Those print publishers who staked the money and allowed time to commission painters to produce life portraits during this period of peak demand deserve much praise. The print portraits that these men produced boasted genuine originality, and their ambitious printmakers spared neither effort nor funds to make them so.[25]

Most printmakers invested considerably less capital and even less time in crafting Lincoln campaign images during this period of intense curiosity about the new presidential nominee. Such publishers were content merely to adapt period photographs into prints, sometimes adding color or new backgrounds to disguise the antecedents. These publishers preferred speed to originality. And because they chose the path of least resistance to creating and distributing their prints, many of their Lincoln portraits reached the public long before the more ambitious prints based on life portraits of the candidate.

A Samuel M. Fassett photograph taken in Chicago in 1859 *(Fig. 53)*, and reportedly a particular favorite of Mary Lincoln's, became one of the most frequently adapted models. Its appeal attracted Chicago lithographer Edward Mendel, who produced a handsome

vignetted oval *(Fig. 54)* that corrected the sole flaw in the Fassett original: an akimbo shirt collar that seemed to have a mind of its own. Similar cosmetic remedies were applied to the adaptation lithographed by the Ehrgott, Forbriger Company for the cover of a campaign songsheet entitled the *Lincoln Polka (Fig. 55)*. For this effort, the printmakers not only straightened out the collar, they added flesh to Lincoln's neck—which had looked decidedly scrawny in the photographic model.[26]

In the fierce competition for customers, printmakers could ill afford to publish only straightforward portraiture, however romanticized. But with little time to create exotic scenes in which to place Lincoln in order to make their prints appear more unique, several printmakers—not only the aforementioned Baker & Godwin—superimposed Lincoln's head on portraits of famous men of earlier eras to create some of the most anomalous hybrid images in 19th century iconography. Another revealing case in point could trace its roots all the way back to a long-forgotten engraving of Daniel Webster by Woodcock & Harvey of New York, published by Charles Thomas & Co. a generation earlier *(Fig. 56)*. The print was designed to celebrate Webster's honesty, and did so by showing the legendary figure Diogenes at last finding in the Massachusetts Senator the honest man for whom he had so long been searching. In the background, a symbolic pillar of state dominated a scene that included the place where Webster earned his fame, the United States Capitol. By 1860, of course, the image had little appeal for American audiences, so one clever printmaker redrew it on a lithographic stone, and replaced Webster's image with Lincoln's, modeling it after

ABRAHAM LINCOLN,

REPUBLICAN CANDIDATE FOR PRESIDENT OF THE UNITED STATES.

an obscure but arresting 1860 Alexander Hesler photograph *(Fig. 57)*, and thus producing a "new" image of Lincoln with Diogenes *(Fig. 58)* that neatly illustrated the candidate's own emerging reputation as "Honest Abe." Here was an even more appropriate discovery for Diogenes than Webster (even if the once suggestive sight of the capitol now had little meaning for a politician who had spent but a single, undistinguished term in Congress).

By mid-campaign, all these photographic models—and all their many adaptations—had become so common that some printmakers began issuing mirror-image variants to give a new "look" to their stale interpretations. They apparently failed to realize, or thought it of little importance, that as a result of such trickery, Lincoln's distinguishing and increasingly recognizable facial mole would appear on the wrong cheek. Nonetheless, the practice proliferated. Even Currier & Ives of New York, the industry leader among American lithographers, issued such reverse images *(Fig. 59)*—sometimes of their very own portraits—in an effort to manufacture "new" poses. Lincoln's familiar facial markings were unavoidably transposed in all of them.[27]

Of all the photographic models adapted by engravers and lithographers during the 1860 campaign, none had as much appeal and ubiquity—at least judging from the vast number and variety of prints it inspired—as the extraordinarily influential photograph taken by Mathew Brady in New York City during Lincoln's February 1860 trip east to speak at the Cooper Union *(Fig. 60)*. Brady later all but claimed

credit for electing Lincoln single-handedly by producing the flattering likeness. What is seldom recalled is that in its own time the image achieved little distribution as a photograph. Its widespread visibility came in its various engraved and lithographed adaptations, not as a camera portrait. The image was copied, with and without permission, by a host of printmakers, and quickly began appearing in media aimed at all tastes and pocketbooks: woodcuts in the picture weeklies, smeary lithographs available for nickels and dimes, elegant (and expensive) engravings, and illustrations for hastily issued campaign biographies—not to mention cartoons and caricatures.[28]

One printmaker who made considerable use of the photograph was John Chester Buttre of New York. Displaying all the nonpartisan commercial zeal typical of his era and his profession, he issued portraits of *all* the 1860 presidential candidates, "beautifully engraved on steel," he advertised *(Fig. 61)*, and nearly all based on "Brady's Celebrated photographs." The prints, the advertisement boasted, were "reliable for their correctness and beauty of execution," and "suitable for framing or preserving in portfolios."[29]

Buttre also produced what he called *The Dime Picture of Hon. Abraham Lincoln (Fig. 62)*, based on the Brady photograph, and now "printed on the finest enamel card, about 4 × 6 inches in size," and available postage free in its own special envelope. "Every member of the LINCOLN CLUBS, throughout the United States," its advertisement trumpeted, "should possess a copy of this little gem." Finally,

Opposite: Fig. 49. **Baker & Godwin after photograph by Alexander Hesler,** *Abraham Lincoln,/ Republican Candidate for President of the United States.* **Woodcut engraving, New York, 1860 (Library of Congress).**

MILLARD FILLMORE,

AMERICAN CANDIDATE FOR PRESIDENT OF THE UNITED STATES.

ENGRAVED BY SAMUEL SARTAIN AFTER THE MINIATURE FROM LIFE BY J.HENRY BROWN, IN THE POSSESSION OF JUDGE READ.

A. Lincoln

Fig. 51. Samuel Sartain after painting by John Henry Brown and photograph by Preston Butler, *A. Lincoln* [facsimile signature]. Mezzotint engraving, Philadelphia, 1860 (The Lincoln Museum).

Opposite: Fig. 50. Baker & Godwin, *Millard Fillmore,/ American Candidate for President of the United States.* Woodcut engraving [model for *Fig. 49*], New York, 1856 (Library of Congress).

Fig. 52. D. C. Fabronius after Thomas M. Johnston, *Lincoln and Hamlin.* Printed by J. H. Bufford, designed by J. N. Hyde, published by C. H. Brainard, Boston, 1860 (Library of Congress).

Buttre offered for 50 cents a 32-page booklet featuring portraits and biographical sketches of all four presidential candidates, highlights from the various party platforms and the full text of the Constitution.[30]

The New York engraver was clearly covering all his bases, but his emphasis was on Lincoln. Proof could be found in Buttre's 50-cent book of biographies, with several pages of advertisements for the publisher's other offerings. While these highlighted something for virtually everyone (a separate portrait of candidate John C. Breckenridge, for example; 10-cent satin portrait badges of all the nominees; and several Washington portraits

as well), much of the space was reserved to promote new Lincoln images.
There was a self-proclaimed "superb"
full-length, 19 by 26 inch mezzotint that
would surely "add much to the appearance of every Lincoln Club room in the
United States," priced from $3 to $6
(the higher price included a pearl-and-
gilt or rosewood-and-gilt frame). Then
there was a 25 cent, 11 by 15 inch
engraving of Lincoln's old Kentucky
home, a vivid "contrast to the White
House," its publisher acknowledged,
and yet "an exquisite picture, engraved
on steel, from an ambrotype, taken on
the spot, of the cabin where Abraham
Lincoln once lived." Not only were
Lincoln images being marketed to decorate the American family hearthplace,
but nostalgic looks at Lincoln's own
ramshackle family homes were taking
their place in these domestic galleries as
well. Not all Lincoln images, however,
would be quite so reverential.[31]

Currier & Ives, for example, seek-
ing advantage for none of the candidates, just for themselves, used the
aforementioned Cooper Union Brady
not only for romanticized portraits
calculated to appeal to his admirers,
but for separate-sheet cartoons that
ridiculed the candidate as effectively as
the portraits flattered him.

This particular genre can be all
too easily overlooked, especially in a
comparative study presenting Lincoln
imagery alongside the portraits of
George Washington, a man who inspired little opposition, and even less
caricature. But the frenzied 1860 campaign, with four nominees in the
field—not only Lincoln and his longtime rival Douglas, but John Bell and
John C. Breckenridge—unleashed a
frenzy of campaign activity nationwide.
Separate sheet cartoons fueled the
heated contest, although iconographers

have been unable ever since to recon-
struct with precision just how such lampoons, with their verbose word bal-
loons, were used (for display at rallies?
at taverns? on billboards?). Whatever
their precise "decorative" purpose—and
these were not cartoons in newspapers
but separately printed display items—
an abundance of examples flowed from
the presses during the 1860 race. And it
was anything but unusual for a firm
such as Currier & Ives to publish not
only display portraits of Lincoln (and
for that matter, opponent Douglas), but
also cartoons comfortably assailing one,
the other, or both. The publisher was
nonpartisan—devoted to only one campaign, the race for profit. Audiences of
all political persuasions were to be provided images they could cherish—or
laugh at.

The Great Exhibition of 1860, for example *(Fig. 63),* its Lincoln likeness
based loosely on Hesler's tousled-hair
photograph, depicted railsplitter Lincoln uncomfortably straddling a symbolic rail (quickly emerging as a
familiar device in Lincoln imagery),
playing the silent monkey to New York
publisher Horace Greeley's organ
grinder, his lips sealed by padlock to
suggest that his campaign was avoiding
the divisive slavery issue (his one-time
rival for the Republican nomination,
William Seward, is relegated to the
background and in female disguise to
keep the public from recognizing who
is cradling the symbolic black infant in
his arms). Yet a quite flattering Currier
& Ives cartoon, *The National Game (Fig.
64),* could convincingly use the same
symbolic rail, this time to mock Lincoln's opponents. In the baseball contest
it portrays, Lincoln's rail has proved
unbeatable against Bell, Douglas, and
Breckenridge. Lincoln (his portrait
again based on Hesler) stands firmly on

Fig. 53. **Samuel M. Fassett, *[Abraham Lincoln]*. Photograph, Chicago, October 4, 1859.**

home plate, "fair ball" in hand, his "good bat" (the rail is labeled "equal rights and free territory") having helped him prevail. Douglas can only lament that he had expected the "fusion" of Lincoln's three opponents to be a "'short stop' to his career."

Currier & Ives' cartoons were among the most sophisticated, clever, and expertly rendered of the campaign, which boasted its share of crude caricature as well. In the pro–Breckenridge *The Undecided Political Prize Fight* **(Fig. 65)**, for instance, an unidentified printmaker depicted Lincoln and Douglas as swarthy boxers, their equally unappealing supporters (racist caricatures of blacks and Irishmen, respectively), filling out the scene. Visible in the background is Breckenridge, thumbing his nose and gesturing decisively toward his own destination—the White House. Conversely, the same unknown artist may have been responsible for an untitled print **(Fig. 66)** showing three of the four presidential aspirants tearing apart a map of the country, each claiming a region for himself at the expense of the whole. It is left to National Union candidate John Bell (far right), to try nobly to use then-popular Spalding's Glue to paste the map back together. Like most period cartoons, especially Currier & Ives', it based its Lincoln portrait on the overused Cooper Union photo, whose rather dignified expression tended to appear all the more ridiculous when attached to a scrawny, long-legged body.[32]

The popular Brady model had other incarnations as well, particularly as the central pose on several campaign banners and broadsides—including one that literally changed the face of history. Publisher H. H. Lloyd of New York used the Cooper Union photograph as a model for Lincoln's portrait in the *National Republican Chart* **(Fig. 67)**, an extraordinary lithographed broadside that printed the entire Republican party platform, along with select Lincoln quotations and key demographic statistics, all in one impressive 3 foot by 2 foot poster. It was a copy of this very broadside that inspired 11-year-old Grace Bedell of Westfield, New York, to write her leg-endary letter to Abraham Lincoln, promising him at least a few extra votes ("part of" those of her father and brothers) were he merely to improve his appearance by growing whiskers. Lincoln politely dismissed the suggestion in a charming letter of response, suggesting that if he were to sprout a beard so late in life people would think him affected. Yet soon after he won the election clean-shaven, he began to grow a beard after all.[33]

The legend that grew up around Grace Bedell's influence on Lincoln is undoubtedly inflated. But the story of the H. H. Lloyd poster's influence on Grace Bedell is well-documented (she particularly liked the split-rail motif that framed the candidate's portrait). It suggests the importance such images held in the picture-hungry society of the 1860s. And there is poetic justice in the fact that Lincoln's revolutionary tonsorial decision (he was the first president to wear a beard) was inspired by a print portrait, because as a result, the printmakers suddenly faced a new challenge to provide up-to-date prints of Lincoln.

The engravers and lithographers no doubt planned to continue marketing their existing campaign prints of the newly elected Lincoln, which would have required only revised captions to reflect the president-elect's new status. In fact, several unsuspecting printmakers had already begun publishing pictures depicting Lincoln as president *without* whiskers. London engraver D. J. Pound issued a prettified version of the clean-shaven Brady Cooper Union pose, and captioned it *President Lincoln.* So did Currier and Ives **(see Fig. 59)**. But Lincoln's decision, in the words of one reporter, to put on "(h)airs," rendered such portraits obsolete, and excited new curiosity among

Fig. 54. Edw[ard]. Mendel after photograph by Fassett, *Abraham Lincoln*. Signed: [Dominique] *Fabronius*. Lithograph, Chicago, 1860 (Library of Congress).

his admirers. The people simply wanted to see what he now looked like.[34]

Even if they knew about Lincoln's beard — which is doubtful — printmakers were so unprepared for, or annoyed by its arrival that none sent artists to Springfield to record the change in appearance. No one even bothered to send artists to sketch the new beard when his train passed through their cities en route to Washington for the inauguration in early 1861. Instead, the graphic artists guessed haphazardly at the style of beard Lincoln ultimately might grow and published their pictorial forecasts in a variety of colors, shapes, and sizes, usually imposing a beard onto existing prints without comparing the results with Lincoln's true appearance.[35]

Perhaps Lincoln had some of the more grotesque beardless print portraits uppermost in mind when he finally made the decision to let his whiskers grow. He certainly had additional letters urging him to do so. Just three days before Grace Bedell wrote her famous note to Lincoln, a New York group signing itself "True Republicans" sent him the following:

> Dear Sir: Allow a number of very earnest Republicans to intimate to you, that after oft-repeated views of the daguerreo-types; which we wear as tokens of our devotedness to you; we have come to the candid determination that these medals would be much improved in appearance, provided you would cultivate whiskers and wear standing collars.
>
> Believe us nothing but an earnest desire that 'our candidate' should be the best looking as well as the best of the rival candidates, would induce us to trespass upon your valued time.[36]

No one knows what the clean-shaven Republican nominee said or

thought when he read this carefully worded suggestion. The anonymous letter-writers had been both respectful and subtle. They did not suggest that Lincoln himself needed to improve his appearance; they suggested only that his campaign *likenesses* would look far better if *they* had a beard.

Surely this was not the first time the lantern-jawed politician had been told he was not the handsomest man around. Posing for one painter during the campaign, he had pleaded jocularly to be painted with false whiskers to hide his jutting chin, lamenting with mock-seriousness, "it is allowed to be ugly in this world, but not as ugly as I am."[37]

Lincoln could afford such jokes in his circuit-riding or local political days. But by the time he was nominated for the presidency, national campaigns had changed. They demanded of their participants a curious blend of public silence and public visibility (through the circulation of photographs, prints, and campaign tokens). And in the 1860 campaign, with Republicans eagerly celebrating Lincoln's inspiring rise from poverty and his prowess as a frontier railsplitter — far more often than they celebrated his political views — such images became more crucial than ever. Nevertheless, while encouraging artists who wanted to pose him — most of whom created flattering images upon which appropriately misleading popular prints were crafted and circulated — Lincoln apparently resolved to do nothing to make a drastic change. And then came the October letters from his supporters.

Respectful as it was, the letter from the group of "True Republicans" ended with an ominous postscript: "We really fear votes will be lost to 'the cause' unless our 'gentle hints' are

Fig. 55. [Peter E.] Ehrgott, [Adolphus] Forbriger & Co. after photograph by Fassett, *Lincoln Polka*. Lithographed songsheet cover, published by J. Church, Jr., Cincinnati, 1860.

attended to." Three days later came yet another "gentle hint"—this the famous letter from Grace Bedell, moved to write to the candidate after her father brought home a homely picture of Lincoln and his running mate, Hannibal Hamlin, from a local county fair.[38]

I "want you should be President of the United States very much," she wrote in her charming letter. "I hope you won't think me very bold to write such a great man as you are.... I have got 4 brother's [sic] and part of them will vote for you any way and if you will let your whiskers grow I will try and get the rest of them to vote for you. [Y]ou would look a great deal better for your face is so thin. All the ladies like whiskers and they would get their husband's [sic] to vote for you, and then you would be President." Just four days later, Lincoln replied with his classic note. "As to the whiskers," he asked gently, "do you not think people would call it a piece of silly affect[at]ion if I were to begin it now?"[39]

And yet, as every school child then and since well knows, "begin" it did. Only a few weeks after his election in November, Lincoln began letting his whiskers fill in, affectation or not. Photographs made on November 25 and February 9, the latter two days before he left Springfield on his train trip to Washington for his inauguration, record the progress of the tonsorial change, and suggest that his correspondents were right. Lincoln did look better with a beard. Overnight, he transformed himself from the railsplitter who attracted widespread enthusiasm from voters, to the dignified statesman meant to attract widespread confidence from the nation. He was the first Republican president. He would also be the first bearded president.[40]

But Lincoln's decision to grow a beard was far easier reported than recorded. As a presidential candidate eager to see his image widely distributed during a campaign (and with not much else to occupy his time while waiting for the campaign to end), Lincoln was a willing sitter to artists and sculptors. He became increasingly unavailable as the date for his departure neared. (A bust by Thomas D. Jones, made in Springfield during these last days as president-elect, was the first to show him with a beard, and the last to depict him in his home town.)

Now picture publishers experienced another surge of audience demand, but had not so willing a model. Just as in the campaign, when Americans eagerly sought pictures of the dark horse aspirant who somehow had won the Republican nomination, now they sought new pictures of his new image. But with no original paintings or widely distributed photos to work from, printmakers had little choice but to make feeble artistic guesses at Lincoln's new appearance. Most had clearly only read about Lincoln's beard. They had not seen it.

Thus, while the first photograph of Lincoln in Washington *(Fig. 68)*, later a favorite model for printmakers, especially in Europe, showed him wearing the bushiest beard he would feature for the rest of his life, prints of the same period offered wildly divergent impressions of the new presidential whiskers. The comical surviving results offer glimpses into the way in which 19th century printmakers were able to deceive 19th century audiences long before the modern media—instantaneous photography, rotogravure printing, film and television—made a president's slightest alteration in image instantly visible to millions, and instantly subject to study, analysis, and criticism. (One

Fig. 56. Woodcock & Harvey after James Frothingham, *Diogones his Lantern needs no more./ An honest man is found! the search is o'er.* Engraving, printed by Charles Thomas & Co., 1838 (National Portrait Gallery, Smithsonian Institution).

recalls, for example, the hasty explanations required of modern White House spin doctors when Ronald Reagan showed up unexpectedly one day with a tiny abrasion on his nose, where a small skin cancer had been quietly—or such was the plan—removed.)

The "bearding of the president," oddly enough, gave new life to the now four-year-old Hesler "Wigwam" image. Only now, Thomas Doney was obliged to alter his 1860 adaptation *(see Fig. 48)* with the superimposition of a devilish-looking goatee *(Fig. 69)*. It was but one of many such Lincolns—coarsely bearded, side-whiskered, and fuzzychinned—suddenly circulated to a curious and apparently gullible and undiscriminating public.

Did the "new" Lincoln really take America by such surprise? Schooled only by the relentless 20th century media, and its incessant close-up look of our leaders, modern audiences may find it difficult to imagine such a response. But as Lincoln slowly made his way east, and then south toward Washington and his inauguration in 1861, there was ample evidence that his whiskers did indeed create attention as well as perplexity.

At one point his train pulled into Albany, the capital of New York State, causing a riot of "confusion, hurry, and disorder" as residents thronged the railroad tracks to get a look at the newly elected president. But even with excitement "intense," Lincoln's first appearance outside his railroad car served only to elicit befuddled stares and "a faint cheer." "Standing uncovered there," a reporter on the scene explained, "the President was barely recognized by the crowd, and anxiety to see him and to be certain that they saw the right man overcame any disposition to cheer. When the eyes of the people were so very wide open it is no wonder that their mouths remained shut and that Mr. Lincoln was not cheered. . . . Lincoln, tired, sunburned, adorned with huge whiskers, looked so unlike the hale, smooth shaven, redcheeked individual who is represented upon the popular prints and is dubbed the 'rail-splitter' that the people did not recognize him until his extreme height distinguished him unmistakably."[41]

In the intense competition that followed—an effort virtually to reintroduce Lincoln pictorially—printmakers rushed out an astonishing variety of pictures, in the process occasionally compounding one piece of trickery with another, one bit of artistic piracy with a second, in an almost shameless effort to reach the public speedily, however inaccurate the results.

A good example can be found in the laughable genesis of a print called *Union,* which was first issued in 1852—eight years before Lincoln became a major subject in American prints. In fact, the central figure of *Union (see Fig. 100)* was not Lincoln at all, but John C. Calhoun, a man whose ardently held pro–Southern view on the acceptability of secession were antithetical to Lincoln's. But the print was originally issued to celebrate political compromise, not political confrontation, and thus Calhoun was given prominence, along with Henry Clay and Daniel Webster, the other United States Senate giants of that era.

For nearly a decade after its initial publication, the print *Union* was all but forgotten, the steel plate on which it had been engraved no doubt stored away. Then came the campaign of 1860, and a printmaker hatched an extraordinary, almost comical scheme to revive it. Relocating the long-forgotten

Fig. 57. Alexander Hesler, *[Abraham Lincoln].* Photograph, Springfield, Illinois, June 3, 1860 (The Lincoln Museum).

plate, the enterprising printmaker simply dusted it off, burnished out Calhoun's head, and superimposed Lincoln's (based on Brady) onto what was left of the long-dead Senator. Overnight, a new *Union* was born *(see Fig. 101)* with Lincoln suddenly the central character in the group, some modern-day celebrities added, but the old notables of the previous decade (Clay and Webster among them) still visible.

It must have been a source of great curiosity to Lincoln, if he saw this print. Henry Clay was his "beau ideal" of a statesman. Lincoln had given a memorial oration for him when he died. While some of his recent psychobiographers have asserted that Lincoln had a healthy enough ego to permit him early to view himself as a natural successor to the founding fathers, surely it would have startled him to see himself standing alongside one of his own mid-century heroes in the second state of the stubbornly long-lived print called *Union.*[42]

But the story did not die there. Once Lincoln grew his beard, this bizarre revision was also rendered obsolete. But with so much time and effort already invested, the printmaker could hardly afford to allow the mere addition of post-election whiskers to make his reprint unsaleable. Inevitably, *Union,* too, grew a beard, in a third version of the scene still featuring the celebrities of the bygone era, now alongside the curiously dressed, now-unconvincingly bewhiskered Lincoln. In fact, if viewers looked closely at Lincoln's head, they could perhaps make out an odd halo encircling his head like a bloated nimbus. This was no artistic flourish. It was the burnished-out remains of John C. Calhoun's impressive mane of white hair, vaguely visible in this unusual "bearded" Lincoln image *(see Fig. 102).*

For a surprisingly long time—even after more accurate models became available to them courtesy of Lincoln's frequent visits to photographic galleries in Washington during the Civil War—many American printmakers and photographers persisted in issuing endless variations on the clean-shaven Lincoln, with beards superimposed.

Even after his assassination, mourning photographs flooded the nation showing Lincoln as he had looked in an outdated 1858 C. S. German photograph, for one, with an uncharacteristic blob of a beard added. These efforts now seemed especially unrealistic, since during the war Lincoln aged markedly, grew more weary-looking, lost considerable weight in his face, and trimmed his beard down to little more than a goatee. Nevertheless, with a public apparently insatiable in its appetite for Lincoln portraits, yet undiscerning in its choices, the beard-on-beardless pictures remained viable and popular.

Long before then, Lincoln surely understood the intense curiosity his decision to grow a beard had inspired among Americans. In a masterful public relations move, he even reached out personally to acknowledge the person whom historians have since embraced as the single greatest influence on Lincoln's altered image.

On his inaugural journey east in 1861, Lincoln's train pulled into Westfield, New York. Grace Bedell was part of the throng on hand, no doubt as eager as the rest of the community to catch a brief glimpse of the next President. Conceivably, like the citizens of Albany a few days later, she did not even know that Lincoln had belatedly taken her tonsorial advice. But when the train pulled in and Lincoln made his appearance, she undoubtedly approved of what she saw. Here was the

Fig. 58. Printmaker unknown after Woodcock & Harvey and photograph by Hesler, *Diogenes his lantern needs no more./ An honest man is found! the search is o'er.* [2nd state of *Fig. 56;* a third state, with Lincoln bearded, was issued by H. B. Hall in 1865] (Library of Congress).

Fig. 59. Currier & Ives after photograph by Mathew B. Brady, *Abraham Lincoln,/ Sixteenth President of the United States.* Lithograph, New York, 1860 (The Lincoln Museum).

Fig. 60. Mathew B. Brady, *[Abraham Lincoln].* Photograph, New York, February 27, 1860 (The Lincoln Museum).

PORTRAITS AND SKETCHES

OF THE

Hon. J. C. BRECKINRIDGE

AND THE

Hon. JOSEPH LANE.

IN ONE NEAT 8vo. PRICE 25 CTS.

IT CONTAINS

TWO PORTRAITS BEAUTIFULLY ILLUSTRATED ON STEEL, FACTS IN THE LIFE
OF EACH, THE NATIONAL DEMOCRATIC PLATFORM , THE
CINCINNATI PLATFORM, AND

THE CONSTITUTION OF THE UNITED STATES.

Published by J. C. BUTTRE,

48 FRANKLIN STREET, NEW-YORK.

Copies sent by mail, postage prepaid, on receipt of the price.

AGENTS WANTED.

THE DIME PICTURE

OF

Hon. ABRAHAM LINCOLN,

Beautifully engraved on steel, and printed on the finest enamel
card, about 4 x 6 inches in size. It is neatly enclosed in an envelope, ready for delivery, or to send by mail.

Every member of the LINCOLN CLUBS throughout the United
States should possess a copy of this little gem.

It is sent free by mail on receipt of the price,

ONE DIME.

Engraved and Published by J. C. BUTTRE,

48 Franklin Street, New-York.

☞ A GOOD PICTURE FOR AGENTS TO SELL.

Fig. 61. Advertisement for *THE DIME PICTURE of Hon. ABRAHAM LINCOLN,* published
by J[ohn]. C[hester]. Buttre, New York, 1860.

Fig. 62. J. C. Buttre after photograph by Mathew B. Brady, *A. Lincoln* [facsimile signature]. Engraving, New York, 1860 (The Lincoln Museum).

once painfully thin face, covered with luxuriant whiskers, just as she had advised. "I am glad to see you," Lincoln told the crowd. "I suppose you are to see me, but I certainly think I have the best of the bargain." Applause rang out. Then he added: "Some three months ago I received a letter from a young lady here; it was a very pretty letter, and she advised me to let my whiskers grow, as it would improve my personal appearance. Acting partly upon her suggestion, I have done so; and now, if she is here, I would like to see her." The crowd quickly pointed out Grace Bedell, and Lincoln invited her to come forward to meet him. When he met her face to face, he lifted her in his arms, kissed her repeatedly, and then, bidding Westfield farewell, returned to his car "amid the yells of delight from the excited crowd."[43]

America's image-makers had a difficult time contending with the results of Grace Bedell's advice, but surely they wound up profiting by it. Had Lincoln not given them a new reason to issue pictures, the demand for Lincoln images would have dwindled after the 1860 election. His new beard gave rise to new curiosity, and much as it confounded the image-makers, it revived a dormant marketplace. Lincoln profited, too. His image was permanently changed, from that of the frontier hero to national paterfamilias. At last he was ready to take his place alongside the founding fathers. And in post-assassination pictures that portrayed him side by side with Washington, as the "founder and preserver of the Union," he would do so.

Yet it must have been something of a relief to the printmakers that by the time Lincoln's whiskers and administration were finally in place, public demand for the president's image

slackened again. In fact, interest ebbed to such a degree that one early Currier & Ives Civil War print, *Soldier's Memorial,* depicted as the central figure not the president, but General-in-chief Winfield Scott. Lincoln was relegated to the left-hand corner of the lithograph—almost as an afterthought, or a reluctant concession to protocol.

There were exceptions to the sudden indifference, but they were neither memorable nor, judging from their rarity today, particularly popular. J. H. Bufford's group, *President Lincoln & Cabinet (Fig. 70),* issued as a premium for subscribers of the *Watchman & Reflector,* did depict the new president slightly larger, and in the central position among his ministers—the Lincoln portrait based on an aforementioned Alexander Gardner photograph *(see Fig. 68).* Yet it managed to make the new chief executive appear dreamy and rather detached, not inspiring, his vapid expression contrasting with the grim visages of his cabinet secretaries. Far more memorable was the hostile image *(Fig. 71)* crafted by Copperhead Baltimore dentist-etcher, Dr. Adalbert Volck, whose anti–Union, pro–Confederate prints were printed secretly during the war, and distributed to a small core of like-minded friends in that city. Their reputation was made by postwar circulation and later accolades for their obvious skill.[44]

Volck seized on the story that Lincoln had donned a disguise—a scotch cap and military cap—to pass secretly through Baltimore en route to his 1861 inauguration in order to foil a rumored assassination plot. In truth, Lincoln had merely exchanged his familiar stovepipe hat for a slouch hat, but by the time Volck was finished interpreting the scene, Lincoln was in full disguise, cowering pathetically in a

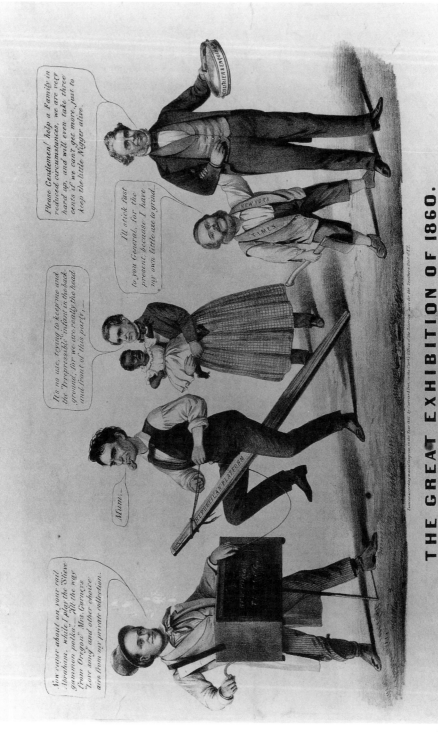

THE GREAT EXHIBITION OF 1860.

freight car at the mere sight of a hissing cat.

However clever, it is questionable whether even Volck's masterful lampoons, had they been openly available, would have found a particularly interested audience in 1861. For when the first guns of the Civil War were fired, not only did Lincoln immediately and automatically lose whatever small, curious audience he might have retained in the South, but for a time he lost appeal as well for Northerners now stated with Lincoln pictures, and far more fascinated with the early heroes and martyrs of the Rebellion.

Lincoln picture production came to an abrupt, albeit temporary standstill. In their place, portraits of "newer faces" abounded. Engravings and lithographs of Major Robert Anderson, the brave defender of Fort Sumter; the Napoleonic Union commander George B. McClellan; and Elmer E. Ellsworth, the handsome young Zouave who became the Union's first casualty, shot dead during a valiant effort to take down a Confederate flag near Washington, now flooded the North. Lincoln print production all but ceased. But not for long.[45]

The situation changed abruptly in September 1862, when Lincoln publicly announced that he had written a preliminary draft of a proclamation of emancipation. The president's response to Horace Greeley's plea for immediate abolition had recently been published in the *New York Tribune*. In it Lincoln implied that such would not be his immediate policy. His subsequent reversal of policy took publisher Greeley, the public, and the printmakers by surprise.[46]

To their credit, the engravers and lithographers at once realized the importance — to the slaves, to the war effort, and not least of all, to themselves — of Lincoln's edict. Having triggered the mechanism that ultimately would free an entire race, having redefined the war both militarily and morally into a crusade against human bondage, Lincoln now inspired a number of worshipful new print portraits. He had secured for himself a place in history and the printmakers would move to market it. The new image of Abraham Lincoln as the "great emancipator" was nurtured in prints, with an impact against which no other medium could compete.

July 22, 1862, was the historic day Abraham Lincoln first read the Emancipation Proclamation to his Cabinet. Exactly two years later — on July 22, 1864 — Lincoln was presiding over yet another Cabinet session, and yet again, the subject of the Emancipation Proclamation came up, this time in a different but related way.

Lincoln adjourned the meeting and led the Cabinet into the State Dining Room. There, set up on display for their inspection, was artist Francis B. Carpenter's newly completed painting of the momentous session two years earlier: *The First Reading of the Emancipation Proclamation Before the Cabinet.*

There were a few grumbles from the ministers — Secretary of the Treasury Salmon P. Chase, for example, reportedly did not like the prominence the artist assigned to Secretary of State William H. Seward — but artist Carpenter remembered that Lincoln told him that there was "little to find fault with.

Opposite: Fig. 63. **Currier & Ives after Mathew B. Brady,** *The Great Exhibition of 1860* [probably drawn on stone by Louis Maurer]. **Lithograph, New York, 1860 (The Lincoln Museum).**

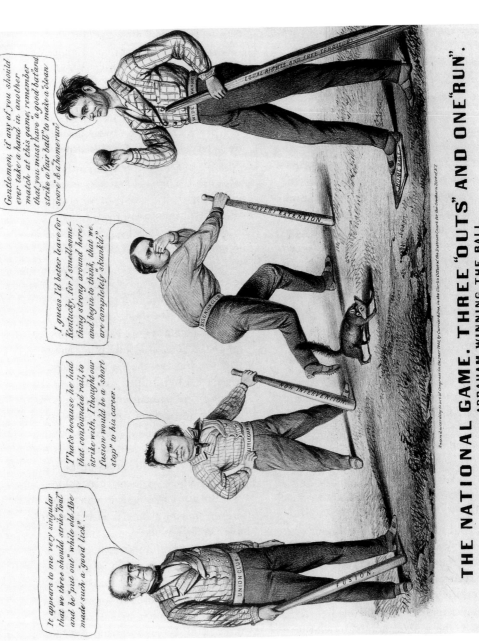

THE NATIONAL GAME. THREE "OUTS" AND ONE "RUN".
ABRAHAM WINNING THE BALL.

The portraiture is the main thing, and that seems to me absolutely perfect . . . it is as good as it can be made." With Lincoln's approval, the private viewing for the Cabinet was followed by a two-day public exhibition in the East Room. Carpenter remembered a White House "thronged with visitors." Or so Carpenter — a far better self-promoter than he was a painter — would later claim.[47]

One visitor who came to have a look at the canvas was journalist Noah Brooks. And while he admitted in his published review that the painting was exciting "considerable attention," he found fault with it too: "rawness, lack of finish, and commonplaceness — such as might be expected in the work of a young artist who has grappled with a subject so difficult."[48]

Looking at it, Brooks saw "a group of men, wearing the somber-hued garments of American gentlemen. No amount of accidental lights, warm coloring, and dramatic pose," he wrote, can invest Seward, [Postmaster General Montgomery] Blair, and the 'Marie Antoinette' of the Navy Department [Gideon Welles] with the supernal glories which gleam on the canvas of painters who had for their subjects kings and emperors in gorgeous robes."[49]

But Brooks learned that the picture "will soon be popular and familiar with all people through the medium of engravings," and this seemed to open up entirely new possibilities. "The artist has anticipated an inevitable demand (and perhaps abler hands) in executing . . . the picture," he wrote, predicting:

The chief faults which are not noticeable will be remedied in engraving, and when this large, life-size painting is reduced to a fine, clear engraving of the size of the Signing of the Declaration of Independence [an early but unmistakable comparison to Washington], there will be furnished a picture which will be prized in every liberty-loving household as a work of art . . . a perpetual remembrance of the noblest event in American history.[50]

Brooks had perceptively calculated the potential power of political prints — not only to mask the flaws of original art, but to achieve a widespread distribution for such pictures in an era in which art museums were still rare. Only prints, Brooks understood, could provide the kind of "perpetual remembrances" which historical milestones deserved.

What Brooks didn't realize at the time was that the engraving of the Carpenter painting would, when issued two years later, also solidify an iconographical metamorphosis that helped transform Lincoln into a modern Moses in the popular consciousness — a transfiguration given strong visual enhancement by popular prints. Eventually such prints would make the Great Emancipator seem even more important than the Great Emancipation. But it took longer to reach that point in image-making than historians have heretofore noted.

To be sure, the Proclamation sparked immediate public interest. Yet it took American printmakers a surprisingly long time to find a way to market both the document and its author, and it is no accident that the vast majority of emancipation graphics appeared after Lincoln's assassination

Opposite: Fig. 64. **Currier & Ives,** *The National Game. Three "Outs" and One "Run."/* *Abraham Winning the Ball* **[probably drawn on stone by Louis Maurer]. Lithograph, New York, 1860 (Library of Congress).**

THE UNDECIDED POLITICAL PRIZE FIGHT.

automatically made palatable even the most controversial policies with which Lincoln had been involved in life.

True, announcement of the Emancipation Proclamation in large measure changed the Lincoln image overnight, but the response from the graphic arts industry lagged. It took printmakers two years to catch up with the potential it offered for the marketing of a new body of Lincoln portraiture.

There are several possible explanations. While Noah Brooks, for one, noted an overnight "grand rush" for texts of the document, it may well have seemed too controversial at first for translation into pictures for the home. The Northern Democratic press quickly attacked it, expressing "alarm and dismay." The atmosphere may have seemed too charged to inspire domestically acceptable "Moses" images. At its most obvious level, of course, the Proclamation was to affect black people — and another point worth noting is that from all that is known, whites did not then display pictures of blacks in their homes. Since whites were surely the ones who bought most prints, this likely also worked to delay a pictorial response to the Proclamation (and help explain why Carpenter's picture, which portrayed *only* whites, became so popular).[51]

Finally, its immediate effect on the South was negligible, certainly still unknown as of January 1, 1863, the date it took effect. Even then, it required more years of military effort to make Lincoln's declaration of freedom come true: so perhaps, as far as the printmakers were concerned, the Proclamation really seemed, as Lincoln first feared, as hollow as the Pope's "bull against the comet."[52]

As for the words themselves, they were hardly the stuff to inspire great art. Senator Charles Sumner had hoped Lincoln would include in it "some sentiment of justice and humanity," but in the end, as the *New York Times* put it, he decided not to "place the Proclamation upon high moral grounds." Instead, he wrote it "as a war measure, and not a measure of morality," so slaves could later "plead the Proclamation . . . to establish judicially their title to freedom. They can do this, the President says, on a proclamation *proceeding as a war measure from the Commander-in-Chief . . . not on one issuing from the bosom of philanthropy.*"[53]

All these factors may have combined to inhibit the prompt production of Emancipation portraiture, widespread interest or no: it was immediately controversial, and except for caricature, printmakers usually steered clear of controversy; its ultimate effect was still not known; it required portrayals of blacks; and, finally, its soporific legal language hardly suggested evocative graphic interpretation.

Not that some publishers did not immediately make the proclamation an immediate staple of their business. Historian Charles Eberstadt, in a definitive 1950 bibliography, maintained that separately printed texts in pamphlet and sheet form began appearing as early as 1862. "Framed and displayed in thousands of homes and prominent places," Eberstadt claimed, "Emancipation became a watchword of almost hysterical power and incalculable effect . . . it provided an ever-present reminder of the war's true justification, and thus was important as a propaganda and morale factor."[54]

Opposite: Fig. 65. **Printmaker unknown [possibly F. Welcker, Cincinnati],** *The Undecided Political Prize Fight.* **Lithograph, 1860 (Library of Congress).**

Fig. 67. H. H. Lloyd after photograph by Mathew B. Brady, *National Republican Chart/ Presidential Campaign, 1860.* Woodengraving broadside, New York, 1860 (The Lincoln Museum).

Opposite: Fig. 66. Printmaker unknown, *[Splitting the] National ... Map of the United States.* Lithograph, 1860 (Library of Congress).

Fig. 68. Alexander Gardner, *[Abraham Lincoln]*. Photograph, Washington, D.C., February 24, 1861 (The Lincoln Museum).

But if Eberstadt was correct, publishers would have done more than issue beautifully engraved and lithographed texts. They would have created graphic images as well, and this they would not do for years. Lincoln's words alone, even if a few buyers did hang them on their walls, couldn't conceivably have inspired the passions Eberstadt claims.

Things finally began to change as the 1864 election loomed. Iconographers have noted the dearth of 1864 campaign prints compared to the flood of them published for 1860. They have largely attributed the difference to the fact that Lincoln was better known in 1864, and thus required fewer pictorial introductions. But another factor might have been the growing number of prints celebrating the Emancipation, and finally connected its author to its increasingly acceptable goals.

Lincoln personally helped advance at least two such projects. This supposedly modest and self-deprecating president welcomed two different artists-in-residence to the White House to work on paintings celebrating Emancipation. Significantly, both projects were to be engraved for mass distribution to the electorate. While there is no hard evidence to suggest that Lincoln understood the image-building potential of such pictures, and while all of them were commercially inspired, unlike today's campaign-produced media, it is significant that he proved so willing to sit still to make possible these historical records.

The first of these artists-in-residence was Edward Dalton Marchant (1806–1887), who arrived in Washington in 1863 to paint an Emancipator portrait for Independence Hall. His neoclassical work showed Lincoln emancipating the slaves both legally — signing the proclamation with a quill — and figuratively as suggested by broken shackles on a symbolic Liberty statue over his left shoulder.

Marchant's Lincoln was quickly engraved by John Sartain of Philadelphia and published in time for the 1864 campaign. The print must have proven popular; it was promptly pirated in a cheaper, lithographed version. Even though the original canvas never made it to Independence Hall, its impact was secured by the widespread distribution of the adaptations of it. It clearly marked a sea change in artistic appreciation of the Emancipation.[55]

Large renderings of the Emancipation text were already commonplace by 1864. Now some began to feature pictures. Martin & Judson of Milwaukee and Chicago's Edward Mendel, among others, issued so-called "facsimile" editions of the Proclamation boasting lithographed portraits of its author. A copy of Mendel's print was sent to Lincoln himself in January 1864. And on March 6, 1865, publisher L. Franklin Smith of Philadelphia personally presented Lincoln with what he immodestly declared "The Greatest Novelty of the Age." It was a broadside reproducing the Proclamation and surrounding the text with 32 portraits and 120 symbolic illustrations, including metaphorical vignettes variously representing "the curse of Slavery and the blessings of Liberty." To its publisher, it was nothing less than "unsurpassed" — an "elegant historical memorial."[56]

On the other side of the political spectrum — Adalbert Volck's vision of Lincoln writing the Proclamation suggested influences ranging from the devil himself (made to hold the inkstand Lincoln uses), to too much liquor (in depictions of a decanter and drinking glasses). American anti-Emancipation

Fig. 69. **Thomas Doney after photograph by Alexander Hesler [beard added],** *[Abraham Lincoln.]* **Mezzotint engraving [2nd state of** *Fig. 48*]**, Elgin, Illinois, 1861 (Illinois State Historical Library).**

caricature is all but unknown, at least from pens other than Volck's, suggesting again that this was one subject quite too hot to handle during the war.

To the racist Marylander, as he made clear in yet another etching, Lincoln's policies constituted nothing less than "negro worship" *(Fig. 72)*. Lincoln

Fig. 70. J. H. Bufford after photograph by Alexander Gardner, *President Lincoln &
Cabinet.* Lithograph with tintstone, published by Elliot & White, Boston, 1861 (The
Lincoln Museum).

would be ruthlessly and hilariously parodied during his reelection campaign, but such cartoons generally steered clear of the slavery question once Lincoln's thunderbolt was finally hurled.

The best known and most widely reported emancipation image (it inspired many newspaper articles and two separate books) was the work of the aforementioned Francis B. Carpenter (1830–1900), who began his project by commissioning photographs, both in nearby galleries and in the White House itself. From these he then sketched out the models he proposed to fit into his famous group portrait, now in the U.S. Capitol. He made separate model heads of each person in the Cabinet, including a beautiful study of Lincoln which the painter was later clever enough to have engraved as a separate image *(Fig. 73)*.

Mary Lincoln called the resulting portrait engraving by Frederick Halpin a "most perfect likeness," and her son, Robert, pronounced it "the best likeness I have ever seen." Wrote Lincoln's old Illinois law partner, William H. Herndon:

> When I opened the box and unrolled the portrait, Mr. Lincoln *flashed* on me as never from picture. As a portrait—a likeness—it is Lincoln.... Now let me give you a thousand thanks.

Advertising it as "the standard portrait," the publishers offered the 24 by 20 inch line-and-stipple engraving for prices ranging from $4.75 for plain prints, to $7.75 for india proofs, to $15 for artist's prints. Judging from the considerable number of surviving copies, the portrait was an enormous commercial success.[57]

Ever the clever merchandiser, Carpenter found a novel way to market his portrait engraving, engaging in a campaign quite familiar in the commercial world of today, but unprecedented in the world of Lincoln iconography: negative comparative advertising. Before Carpenter's print appeared, rival New York publisher Ticknor & Fields had issued a widely promoted portrait based on a rather stiff-looking painting by William Edgar Marshall *(Fig. 74)*, an artist who, unlike Carpenter, had never enjoyed the advantage of studying Lincoln from the flesh. At its publication, however, many of the same Lincoln intimates who later praised Carpenter's portrait—including son Robert Lincoln and William Herndon—enthusiastically lauded the Marshall effort. Then, when Halpin's engraving appeared, a worried Ticknor & Fields hurled what one group of professional engravers labeled "an unwarrantable fling at the character" of the Carpenter portrait, backed up by the considerable editorial clout of the influential *Atlantic Monthly* which happened to be published by the very same Ticknor & Fields.[58]

Now Carpenter sent to many of Marshall's admirers his own work, together with a specific request to compare the two. Herndon replied: "If art is perfection of likeness and exquisite culture of execution, then I give your picture the decided preference." And conceding that "Mr. Marshall made a very good picture," Robert Lincoln now admitted: "There is something unsatisfactory about it which I can not explain, and I would have no hesitation in choosing between the two." A period advertisement for the Carpenter effort, which appeared as an appendix to a book that described the making of the artist's Emancipation painting, featured a statement by a consortium calling itself the "New York Steel Plate Engravers," and boasting such prominent names as A. H. Ritchie (whose

Fig. 71. V. Blada [Adalbert Johann Volck], *Passage Through Baltimore.* Etching, London [Baltimore], 1863.

WORSHIP OF THE NORTH.

relationship with Carpenter made his testimony suspect), J. C. Buttre, and George E. Perine, all veteran Lincoln image-makers. Their statement said, in part:

> ...After a careful examination, we unhesitatingly say that your engraving of Lincoln is the finest and most artistic piece of portraiture-engraving ever executed on this continent, and is decidedly superior to Marshall's engraving of Lincoln, published by Ticknor & Fields. We say this without any unfriendly feeling toward Ticknor & Fields or Mr. Marshall, but simply as an act of justice to you.[59]

Francis B. Carpenter had won the battle of words and pictures, and more importantly, scored a small triumph in the war for the collective memory of the American people. And for this supreme Lincoln image-maker, it would not be the last such battle in which he would triumph. All the images that were issued in the Lincoln era to commemorate and celebrate emancipation—all the gaudy, imaginary scenes of Lincoln breaking shackles and pointing heavenward, all the fancy reproductions of the document's formal text—withered in a marketplace dominated by Carpenter's stately scene depicting Lincoln's cabinet hearing those words for the very first time. Pallid as the representation may seem to modern eyes—not very much unlike the insipid results of the brief photo opportunities White House *paparazzi* enjoy at the start of modern presidential cabinet meetings—Carpenter's group scene had a strong appeal to 19th century audiences unfamiliar with such eye-opening glimpses into White House routine. Condemn him for mediocre

artistic talent and shameless hustling, but Carpenter knew precisely what his audience wanted—and satisfied its needs accordingly.

Carpenter, surely the most skillful marketer ever to portray the public and private Lincoln, quickly arranged for his Emancipation canvas to go on national tour. He also contracted with a New York publisher to pay A. H. Ritchie $6,000 to engrave the popular print. By the time the project came to fruition two years later, it had been so well publicized that Carpenter's fame and fortune had been all but assured.[60]

The final Ritchie Emancipation engraving *(Fig. 75)* proved, just as Noah Brooks had predicted, a vast improvement over the original. It was also an immediate and overwhelming success, boosted immeasurably by the appearance of Carpenter's bestselling memoirs, as well as detailed advertisements on page one of the *New York Times,* featuring rave reviews of the print by the men portrayed in it—endorsements Carpenter had solicited himself. Its publisher later recalled that 30,000 impressions were printed altogether, eventually wearing out the steel plate. The print set new longevity records even in an age of rapidly changing publishing technologies. New variant editions appeared as late as 1895.[61]

In a way it is a shame that Carpenter's print did not appear earlier than it did, thus guaranteeing him the place he deserved as Lincoln's principal image-maker. But by the time the painstakingly slow Ritchie effort was completed, Lincoln had died, unleashing a flood of portraits, among which came the first real rush of overt "Great

Opposite: Fig. 72. **V. Blada [Adalbert Johann Volck],** *Worship of the North.* **Etching, London [Baltimore], 1863.**

Fig. 73. F[rederick]. Halpin after Francis Bicknell Carpenter and photograph by Anthony Beger, Washington, D.C., April 20, 1864, *Abraham Lincoln* [facsimile signature]. Engraving (1865). Signed: *From life by/ F. B. Carpenter/ 1864* (The Lincoln Museum).

Emancipator" images, including so-called "Emancipation Moment" images that colorfully, if improbably, portrayed Lincoln personally liberating slaves.

It was almost as if a national catharsis had been required before the printmakers themselves could be liberated sufficiently to celebrate uninhibitedly and fearlessly the emancipation of the slaves two years earlier. Finally, in 1865, as printmakers searched desperately for original ways in which to memorialize Lincoln, came the body of Great Emancipator images that by all rights should have first come off the presses in 1862 or 1863. Finally, Lincoln, the Christ figure who died for his nation's sins on Good Friday, could also be memorialized as a modern Moses. Before long, even straightforward memorial portraiture was featuring marginal, allegorical scenes belatedly acknowledging Emancipation as the principal act of Lincoln's life. Such symbolic efforts, some of the later ones designed to appeal to black audiences, remained popular for 30 years.

But between 1863 and 1865 — after the first rush of illustrated reproductions of the Emancipation — the market for Lincoln prints again grew sluggish. Dominique Fabronius' 1863 lithograph, *The Mower* (**Fig. 76**), contrasting the glories of free black labor (left) to the tyranny of slave labor (right), presented as its central character a bearded, scythe-wielding farmer, evidently intended to represent Lincoln, since he has literally just uncovered a Copperhead snake in the grass — symbol of the Northern anti-war movement. But the caption to the print did not bother even to make clear that the figure represented the President (which might also be construed as a tribute to the man so familiar by then that he

needed no introduction). As a poem in the caption put it:

> We have battles to fight, we have foes to
> subdue[;]
> Time waits not for us, and we wait not
> for you!
> The mower mows on, though the adder
> may writhe
> And the copperhead coil round the blade
> of his scythe.

One might have expected the 1864 presidential campaign to inspire almost as many graphics as the contest four years earlier. Such, however, would not be the case. For whatever combination of reasons — and one compelling factor was surely the absence of an urgent need to introduce visually either Lincoln or his much-photographed opponent, former Union General George B. McClellan — the output in 1864 did not even approach the volume of 1860.

Some printmakers did attempt to create new graphics targeted specifically to the new campaign. George E. Perine, the New York–based engraver, wrote to Lincoln on May 6, 1864, to ask for help in producing a worthy portrait.

> I desire Engraving in best style & large
> size *your Portrait* on Steel — and wishing a
> reliable Photograph to copy from — I have
> taken the liberty to address you for the
> purpose of obtaining one pleasing to
> yourself & family. Will you please favor
> me with the same — together with your
> autograph to engrave on the Plate — by
> mail or otherwise.[62]

There is no record of Lincoln's reply, but it is likely that the President or one of his secretaries filled Perine's request. By 1864, the printmaker had issued a handsome portrait (**Fig. 77**) based on a flattering period photograph (**Fig. 78**), featuring a facsimile autograph, and not surprisingly placing suggestively in Lincoln's hands a copy of the Emancipation Proclamation.

Fig. 74. William Edgar Marshall, *Abraham Lincoln.* Engraving, published by Ticknor & Fields, Boston, 1866 (The Lincoln Museum).

But Perine's effort proved the exception, not the rule. Most of the visual battle of 1864 was fought in caricature, not portraiture. New York lithographer M. W. Siebert, for example, highlighted Lincoln's and Mc-Clellan's contrasting visions of the Union with a pro–Republican cartoon *(Fig. 79)* that warned that Democrats were ready to accept slave auctions and shake hands with Rebel President Jefferson Davis. To a like-minded printmaker, Lincoln was the slow but steady "Union Roadster," McClellan all "brag and bluster," balancing himself between a "war horse" and a cringing "peace Donkey" *(Fig. 80)*.

Yet Bromley & Co. of New York could counter, in its anti–Lincoln campaign caricature, *The Abolition Catastrophe,/ Or the November Smash-Up (Fig. 81)*, that the new National Union Party, whose platform boasted a plank calling for a constitutional amendment banning slavery everywhere, was pointing the nation in the direction of public debt, European military intervention, and miscegenation (the new word for racial amalgamation). "Lor'Amighty, Massa Linkum," cries a black man exploding skyward in a symbolic train wreck along with the President, "Is dis wot yer call 'Elewating de Nigger?'"

In the end, what few prints were issued in 1864 tended to elevate Lincoln, who triumphed over McClellan in the November Election. But neither his triumph nor his rhetorical zenith at his second inauguration in March 1865 inspired further graphic tributes (the sole known exception being an inaugural address commemorative clearly not issued until after Lincoln's death).

Needless to say, no rush of demand for Lincoln prints surpassed the one that began the day the nation's 16th president died at the hands of an assassin. Nothing Lincoln ever did in his life quite so inspired (or profited) America's engravers and lithographers as did his death. The shot that killed Lincoln revitalized the print industry. It ignited an insatiable national appetite for images of the man who became, in death, bigger than life — a distortion that seemed to please the American audience immensely.

Although many of these post-assassination prints suffered from indifferent

artistry, limited imagination, incredibly poor research, and even outright fakery (more were products of dizzying commercial competition than art), they were nonetheless extremely popular. And they played a significant role in iconographical history despite their shortcomings. The Lincoln myth — the roots of Lincoln's unique and permanent hold on the American consciousness — was shaped in these prints, the first of which gave Americans their initial glimpse (although it was usually inaccurate) of the shooting on April 14, 1865, and Lincoln's last breath the following morning.

Innumerable engravings and lithographs of the assassination itself appeared virtually overnight, nearly all contrived and stilted. Most featured inept portraiture, ludicrous proportion *(Fig. 82)* a poor sense of drama, and some an inability even to position correctly the occupants of the presidential box in Ford's Theatre at the moment of the shooting. One particularly absurd unsigned lithograph *(Fig. 83)* depicted Lincoln collapsed in a chair upholstered in American flag pattern, included an extra figure in the presidential box, and showed curtains surrounding their seats that were so thick they would have obscured their view of the play. The same print failed to include the bunting that draped the front of the box, although it played an important part in the assassination story. Leaping from the box after shooting Lincoln, John Wilkes Booth caught his spur in the flag drapery, and broke a bone in his foot when he landed on the stage below. The injury probably slowed him down enough to permit his capture by federal troops 12 days later (and fatefully involved Dr. Samuel Mudd).[63]

Many printmakers who published murder scenes also issued deathbed

THE FIRST READING OF THE EMANCIPATION PROCLAMATION BEFORE THE CABINET

views as companion pieces. The variety among them demonstrates the printmakers' confusion over which prominent figures of the day should be included and which excluded from these creations. Currier & Ives depicted Mary Todd Lincoln weeping at her husband's bedside even though Secretary of War Stanton had at one point barred her from the chamber because of his disconcerting outbursts. She was not present at the moment of Lincoln's death, so her appearance in this and other prints may have been a concession to propriety. Less understandable was the frequent inclusion of her son Tad, who was not brought to the scene at all during his father's final hours. Still another celebrity whose presence confounded the printmakers was Vice President Andrew Johnson. Currier & Ives omitted him initially, but included him in a revised print. Perhaps early customers complained because the new president was left out of the original. Yet his actual visit to Lincoln's bedside was perfunctory, and there was little possibility he would have been present at the same time as Mrs. Lincoln, as he was frequently portrayed in prints. The First Lady so despised Johnson that it was beyond comprehension that she would have allowed it. Some printmakers solved the dilemma by including Johnson and omitting Mrs. Lincoln. The publication of these prints coincided with her widely reported and frequently criticized inability to attend any of the funeral services for her husband; besides, with the new president included they became Johnson prints, too, that testified to the peaceful succession of office—to presidential continuity.[64]

One Philadelphia printmaker, John L. Magee, who achieved his greatest fame producing baseball lithographs, placed both controversial figures in his improbable deathbed scene. Magee went so far as to portray Johnson holding Lincoln's hand, while Mary Todd Lincoln collapsed in an awkward, almost incestuous, embrace with her eldest son, Robert. The portraiture lacks scale and depth; Stanton, for example, is dwarf-sized, so reduced in stature that, standing, he is barely as tall as the seated vice president.

The Magee print typifies the deathbed views rushed to market at the height of the morbid national curiosity over Lincoln's expiration. The printmakers sensed that practically any Lincoln effort would sell, and many of their productions display a resulting carelessness and insensitivity. The public demanded only that the death scenes reflect the same kind of noble dying that heroes like Washington had supposedly experienced.

One of the most skillfully marketed of the deathbed scenes—even if it was not appreciably more precise historically—was produced by Alexander Hay Ritchie, the same engraver who was responsible for adapting Carpenter's crucial image of Lincoln as Emancipator. Ritchie was by profession an engraver, but evidently a gifted painter as well. We know, for example, that Carpenter entrusted him with the task of touching up his original canvas after the painter made so many revisions to the portrait of Lincoln that it was barely recognizable.[65]

Opposite: **Fig. 75.** Alexander Hay Ritchie after Francis B. Carpenter, *The First Reading of the Emancipation Proclamation Before the Cabinet.* **Engraving, published by Derby & Miller, New York, (Library of Congress).**

THE MOWER.

N. 263.

Designed & Lith by D. C. Fabronius.

ENTERED ACCORDING TO ACT OF CONGRESS, IN THE YEAR 1861, BY D.C.FABRONIUS, IN THE CLERKS OFFICE OF THE DISTRICT COURT OF MASS.

We have battles to fight, we have foes to subdue,—
Time waits not for us, and we wait not for you!
The mower mows on, though the adder may writhe
And the copperhead coil round the blade of his scythe.

In 1867, Ritchie produced an ambitious oil of *The Death of President Lincoln,* in which he portrayed no less than 26 onlookers on all sides surrounding the mortally wounded president as Assistant Surgeon General Charles Crane checks Lincoln's fading pulse and notes the precise time of death on his pocket watch. As history, although Ritchie claimed to have visited the house where Lincoln died and made faithful sketches of the carpeting and furniture, the record was deficient. The tiny bedroom could hardly have accommodated such a throng of attendants at one time as the artist portrayed. On the other hand, Ritchie was scrupulous enough about detail to exclude both Vice President Johnson, whose visit to the scene had been so brief, or Mrs. Lincoln, whose outbursts during the death struggle had emboldened Secretary of War Stanton to order her from the room.

Ritchie advertised that he had "cleverly evaded the difficulty common to portrait-pieces in which a number of faces have to be arranged with a view to recognition. There is much variety of pose throughout the composition, nor is there to be seen anywhere in it the unpleasing formality that so often repeats the horizontal line of the frame with a parallel line of heads." A promotional brochure explained: "Every mind is absorbed by one idea, and we read it on every face." The result was not only a canvas whose portraits boasted "striking character and individuality," but a valuable "record of the passing history of the nation."[66]

Eyewitnesses to the tragedy apparently shared this enthusiasm. Invited to an exhibition of the painting at the U.S. Capitol and then petitioned for testimonials, attending physician Robert King Stone, for one, wrote Ritchie to praise "the minute faithfulness and feeling of the picture—the pathos of which is unsurpassed—and most sincerely congratulate you on your fidelity to truth, and as an historical painter, your perfect success." Rev. Phineas T. Gurley, who spent three hours beside the deathbed, confessed: "It renews to my eye and heart with surprising vividness, the scenes and impressions of that sadly memorable morning." And Quartermaster General Montgomery Meigs also praised the effort, adding: "I hope that the engraving may well have a place in thousands of American Homes."[67]

As Meigs' comment suggests, by the time it was written—March 1867— plans were already underway to engrave the painting. And no better engraver was at work at the time than artist Ritchie himself.

By 1868 a mammoth, 32½ by 21½ inch engraved adaptation *(Fig. 84)* was being offered by Ritchie for $30 for artists' proofs and $20 for plain proofs— hefty sums in postwar America. Ritchie also produced a ten-page brochure to help salesmen attract buyers. The advertising pamphlet included the celebrity testimonials, a brief history of the assassination and the painting, and a key to the picture *(Fig. 85)*. Whether or not the final result was, as the Rev. Gurley put it, "a work of surpassing merit," the engraving was unquestionably influential. It was quickly pirated by photographers and issued as *cartes-de-visite* for family albums.

But judging from the dearth of surviving copies of the engraving, it may not have been a popular success.

Opposite: Fig. 76. **D. C. Fabronius,** *The Mower.* **Lithograph, printed by A. Trochsler, Boston, 1863 (Library of Congress).**

Fig. 77. Cameraman unknown, *[Abraham Lincoln].* Photograph, Washington, D.C., *ca.* June 1861 (The Lincoln Museum).

Its unwieldy size may have mitigated against its appeal (although the Ritchie engraving after Carpenter, only slightly smaller, was a best-seller). Not long ago, a cache of mint-condition signed artists' proofs was unearthed in the John Hay Library of Brown University — unseen, and presumably unsold, for more than a century. Their discovery suggests that Lincoln's death

Fig. 78. Geo[rge]. E. Perine after "photograph by Fredericks," *A. Lincoln* [facsimile signature]. Engraving, New York, *ca.* 1864 (Illinois State Historical Library).

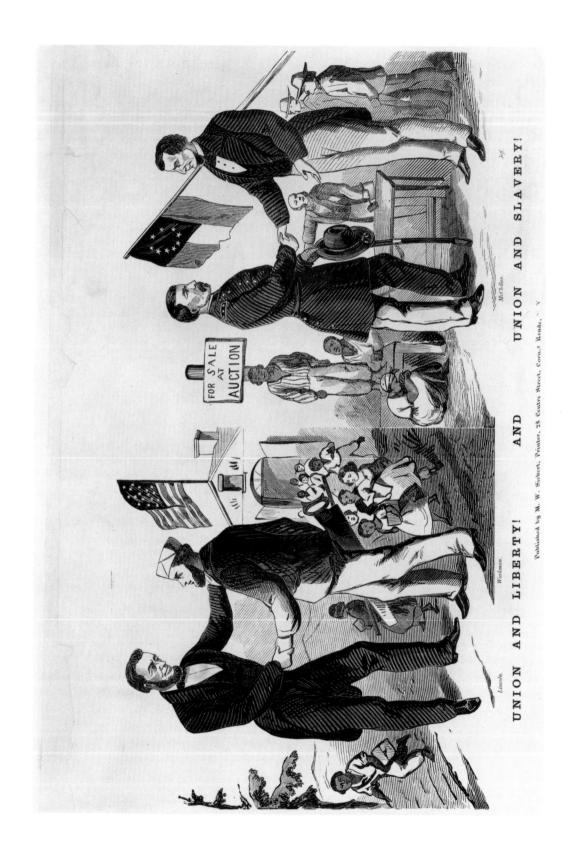

Workman.   Lincoln.

UNION AND LIBERTY!   **AND**

Jeff.   McClellan.

UNION AND SLAVERY!

Published by M. W. Siebert, Printer, 23 Centre Street, Corner Reade, N. Y

inspired a flurry of interest in pictorial evocations of the murder and final moments; printmakers who responded to the news value of the extraordinary event and issued interpretations quickly received the maximum commercial return for their work.

On the other hand, the more ambitious printmakers, like Ritchie, who invested generously in their interpretations, exhibited the most originality, researched most carefully, and labored most prodigiously, took so much time to produce their works that they may have found audiences indifferent. Ritchie's work may boast value as the historical record which its advertising brochure claimed for it, but as a popular print it was found wanting: too much, perhaps and certainly too late. Printmaking in the 1860s was an ephemeral business. And publishers who overestimated public appetites and underestimated need for timely, newsworthy pictures were usually greeted with marketplace indifference.

By 1868, the year Ritchie's deathbed scene appeared, Lincoln was no longer the American president who had died. He was the American myth who had been reborn. Photographs *(Figs. 86, 88)* were quickly adapted into a staggering variety of memorial portraiture *(Fig. 87)*, and mourning envelopes **(Fig. 89)**. In the inevitable retrospective tribute to Lincoln's final triumphant days, it was anything but surprising that such accurate but uninspiring portrayals as J. C. Buttre's original and worthy depiction of Lincoln's 1865 meeting with Alexander H. Stephens and other Confederate leaders *(Fig. 90)* in a last-ditch effort to end the war, was never completed, and survives only in rough proof form. Apparently Americans wanted only post-assassination graphics that emphasized Lincoln the victor, not the peacemaker, and in that culture Buttre's print of Lincoln's triumphal entry into the conquered Confederate capital of Richmond *(Fig. 91)* better satisfied the public need to cherish the memory of Lincoln as a conquering hero.

The assassination also gave rise to intense national curiosity about the star-crossed Lincoln family. The successive tragedies endured by the Lincolns—deaths first of a son, Willie, and then the father—mirrored the catastrophes that so many families suffered during the war. The harmonious domestic scenes that became popular after Lincoln's assassination seemed to touch a responsive chord with a sympathetic audience.[68]

Some Lincoln family prints were quite good and were either based on stylish paintings or skillfully pieced together from separate photographs. But since Lincoln had posed before the cameras with only one of his sons, and never with his wife, many printmakers encountered difficulty assembling well-proportioned composites, so the results suggest.

A generation before the Lincoln family moved into the White House, an influential Philadelphia clergyman had bestowed his official blessing on a new style of decorations for the American home. "They are like cherished plants in the window, the green creepers in the yard, or the caged singing bird on the wall," he said approvingly, "signs of a fondness for home and a desire to cultivate those virtues which make home peaceful and happy." What he

Opposite: Fig. 79. **M. W. Siebert,** *Union and Liberty! And Union and Slavery!* **Woodcut engraving, New York, 1864 (Library of Congress).**

was describing were lithographs: "rude and gaudy" mass-produced popular graphic art design to adorn the family parlor.[69]

Before many years passed, prints had indeed become decorating fixtures, to such a degree that one art critic complained: "There seems to be a prejudice on the part of women, against leaving any considerable portion of the wall space uncovered.... No lithographed ... plaque is too atrocious in design or coloring to prevent its being used ... to disfigure house walls." But in an era whose decorating ethic dictated that "whatnots groaned under bric-a-brac," walls were meant to be covered—from chair rail to ceiling, if possible—with pictures that not only decorated, but testified to their owners' pious aspirations and refined taste.[70]

Prints provided their buyers with something far more resonant than mere objects to take up space. During the Civil War, print portraits of political and military heroes attained a status within the home once reserved only for religious pictures, occupying honored places above family hearths. Like the popular, early engraved adaptation of Edward Savage's *Washington Family,* many of these prints portrayed families grouped in domestic settings that looked much like the rooms in which their customers devotedly displayed them. And what better print for a family parlor, after all, than a print of the *nation's* family—its First Family—posing in its own family parlor?

To a generation like ours, weaned on such indelible images as little John-John Kennedy saluting his father's coffin, or Ron Reagan, Jr., dancing on national television in his jockey shorts to parody a Tom Cruise movie, it is nearly impossible to imagine that there wasn't always a cult of the First Family, as well as a glut of pictures to feed it. But before *paparazzi* and *People Magazine*—before pictures could move or talk or even be reproduced in the newspapers—the cult did not yet exist. It began with the Lincolns.

How and when it began—and what cultural yearnings it satisfied—tell us much about the age in which these first First Family images emerged: both the audience that thirsted for them, and the commercial skills that so effectively slaked that thirst. What they tell us least about, ironically, is the Lincolns themselves.

For as surprising as it is that it took so long for America to create its First Family cult is the fact that it was the Lincolns—for whose unhappy era Lincoln himself aptly chose the metaphor of a "House Divided"—around whom it grew. Their domestic sphere, too, was a house divided—by war, personal tragedy, and perhaps most of all by the exhausting demands of the high office that stimulated the cult in the first place. Yet like all his predecessors, not to mention each of his successors until Theodore Roosevelt, Abraham Lincoln failed to grasp his family's potentially ameliorating impact on his image. Presidents from Washington to Pierce can be more easily forgiven for their short-sightedness, since the printmaking during their administrations was still a young industry. Lincoln, on the other hand, reached the White House at the crest of a new era in the graphic arts; he and printmaking came of age together, and proof could be

Opposite: Fig. 80. **Printmaker unknown,** *Slow & Steady/ Wins the Race.* **Lithograph, 1864 (Lincoln Memorial University).**

POLITICAL CARICATURE Nº 3

THE ABOLITION CATASTROPHE,
Or the November Smash-up.

found in the widespread distribution of Lincoln graphics during the 1860 campaign. Still, it did not dawn on him—nor, in all fairness, on the nation's printmakers—that family images would be as marketable as straightforward political portraiture. Lincoln failed even to provide the models on which printmakers were accustomed to relying in order to create their derivative works: as noted, he posed for the camera only twice with one of his four sons, and never posed at all with his other children, or even with his wife.

The gaping photographic void testifies to the painful fact that there were really two Lincoln families: the President, First Lady, and sons who lived a life of misery in the bustling but lonely, and occasionally tragic White House; and the idealized group which was nonetheless portrayed subsequently by printmakers basking in warmth and contentment.

The presidency did not bring the Lincolns closer; it drove them further apart. Husband, wife, and children were almost never together during the war years, even though the printmakers would later portray them so.

The presidency was destructive of the family circle, a circle made lonelier still by family tragedy and the nation's own fratricidal war. Between the rebellion and the death of their son, Willie, Mary remembered Lincoln telling her on his last day alive, "we have been very miserable."[71]

Eldest son Robert was seldom on the scene to make the misery more endurable. He returned to school in Massachusetts at the start of his father's presidency, and joined the army at the end, confiding later that even when he

was home for brief visits, his father was too busy to give him much attention, and "intimacy" between them became "impossible." When Willie died in 1862 at the age of 11, Mary plunged into a prolonged mourning that drove her to the edge of a breakdown: she called it her "fiery furnace of affliction." Even after she recovered enough to talk about it, she pronounced her life "heavily visited by affliction," and thereafter seemed almost to relish her misery. With one son, Robert, "sick of Washington and glad to get back" to school and another dead less than a year into his father's first term, little Tad Lincoln's "gayety and affection," in the words of White House secretary John Hay, became the only effective medicine for "the worn and weary heart of the great President through the toilsome years of war." But what Hay referred to as Tad's "uncontrollable boisterousness" probably signaled deep emotional problems, causing his parents pain as well as pleasure. Tad never learned to read or write during his White House years, and the volatile temperament he exhibited along with his indifference to education would have probably earned him, in our own era, the label of "learning disabled." Yet even Tad could summon up the perceptiveness to lament of his father's life in the White House: "He was never happy after he came here. This was not a good place for him."[72]

Nonetheless, reality was no match for the Victorian era's idealized reverence for family and home life and the society's eagerness to embrace its emblematic models. Victorians glorified the family. The family parlor was a haven from the trouble-plagued worlds

Opposite: Fig. 81. **Bivinley & Co.,** *The Abolition Catastrophe./ Or the November Smash-up.* **Engraving, New York, 1864 (Lincoln Memorial University).**

ASSASSINATION OF PRESIDENT LINCOLN,

AT FORD'S THEATRE APL. 14TH 1865.

"TREASON AND MURDER WORK TOGETHER."

Published by H.H. Lloyd & Co. 21 John St. New York.

of work and war. Family was a holy sanctuary — practically a heaven on earth — and its parlor was its cathedral, a shrine to the serenity and moral replenishment to be found at the hearthside. As future President James A. Garfield would later attest: "There is safety — there is rest — as well as inspiration" in the "sphere of domestic love."[73]

Where Lincoln was concerned, printmakers were astonishingly slow to comprehend, much less market this sensibility. Without exception, they did not appreciate the viability of Lincoln family images until after the family had been completely destroyed by the assassination.

When artist Francis B. Carpenter worked in Lincoln's White House for six months painting his Emancipation canvas, he did begin to sense — perhaps alone among the image-makers during Lincoln's lifetime — that there was potential magic in this untapped image resource. It was Carpenter who probably arranged that the best-known Lincoln-and-Tad photograph *(Fig. 93)* be made at Mathew Brady's Washington gallery on February 9, 1864. We know that Carpenter accompanied Lincoln to the studio that day, and that the President posed there at the artist's request. And we know, too, that to Carpenter, the image of Lincoln alongside his son provided "a gauge of his domestic character," which the painter believed would have "melted the hearts of the worst of his adversaries" could they but glimpse it. Despite Carpenter's insight, glimpse it they never did — not while Lincoln lived. For while copies of the photograph were almost certainly available from Brady's over the next 14

months, the picture failed to inspire a single engraved or lithographic adaptation until Lincoln died. Printmakers and artists alike, Carpenter included, failed utterly to comprehend its commercial potential.[74]

The veil inhibiting the market for family prints was abruptly and permanently lifted on April 15, 1865. As demand skyrocketed for Lincoln prints in all categories, the assassin's victim would finally be portrayed, too, as the quintessential parent — devoted, patient, and loving — in a new image made especially appealing in the warm mist of national mourning.

We even know the exact date the image of the Lincoln family was born — May 6, 1865 — the day *Harper's Weekly* published on its cover, over the title *President Lincoln at Home,* a full-page woodcut of the Brady Lincoln-and-Tad photograph. It was this breakthrough that finally inspired faithful, if inaccurately labeled display-print adaptations. Suddenly, the Brady photograph seemed to suggest immeasurable possibilities to the printmakers as a mourning emblem that suggested that somehow in his busy life the martyred president had found ample time to instruct his child in educational and moral values.

That impression was helped along by the fact that the photograph conveniently showed Lincoln and Tad examining a large book. In reality, it was only Brady's oversized sample photograph album. But as early as May 13, a newspaper carried an advertisement for a print adaptation depicting "President Lincoln Reading the Bible to His Son Tad" *(Fig. 94)*. Apparently the large

Opposite: Fig. 82. **H. H. Lloyd & Co.,** *Assassination of President Lincoln,/ at Ford's Theatre Apl. 14th 1865./ "Treason and Murder Work Together."* **Engraving, New York, 1865 (Library of Congress).**

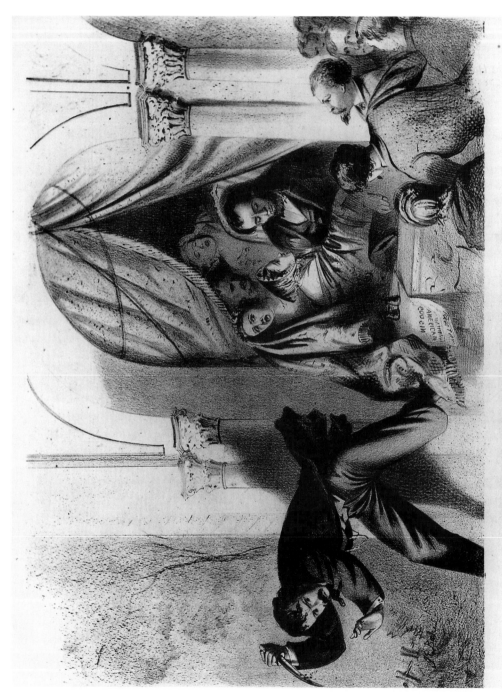

ASSASSINATION OF PRESIDENT LINCOLN.

AT FORD'S THEATRE WASHINGTON D.C APRIL 14.1865.

book had undergone a religious conversion even Lincoln himself, at least judging from his reluctance to join a church, never experienced. It was literally born again. Another print of *Lincoln at Home* went so far as to label the album pages as "Psalms." While Lincoln himself had worried during his lifetime that people would consider it "a species of false pretense" if audiences incorrectly assumed the prop to be a holy book, it was a rare posthumous print of Lincoln with Tad that did not disguise the photo album and either implicitly or brazenly redraw it to make it look like a bible. As recently as a few years ago, our own, modern U.S. Post Office engravers reverted to the same tricks as their 19th century counterparts by issuing a postage stamp based on the old pose, and captioning it "A Nation of Readers." Now, as then, the core photographic model of Lincoln and Tad seemed to offer all things to all people.[75]

The doors to the private quarters of the Lincoln White House were now symbolically thrown open. There was no quenching the public hunger for images, and no stopping the printmakers from inventing new designs to distinguish their efforts from those of the competition. Straightforward adaptations of the Lincoln-and-Tad model quickly became so commonplace that many printmakers began searching for ways to amplify the scene. Many did so by superimposing portraits of additional family members, both living and dead, creating clever and convincing composites *(Fig. 92)* that filled the gap the Lincolns had never thought to fill themselves by posing as a family while they still could. The final irony was

that America did not get to see all the Lincolns together for the first time until, as Tad put it, there were "three of us on earth, & three in Heaven."[76]

Historian James Thomas Flexner has properly complained that even in their more accurate incarnations, all such rigidly posed family scenes merely trivialized the sacred family parlor — what he decried as the "room on which opulence had been lavished to create a domestic 'corporate image.'" Flexner particularly loathed celebrity prints that showcased famous men and their families in such settings, condemning their sprawling designs, lack of artistic unity, heterogeneous ornamentation, and absence of either realistic expression or emotional tension. Flexner actually believed that the proliferation of such efforts all but killed portraiture as an American art form. But not before countless more Lincoln family prints, for all their shortcomings and imperfections, won widespread public acceptance. For as another historian, Wendy Wick Reaves, has astutely pointed out, these uninspired images of the Lincoln family offered their buyers the assurance, however fanciful, that their beloved leader had found "refuge from the horrors of Civil War." What is more, by so suggesting, Reaves argued, the pictures provided the same refuge to those who displayed them. Their owners "welcomed the sight of heroes and presidents in the comfortable security of the family circle."[77]

Perhaps no example of the genre more successfully answered this yearning than William Sartain's beautifully rendered 1866 mezzotint engraving *(see Fig. 124)* designed by painter Samuel B. Waugh and published in Philadelphia

Opposite: Fig. 83. **Printmaker unknown,** *Assassination of President Lincoln./ At Ford's Theatre Washington DC April 14th 1865.* **Lithograph, 1865 (The Lincoln Museum).**

1 President Lincoln
2 Hon Gideon Welles Sec'y the Navy
3 John Hay Esq Pres Private Sec't
4 Hon E M Stanton Sec'y War
5 Rev Dr Gurley
6 Gen Farnsworth M.C. from Ill
7 Gov. Ogilsby of Ill

8 Gen. Todd
9 Rufus Andrews Esq
10 Hon. W.T. Otto Ass. Sec'y the Interior
11 Hon M. Denison Post Master Gen'
12 Judge D.K. Cartter
13 Maj. Gen Halleck
14 Cap't Robert Lincoln

15 Dr Leale
16 Hon Charles Sumner
17 Dr Crane Ass Surg Gen
18 Gov Farwell of Wis.
19 Hon J.P. Usher Sec'y the Interior
20 Maj Gen Augur
21 Maj Gen Meigs

22 Maunsel B Field Esq
23 Hon Schuyler Colfax
24 Hon James Speed Att'y Gen
25 Dr R.K Stone
26 Hon H M Cullough Sec'y the Treas'y
27 Surg Gen Barnes

Opposite page: Fig. 84. A. H. Ritchie, Death of President Lincoln. Engraving, New York, 1868 (The Lincoln Museum). This page: Fig. 85. A. H. Ritchie, Key to Ritchie's Death of President Lincoln. From Ritchie's Historical Picture, New York, 1868.

WASHINGTON, D. C.

in 1866. Mary wears mourning garb, and Willie reappears as a revered portrait on the wall. Cleverly, the parlor table is reduced in size to suggest greater intimacy, an effect heightened by Tad's draping his arm informally over his father's knee.

In its day, this print was deservedly considered the finest of the Lincoln family graphic portraits. A circular declared it "a great triumph of art," adding: "In accuracy of portraiture and excellence of execution, [it] is acknowledged to be unsurpassed." Not least among its virtues was the fact that it subtly advanced appealing ideas, like the vase of flowers, overflowing with roses of the North and Virginia creepers of the South—"wreathed in harmony," in the words of the brochure, "emblematical of the friendly feeling that should exist between the people of the North and South in the great vase of the union." Newspaper critics loved this print. The Boston *Post* predicted it would be "almost universally sought for [as] a desirable picture for thousands of homes in the land." Yet it was probably affordable only to the elite: plain prints cost $7.25, plain proofs $10, india proofs $15, and signed artist's proofs $20, hefty sums for popular art in 1866.[78]

Another notable effort of the period was created by the man who had started it all: Francis B. Carpenter. His picture might have become the definitive portrait of Lincoln as a husband and father, had he not typically delayed its creation so long he did not win the audience, much less the reputation, he deserved for inventing the genre in the first place. Using the Brady photographic model for which he could justi-

fiably claim some credit, along with a flattering photograph of Mary which she herself suggested he adapt, Carpenter fashioned a beautiful painting in shades of black, white and grey—color omitted to "facilitate" its adaptation into an engraving, as Carpenter put it.[79]

But by the time the artist got engraver J. C. Buttre to offer him $500 to produce a print adaptation, the American marketplace had been flooded with Lincoln "families," and Carpenter's version did not seem sufficient to distinguish it from the others, despite the artist's personal access to the Lincolns. One critic said his composition had merely been copied "in a servile manner" from photographs. More damaging to its reputation, it arrived too late to earn Francie B. Carpenter the additional title he deserved: originator of the Lincoln family image.[80]

Thanks to no one print in particular—none had made the singular impact of Savage's *Washington Family*—but, rather, to the cumulative impact of all the family prints, Lincoln would be remembered at the heart of a formal, ritualistically grouped private circle, from whose intimacy he had, in truth, been all but driven by the demands of the presidency and the heartbreak of death and emotional instability. Yet even if the living Lincoln had become increasingly remote to his family, American audiences would be able to treasure the reassuring glimpses of their martyred leader in the safe and inspiring haven of domestic bliss. There would be no more sentimental tributes to the dead president than the pictures that suggested that he had preserved his personal union as successfully as he had preserved the federal union.

Opposite: Fig. 86. **Anthony Berger,** *[Abraham Lincoln].* **Photograph, Washington, D.C., February 9, 1864 (The Lincoln Museum).**

ABRAHAM LINCOLN,
SIXTEENTH PRESIDENT OF THE UNITED STATES.
Born Feby. 12th 1809.   Died April 15th 1865.

Published by Chr. Kimmel & Forster 254 & 256 Canal St. N.Y.

Fig. 87. [P. K.] Kimmel & Forster after photograph by Anthony Berger, *Abraham Lincoln,/ Sixteenth President of the United States./ Born Feby. 12th 1809. Died April 15th 1865.* Lithograph, New York, 1865 (The Lincoln Museum).

Fig. 88. Anthony Berger, *[Abraham Lincoln].* Photograph, Washington, D.C., February 9, 1864 (The Lincoln Museum).

WE CHERISH HIS MEMORY.

A NEATLY PRINTED

Mourning Envelope

With the above excellent Likeness of

OUR BELOVED DEPARTED,

IS NOW READY FOR THE TRADE.

Orders may be sent to S. O. THAYER, over Boylston market, Boston ; or to B. B. RUSSELL & Co., No. 55 Cornhill, Boston.

☞ All orders by Mail, Express, or Telegraph, promptly responded to.

Fig. 89. B[enjamin]. B. Russell after Anthony Berger, *We Cherish His Memory*. Advertisement for a mourning envelope, engraving, published by S. O. Thayer, Boston (1865).

As the brochure for William Sartain's engraving had perceptively noted, such icons testified to "love of home and devotion to country." As such, not just Sartain's but all the prints of the Lincoln family—good, mediocre, even dreadful—became, in the words of the brochure, "desirable pictures for thousands of homes in the land."[81]

Sadly, around the time the Sartain print first appeared, a bitter, "bowed down and heart-broken" Mary Lincoln was complaining that the surviving members of her tragic family, whom she now imagined destitute and abandoned, had become little more than "Living Monuments of a Nation's ingratitude." Frantically uncertain about

Fig. 90. J. C. Buttre, *Lincoln & Stephens in Hampton Roads.* **Proof of an Engraving, New York, 1865 (Brown University Library).**

her future, the widow believed that "the councils of the nation" had "denied the family of the man, who lost his life in their cause — a home." Ironically, in home after home throughout the Union Lincoln preserved, her family was even then dwelling in honored places above the hearthplace in thousands of America's parlor galleries — "Living Monuments" not only to a nation's gratitude, but to an idealized domestic bliss that otherwise lived on principally in Mary Lincoln's imagination.[82]

As Americans east and west gathered in their churches on the Sunday following Abraham Lincoln's assassination on Good Friday 1865, they were reminded of many things in the Black Easter sermons which greeted them. Lincoln, they were told, had died for his country's sins; he had saved the republic created by the founding

fathers; he had freed the slaves but, like Moses, died before finding the promised land; and like Christ he had been slain on Good Friday — and taken to his country's bosom on Easter.[83]

But most often of all, congregants were reminded, again and again, wherever they worshipped, that Abraham Lincoln had been, much like them, thoroughly and proudly — perhaps in his case quintessentially — American. As one Episcopal minister in Philadelphia put it, Lincoln had personified "truth . . . honesty . . . health . . . sagacity . . . [and] practicalness," native qualities that defined "the best American nature." In death even more than in life, no one but the wise, homespun Lincoln ever seemed so American — and no country other than America seemed capable of producing such an indigenous New World phenomenon.[84]

ABRAHAM LINCOLN ENTERING RICHMOND, APRIL 3ᴰ 1865

Fig. 92. **A. Robin after Anthony Berger, *Lincoln and Family*. Engraving, published by G. W. Massee, Philadelphia, 1869.**

So it surely seemed, too, to observers — even confirmed Lincoln admirers — across the ocean in Europe, to whom Lincoln likely loomed as an entirely alien creation, far less statesmanlike than his Confederate counterpart, Jefferson Davis, who exuded an air of nobility that effectively

Opposite: Fig. 91. **J. C. Buttre after L. Hollis, *Abraham Lincoln Entering Richmond, April 3d, 1865*. Engraving, published by B. B. Russell, Boston, 1866.**

Fig. 93. Anthony Berger, *[Abraham Lincoln and his Son, Tad]*. Photograph, Washington, D.C., February 9, 1864 (The Lincoln Museum).

Fig. 94. A[dam]. B. Walter after Anthony Berger, *President Lincoln and His Son "Tad."*
Engraving, published by Bradley & Co., Philadelphia, 1865 (The Lincoln Museum).

masked the fact that his birthplace was not many miles from Lincolns, and in the very same western state, Kentucky.

That did not stop enthusiasts overseas from clamoring, just as Americans did following the catharsis of the assassination, for Lincoln images they could display in family parlors. Here in the United States, engravers and lithographers answered that need by producing an array of flattering likenesses that softened the martyr's harsh frontier physiognomy and improved his wardrobe, posture, and bearing in the bargain.

Not surprisingly, European artists attempted similar cosmetic alterations. Modern observers may be surprised, however, by the total number of Lincoln images produced in Europe (not particularly large); the variety of portraits (even smaller); and the nations which did and did not produce them.

What is particularly fascinating is that a number of European printmakers gravitated toward one particular Lincoln photograph as the model for many of their engraved and lithographed adaptations. It was not one of the pictures most frequently copied in America, like the much-consulted pre-presidential Cooper Union photograph or the ubiquitous Brady Studio "five dollar bill" pose, but the stiffly formal, rather wooden portrait taken in the nation's capital by Alexander Gardner in February 1861, just after Lincoln's arrival for his first inauguration *(see Fig. 68)*.

On close inspection, it is easy to see what attracted the Europeans to this seemingly unremarkable pose: Lincoln appears statesmanlike in it. His hair, worn at the longest length he would allow it to grow for the remainder of his life, swirled around his head in a style almost reminiscent of portraits of American leaders of the past. An uncharacteristic short-winged collar hid his craggy neck and stayed well within the boundaries of his stiff and billowing dress shirt. A fine new suit completed the package along with (for those who saw the original photo), an elegant top hat on a nearby table. But what one eyewitness to the photographer's sitting remembered as a distant expression caused by complete absorption in "deep thought," evidently seemed to European artists the personification of noble bearing. Somehow this photo found its way across the ocean in wartime and spawned a host of copies to become, in essence, the European image of Abraham Lincoln.

Unlike its counterpart in America, Lincoln's image did not truly proliferate in Europe outside the picture press until the assassination. Neither the hoopla of the distant American presidential election of 1860, however exciting to Americans and however many pictures it inspired in its wake, nor Lincoln's subsequent decision to create yet another round of artistic demand by changing his appearance with the sudden addition of postelection whiskers, caused much interest in England, France, Germany, or Italy. Not even the well-reported American Civil War was enough to inspire portraits of America's leaders. Only Lincoln's murder proved eventful enough to alter the pattern of indifference.

At the same time, the nations whose populations might ordinarily have demanded more images of Lincoln than others seemed instead to require fewer. England, for example, a country that shared both language and religion with America, produced only a modest number of Lincoln prints — perhaps because there public opinion remained bitterly divided while here the war raged.

In seemingly inhospitable France, on the other hand, where Napoleon III's dictatorship imposed the heavy yoke of censorship on the press and the arts, Lincoln's image bravely flowered. Liberals there cleverly adapted the Lincoln image as a symbol for their aspirations for freedom. Censorship notwithstanding, French image-makers produced a surprising number of known images of the American hero, the bulk of the surviving examples suggesting that as soon as Gardner's 1861 photograph reached Paris, its printmakers immediately made it their indisputable favorite Lincoln model, with varying results.

C. Bornemann's typical lithographed adaptation *(Fig. 95)*, however, succeeded primarily in making Lincoln look not American but French (a phenomenon—call it adaptable nationality—that can be discerned in other European Lincolns as well).

Other nations found in Lincoln inspiration for additional struggles—and doubtless used his image accordingly. Both Italy and Germany were, at the time of America's Civil War, fighting for unification of their own, a parallel historical development that triggered interest in Lincoln's own struggles to preserve union in America.

A lithograph by Italian printmakers Buono and Borrani *(Fig. 96)* was surely inspired by such comparisons, and clearly modeled—however clumsily—on the same Gardner photograph that had appealed to the English and French. In this case, however, "Abramo" Lincoln appears neither British nor French, and certainly not American, either—but a swarthy caricature of an Italian. When a rival printmaker, known to us only as "Ca-millo," ventured to produce his own Lincoln print, he apparently found the Gardner photographic model equally irresistible, but to disguise his print's origins (and perhaps separate his work from the slavish copying by Buono and Borrani), presented instead a mirror image of the original, whose compounded faults now included the appearance of Lincoln's familiar facial mole on the wrong side of his face. These lithographs also presented the grandest roman nose yet seen on any Lincoln image published to that date.

No country produced as many Lincoln prints of so wide a variety as did Germany, whose printmakers' achievements included the only known European depictions of Lincoln's life and death, including a brilliantly realized portrayal *(Fig. 97)*, of Lincoln parading into the rubble of City Point, Virginia the headquarters of General Ulysses S. Grant's Union invasion army, which Lincoln visited shortly before the end of the war. Although the scene is unrealistic—the discarded enemy cannon belong more suitably in a battlefield print, and the joyous liberated blacks seem lifted from descriptions of the President's subsequent visit to the conquered Confederate capital of Richmond—it was nonetheless imaginatively designed, artistically composed, and richly detailed, an altogether virtuoso effort considering the distance from which it was created. Other German printmakers, like the chromolithographers Berg & Porsch, turned predictably to the apparently irresistible Gardner model.

In retrospect, that Lincoln came to hold appeal for European audiences is anything but surprising. As a universal apostle of democracy he provided a useful symbol in countries, like France, whose own liberties were under siege.

Abraham Lincoln

Fig. 95. C. Bornemann after photograph by Alexander Gardner, *Abraham Lincoln.* Lithograph with tintstone, published by Lemercier, Paris, *ca.* 1861–2 (Bibliothèque Nationale).

Fig. 96. Buono & Borrani after photograph by Alexander Gardner, *Abramo Lincoln/ Presidente della Repubblica degli Stati Uniti.* Lithograph, Florence, Italy, *ca.* 1861 (Illinois State Historical Library).

Fig. 98. C[harles]. Nahl after photograph by Anthony Berger, *To/ Abraham Lincoln/ The/ Best Beloved/ of the/ Nation./ In Memoriam.* Lithograph, printed by L. Nagel, published with "Puck, the Pacific Pictorial," San Francisco, *ca.* 1865.

Opposite: Fig. 97. F. Hartwich after Gustave Bartsch, *Lincoln in City Point.* Lithograph, printed by J. Hesse, published by Oswald Seehagen, Berlin, *ca.* 1865 (Kenneth M. Newman, The Old Print Shop, Inc.).

And as a force for Union he could suggest that equal conviction the national spirit that had gripped both Italy and Germany.

When artists and audiences in Europe focused on the Lincoln image, it remains especially revealing that the resulting portraits reflected the physical characteristics of the countries in which the pictures were made. In English prints, Lincoln looked English. In French portraits he looked French. Italian prints made him look Italian, and German prints made him look German. He was more than an American. As an icon, he was everyman.

It would be something of an exaggeration to suggest that by 1865, Lincoln was already occupying in Europe a place as a universal symbol of democracy and national union. But as engravings and lithographs of the period so strongly suggest, he was well on his way to status as international symbol. European prints of Abraham Lincoln not only point to that direction, they may well have helped inspire the transfiguration.

With all these print portraits — good, bad, and indifferent; original and pirated; clever and commonplace, foreign and domestic — 19th century engravers helped transform an unknown candidate into a familiar face; helped build public support for union and emancipation; and helped build public support for union and emancipation; and helped nurture in strong visual terms the Lincoln legend. As one period author marveled about a post-assassination engraving: "Were all biographies . . . of the president's character to be lost . . . from this picture alone, the distinguishing qualities of his head and heart might be saved to the knowledge of the future." Today,

no face is more indelibly inscribed on the mind's eye than Lincoln's, but this was not always so. It took years of intense productivity by the pictorialists before the association between physiognomy and spirit could evoke such responses. It took an era of inventive image-making to establish a national familiarity with the face that eventually would come itself to symbolize the democracy which Lincoln helped to preserve.[85]

Of all the eyewitnesses to, and participants in, this remarkable image transfiguration, none had seen more than Lincoln's chief staff aide, John G. Nicolay. He could remember all the various artists who besieged Abraham Lincoln for sittings beginning with his nomination to the presidency. And he not only could recall the results, but surely the popular prints so many had inspired. In one case, back in Springfield in 1860, Nicolay had even helped mastermind such an adaptation, offering suggestions on how to make a picture look both "pretty" and "truthful" *(see Fig. 51).*

But years later, looking back on the pictorial archive whose creation he had witnessed, and at least once, influenced, Nicolay professed to be dissatisfied with the results. "Lincoln's features were the despair of every artist who undertook his portrait," he now insisted. The pictures they made were "hard and cold." They were, in a dismissive word, "unsatisfactory." Nicolay did not blame the artists, but the subject. As he put it:

Graphic art was powerless before a face that moved through a thousand delicate gradations of line and contour, light and shade, sparkle of the eye and curve of the lip, in the long gamut of expression from grave to gay, and back again from the rollicking jollity of laughter to that serious, faraway look that with prophetic intuitions beheld the awful panorama of war, and heard the cry of oppression and suffering.

Concluded Nicolay: "There are many pictures of Lincoln; there is no portrait of him."[86]

But Nicolay was wrong. And so, for that matter, was Henry Deming, a Congressman who got to know Lincoln during the last two years of his life, and worried a few months after his death that he might still "descend the ages according to malicious caricature."[87]

Not only had thousands of copies of Lincoln pictures by then made his face familiar in every corner of the union he saved; they had together etched a portrait of Lincoln resonant enough to overcome cartoons, withstand time, survive debunking, and transcend biography into the realm of national myth: Lincoln the poor boy who rose from obscurity to power; Lincoln the honest man; Lincoln the liberator; and Lincoln the martyr of freedom. Popular prints in their crude way effectively wove these strands into the permanent fabric of Lincoln's legend and American culture as well.

In helping transform a politician into a myth *(Fig. 98)*, the graphic artists not only illustrated, but likely inspired, the metamorphosis. In popular prints and in the public mind, then and now, Abraham Lincoln had grown from a man into a monument.

Lincoln's path to national sainthood was neither as swift nor as smooth as Washington's, the iconographical Athena who seemed to spring full-blown into a domestic god. But once there, the savior held a place as elevated and secure as the father. Together, they were peerless. The pedestal would now be shared, but it would remain theirs alone.

Military Commission

IV
Washington and Lincoln: "Columbia's Noblest Sons"

During the most anxious days of the ominous summer of 1861, "His honor the President of the United States" received in the mail, under that breathlessly reverent salutation, one piece of comforting news from an admirer in Indiana.

The correspondent was one Jacob L. Tudor, and he was writing to announce proudly that he had named his newborn son "Abraham Lincoln Tudor." "As a Mechanic and an American," he declared, "I feel that all i can bequeath" to "Little Linky," as he referred to him, "is his good name." Besides, he had called his older son "George Washington Tudor." And "with those glorious names recorded in my Bible," he now predicted, "I feel confident of there [sic] success." The reason for Tudor's confidence went beyond party or sectional loyalties: Abraham Lincoln was not only the nation's "Cheafe Executive," he explained, but "the second father of my country."[1]

We have no record of any reply from Lincoln, so we cannot know for certain how he reacted to the flattering comparison—although it is difficult to imagine that it did not please him. Perhaps it was no coincidence, then, that in his "This is . . . a People's Contest" message to Congress only a few days later, he revealed that he had found new faith in "the patriotic instinct of the plain people. They understand without argument," he contended, "that destroying the government, which was made by Washington, means no good to them."[2]

It was not the first time Abraham Lincoln had invoked the name of George Washington to add luster to his own policies, and it would not be the last. From the very start of his political career—in an era in which Washington's name invited panegyrics, not comparisons—Lincoln had almost impudently placed himself squarely on the side of America's all-purpose hero. And

Opposite: **As the nation awaits the start of the trial of the Lincoln assassination conspirators, members of the military commission who will judge them pose for an 1865 Mathew Brady photograph—dwarfed by the background portraits of the father and the martyred saviour of the republic: Washington (left) and Lincoln (photograph: National Archives).**

when the American graphic arts industry, like Lincoln himself, came of age in the 1860s, printmakers began performing precisely the same service in his behalf: literally placing Washington at Lincoln's side pictorially to create evocative visual reminders of an increasingly apparent connection between the first and sixteenth presidents. Beginning with the 1860 presidential campaign, and with particular force immediately after the assassination, America's printmakers produced a visual record which suggested that Lincoln was not only Washington's natural heir—but his historical equal. By 1865 they had provided pictorial validation of the belief that the Union saved had been preserved according to the principles upon which it had been "brought forth upon this continent."

To comprehend the impact such pictures exerted in their time requires an understanding of the political culture in which they thrived. It was an age in which pictures were rare, precious, and prized, and were not the commonplace, quickly discarded illustrations they have become in today's media-glutted society. And it was an age in which the nation's founders were canonized, politicians were typically revered, voter turnout was nearly unanimous, and politics combined the ferver of religious revivalism with the entertainment value of theater. In this inviting milieu, 19th century publishers flooded the market with best-selling display images of current and past leaders alike, which understandably became icons in the American family parlor.[3]

It should come as no surprise that Washington's image dominated the genre, even fifty years after his death. As noted, foreign visitors had taken note of its ubiquity when Lincoln was still a baby growing up in the Kentucky backwoods. Americans like Emerson and Whitman later embraced the tradition of gracing their parlors with Washington portraits, carrying the practice into a new generation, apparently finding in the first president's comforting presence crucial reassurance about the durability of the American experiment, even as the nation itself was engulfed in rebellion.

That Lincoln's image eventually came to be associated with, and later even to rival Washington's, for dominance in patriotic homes, testifies convincingly to both the appeal of the Lincoln reputation and the resonance of the Lincoln legend. And it also confirms the market acumen of the publishers who fed public demand not only for straightforward Lincoln portraiture, but for visualizations of the Lincoln-Washington "association," with a flurry of appealing images. Such prints were not commissioned by political organizations or even memorial organizations: by and large they were the invention of their artists and publishers. They were issued in response—or anticipation—of public appetite. And as a result, they not only illustrated; they influenced.

Above all, the pictures confirmed for Lincoln a remarkable ascendancy in the national pantheon. Writing "a little sketch" of his life in 1859, only six years before his death and deification, Lincoln was moved to admit, rather acerbically: "My parents were both born in Virginia of undistinguished familes— second families, perhaps I should say." Hidden in that ironic remark, one might conclude, was a stinging rebuke of Virginia's *first* families—Washington's, presumably, included; a subtle but undisguisable announcement that Lincoln's America now offered the chance, as he would put it a few years later to a regiment of Ohio soldiers visiting the White House, that "any one of your children may look to come here as my father's child has." In truth, Lincoln's attitude toward Washington and the founders was more than one of envy. He also revered them. But his ascendancy in popular prints—and popular opinion—was surely a triumph for the "second families" of which he spoke, and also came to personify.[4]

It was a triumph of sorts, too, for the graphic artists who so quickly perceived and so vividly portrayed these two presidents together—the daunting distance and differences between them notwithstanding.

But while a case might well be made that print artists independently seized upon the idea of presenting Lincoln and Washington together, and in so doing invented the enduring link between the two, in truth their efforts were but a part of a more widespread canonization that took root from the pulpit, in newspapers, and in literature as well as the arts after Lincoln's assassination. What is more, Lincoln himself, long before his presidency, took a sure hand in forging the association by periodically invoking the father of his country to support what he suggested were their shared purposes. Henry Clay may have been his "beau ideal of a statesman." Jacksonian resolve in the Nullification crisis offered him the safe harbor of precedent in resisting secession. The Jeffersonian spirit of democracy echoed in his own pen. But Washington, remote as he seemed personally served as a universal, all-purpose symbol for Lincoln as well as his contemporaries: the reluctant, stainless hero who shunned a crown to forge a republic. "Getting right" with Washington became as crucial a ritual of passage for politicians

of mid-century as was waving the bloody shirt for the Reconstruction generation. And Lincoln was not immune to the tradition.[5]

In the beginning, Washington seemed to Lincoln "the mightiest name on earth." In his Temperance Address before a hometown audience in Springfield on Washington's birthday in 1842, Lincoln held that "to add brightness to the sun or glory to Washington, is alike impossible," adding: "In solemn awe we pronounce the name, and in its naked deathless splendor, leave it shining on." Even the garbled peroration to his speech at the Springfield Lyceum in 1838 made clear Lincoln's hope that "no hostile foot" ever desecrate the sacred resting place of "our WASHINGTON." Had John Adams been alive, he might well have found such allusions presumptuous, having years before railed against "one of the national sins of our country ... [the] idolatrous worship paid to the name of George Washington by all classes and *nearly* all parties ... manifested by the impious application of names and epithets to him which are ascribed in scripture only to God and Jesus Christ." Adams' complaints predictably did little to inhibit the idolatry, from Lincoln or others.[6]

It was one thing to praise Washington, and quite another to use him— and notwithstanding the dangers posed by recklessly calling up the ghost of "the great ornament of human kind," as a Washington contemporary gushingly called him—Lincoln became as adroit at the latter as he was at the former. Articulating the Whig line on the National Bank issue in 1844, for example, Lincoln pointed out that Washington had created the bank in the first place, and therefore it had to be right, because "Washington never [did] a wrong thing in his life." Four years later he

Lith. & Published by Edwᵈ Mendel, 162 Lake Street Chicago.

Fig. 99. Edw[ard]. Mendel after photograph by Samuel M. Fassett, *[Abraham Lincoln with Bust of George Washington].* Lithograph, Chicago, 1860 (Chicago Historical Society).

took to the floor of Congress to warn President Polk never to forget that "he sits where Washington sat," urging him "to answer, as Washington would answer." He claimed to be fighting against the 1854 Kansas-Nebraska Act in "Washington fashion"; and in debate with Stephen A. Douglas in 1858, went so far as to equate his opposition to the extention of slavery with a desire to place the institution "where Washington . . . placed it." As Lincoln contended at both New York and New Haven in 1860 — both speeches, it is seldom recalled, delivered near Washington's birthday — Washington not only intended that the spread of slavery be arrested, but even foresaw an irrepressible conflict were it allowed instead to flourish. "The old fathers said the same thing," Lincoln insisted. ". . . Washington said it."[7]

"Some of you delight to flaunt in our faces the warning against sectional parties given by Washington, in his farewell address," Lincoln declared at Cooper Union, conveniently ignoring the fact that Washington himself was a slaveholder. Washington was on record for "a confederacy of free states," he continued, and those who wanted something else were guilty of nothing less than "imploring men to unsay what Washington said, and undo what Washington did." Lincoln's implication was clear: *he* would never be guilty of such political sacrilege, although the mere act of politicizing Washington's name itself reflected a kind of impiety. It was one thing to link on to Washington generically — and in the 1840s and 1850s, it was no longer rare to see engraved and lithographed campaign prints featuring portraits of the first president in suggestive proximity to those of current political candidates. But it was quite another thing to apply

Washington's 18th century example to 19th century problems. Lincoln would attempt the latter long before benefiting from the former.[8]

With such rhetoric on the record — the Cooper Union Address was printed in newspapers and circulated in at least three pamphlet versions — it would have been natural for American printmakers to begin visually echoing these associations once Lincoln catapulted to national prominence in 1860, and his nomination for president triggered a huge public demand for his portraits. What is surprising is that so *few* artists immediately did so — an indication of either a remarkable lack of creativity or an as-yet unique regard for Washington as a sanctified subject still unsuitable for politicization either by or with ordinary mortals. For whatever reasons, only a handful of such images surfaced in 1860.[9]

Lincoln's initial "appearance" with Washington came only a few months after the convention, in an adaptation of an 1859 photograph by Samuel Fassett of Chicago *(see Fig. 53)*, which Mary Lincoln is said to have judged "the best likeness she had ever seen of her husband." Local print and map publisher Edward Mendel issued a crude lithographed version *(Fig. 99)* by June 1860. The following month, the image was being advertised as the "most accurate Portrait yet published," not only "acknowledged by all his friends to be a perfect likeness," but applauded by Lincoln himself, whose letter of praise was reprinted in full in the newspaper advertisement. Mendel had shrewdly sent Lincoln a copy of the portrait, and Lincoln acknowledged it as a *"truthful* Lithograph Portrait of myself" — the word "truthful" underlined — strong praise from a man who only, a few months later, would tell the disappointed engraver of a far more accomplished print that its arrival had first "passed from mind," and didn't inspire an assessment anyway, because he was "a very indifferent judge" of such matters. Yet Lincoln was not at all indifferent about the Mendel lithograph, and what likely attracted the subject to the portrait was the prop visible next to him: a small bust of Washington. By this time the Washington image had long seemed, in the words of one artist, "grand and imposing . . . calculated for public buildings." To Lincoln, there may have been in his own mind, sufficient "truthfulness" in the flattering artistic device to excuse all the picture's obvious artistic shortcomings. He was undoubtedly pleased when in August, the print was proudly displayed from a flagstaff in the yard of a Springfield Republican at a rally for Lincoln's presidential campaign.[10]

So far as we know, Lincoln's letter to Mendel was advertised only once, and in a small town Illinois newspaper. Had it achieved wider visibility, it might well have inspired rival printmakers to take up the Washington-Lincoln genre during the campaign. But the only other known contribution came from the New York firm of H. H. Lloyd, the self-proclaimed "greatest" engraver in that city, which adapted the famous Gilbert Stuart Athenaeum portrait of Washington *(see Fig. 13)*, together with a Mathew Brady photograph taken at the time Lincoln was invoking Washington at Cooper Union *(see Fig. 60)*, for an elaborate Lincoln-Hamlin campaign poster, the *National Republican Chart (see Fig. 67)*. The result clearly suggested that Washington was somehow blessing the Lincoln-Hamlin ticket and their party platform, which was reprinted in

full within the broadside. But the truth is, this was no image-making watershed: the Lloyd firm used precisely the same Washington portrait for a *National Political Chart* that gave more prominence to John Bell and Stephen A. Douglas than to Lincoln. Only after the election had been decided in Lincoln's favor did the firm come out with a *New Political Chart* in which a bearded Lincoln portrait now stood alone, dwarfing the emblematic image of Washington. Iconographically, it was a sure sign of things to come.[11]

And Lincoln did much to speed his own transfiguration. Once elected, he began pointedly and regularly invoking the Washington name. To future Confederate vice president Alexander H. Stephens, he sent reassurances that "the South would be in no more danger [from me] . . . than it was in the days of Washington." But the most extraordinary comments were yet to come. It required a considerable leap of faith, perhaps taste as well, to compare oneself, much less to suggest that one faced greater challenges, than the very founder of the nation—"the eagle, the standard, the flag" himself, in the words of one Washington contemporary, "the living symbol of the Republic." Yet departing Springfield for his inauguration a few weeks later, Lincoln told his neighbors—in words he surely knew would be printed in newspapers throughout the nation—that he had before him "a task greater than that which faced Washington." He ended by asking the guidance of "that Divine Being, who ever attended *him*" [emphasis added], suggesting that he shared with Washington, not only a political legacy, but a special relationship with God.[12]

As his train steamed eastward toward the capital bearing Washington's-name, the president-elect called forth the comforting specter of the American St. George in city after city along his route. In Cincinnati, he promised the South, "we mean to treat you ... as Washington ... treated you." In Columbus, he reiterated his Springfield message, declaring: "Without a name, perhaps without a reason why I should have a name, there has fallen upon me a task such as did not rest even upon the Father of His Country." In Trenton, the day before Washington's birthday, he discoursed nostalgically about the influence exerted on him as a child by Weems' *Life of Washington.* He spoke reverently about the inspiring stories he had heard on the frontier about the heroes of the Revolution. And he admitted that he was "exceedingly anxious that that thing which they struggled for ... that something that held out a great promise to all the people of the world to all time to come ... shall be perpetuated in accordance with the original idea for which that struggle was made." He would be pleased to become but the "humble instrument" to perpetuate "the object of this great struggle." Audiences interrupted him repeatedly with enthusiastic applause. Even in hostile New York, whose Democratic mayor had greeted the disunion crisis with his own proposal to secede from the Union and turn the nation's largest metropolis into a free city, and where Lincoln frankly admitted, a "majority of your people do not support me," the welcoming crowds were nonetheless vast. But as eyewitness Walt Whitman observed, they were at first strangely silent, too, lacking "that indescribably human roar and magnetism ... the glad exulting thunder-shouts of countless unloos'd throats." At a reception inside City Hall, Mayor Fernando Wood politely ushered

Lincoln toward the head of a receiving line near a desk Washington had once used. But the president-elect found the glare from the room's floor-to-ceiling windows oppressive, and suggested that the line be reformed in a new location: in front of a Washington statue on the other side of the room. "Let me stand there with my back to the old General," Lincoln said, loud enough for everyone in the chamber to hear him. "Sustained by Washington, I shall get along better." For a time, Washington continued to sustain him. To allow the Union to disintegrate, he announced once installed in the White House, would violate the very legacy he had inherited. There was neither "manhood nor honor in that," he protested. "There is no Washington in that." The message was clear: Lincoln was not only Washington's political successor, but his spiritual heir as well.[13]

Once again, however, the printmaker's response to the rekindled imagery proved sluggish and uninspired. In their defense, public demand for Lincoln pictures had been sated by then by the plethora of campaign portraits still in circulation, some now with whiskers hastily superimposed to bring them up to date. As a result, only a few wartime prints took note of Lincoln's renewed Washington emphasis—and of these, one was attributable chiefly to convenience and coincidence. A bust of Washington had been the centerpiece of an outdated 1852 engraving *(Fig. 100)*, depicting the leaders of antebellum America gathered around the emblematic symbol. To update *Union,* whose title seemed now particularly appropriate even if its cast of characters wasn't, a printmaker simply dusted off the old plate, burnished out the face of a central figure, John C. Calhoun, and superimposed that of

Lincoln *(Fig. 101)*, his portrait once again based on the Cooper Union photographic model, now shown directly alongside the symbolically potent figure of Washington.

But the revised group was still an anachronism: it showed Lincoln inexplicably posing alongside men who were long dead—including Henry Clay and Daniel Webster. Only a few concessions to the sea change in American politics in the intervening decade were attempted: Robert Anderson, hero of Fort Sumter, inserted where ex–President James Buchanan had stood in the original; General John Wool in place of defeated presidential aspirant John Bell; and three Southerners, W. P. Mangum of North Carolina, William R. King of Alabama, and Howell Cobb of Georgia, replaced, respectively, by Secretary of State William H. Seward, General Benjamin F. Butler, and orator Edward Everett.[14]

When this version, too, became outdated once Lincoln grew his beard, yet another state of the engraving *(Fig. 102)* appeared, with the old Cooper Union Lincoln itself "updated" through the addition of hastily drawn whiskers—but with the implausible 1852 figures still dominating the scene. It is difficult to imagine what Lincoln-era audiences made of this perplexing assemblage. But surely if they purchased the print for their homes, it was not because Lincoln was portrayed with Lewis Cass and General Wool, but because he was all but wrapped around the inspiring, nation-affirming symbol of his predecessor. Printmakers may have been unpardonably craven in taking such commercially inspired shortcuts to produce images, but they were

no fools when it came to gauging audience taste. The fact that the Lincoln updating went through two separate printings indicates its considerable appeal. Further proof could be found in publisher William Pate's catalogue of titles for 1861, in which *Union* was prominently listed at $1 wholesale, just below four different portraits of George Washington. Washington was still the predominant American symbol, occupying a place as *Union* proved, even in those prints which did not directly portray him. But Abraham Lincoln was beginning to catch up.[15]

For a time, Washington's resonating presence remained a staple of early Civil War iconography. It was very much in evidence, for example, in early group portraits of all 16 presidents, prints which powerfully suggested the continuity of the Union and the institution of the presidency in the face of secession and rebellion. Some examples, like A. Feusir's decorative chromolithograph *(Fig. 103)*, clearly cared more for the overall impact of the genre than about the fidelity of individual portraiture; this particular print was so hastily rushed to the marketplace that its Lincoln portrait was still clean-shaven, even though Lincoln had begun sporting whiskers nearly four months before his inauguration. But it was Washington who remained the focus—slightly larger than his successors in the design, placed high atop the evocative oval, above even the figure of Liberty herself. Lincoln was at the very bottom, an unproven successor to the Washington mantle, relegated to low status by virtue of chronology. Other examples, like Middleton, Strobridge & Co.'s 1861 *Peace* print *(Fig. 104)*,

---

Opposite: Fig. 100. **Henry S. Sadd after Tompkins Harrison Matteson,** *Union.* **Mezzotint engraving, published by William Pate, New York, 1852 (The Lincoln Museum).**

granted Washington an even more pronounced dominance, submerging Lincoln's portrait even with respect to illustrations of such virtues as westward expansion, commerce, and the compatibility of free and slave labor. This print even referred to the new president colloquially: "Abe. Lincoln."

Yet another sign of Washington's uninterrupted dominance of national iconography is evident in a *Family Record of American Allegiances* — an 1861 novelty designed to accommodate private oaths of "true and faithful allegiance" to the Union. While Lincoln's portrait crowned the cluster of celebrities that included Anderson, Butler, George B. McClellan and Winfield Scott, Washington's overarching likeness loomed largest, as did the test of his "Sentiment" reprinted in a nearby scroll. As much space was devoted to Washington's vision of "an indissoluble Union of the Streets" as to the sentiments of Lincoln, Stephen A. Douglas, John Hancock, and Thomas Jefferson combined.

As the quotes suggest, Union and the Constitution had emerged as the common thread binding Lincoln and Washington together in prints during the secession crisis, helping to forge the permanent cultural affiliation that was to achieve its greatest visual form once the Union was saved and Lincoln martyred. But for all his earlier efforts to instill such mystic chords of memory, and even to applaud the first effort to portray it, Lincoln himself ceased calling up the ghost after Washington's birthday in 1862, the same year Johnson & Fry of New York issued the first of two versions of an engraving of Lincoln trampling a secession ordinance

into shreds while clutching a copy of the Constitution — at the same time gazing meaningfully at a large bust of the first president *(Fig. 105)*. Lincoln had proclaimed February 22 an official Union holiday that year, urging Americans to use the occasion to re-read Washington's Farewell Address. But when one citizen tried to read it aloud from the galleries of Congress, an over-zealous guard used excessive force to restrain him. Lincoln offered to pay the guard's fine, convinced he was only trying to perform "his official duty." The incident proved not only an embarrassment but an epiphany. Abraham Lincoln never publicly invoked the name of George Washington again. He did not have to. In historian James M. McPherson's words, he had supplanted the enduring glory of the first American Revolution with a second American revolution. But their goals were in many ways incompatible.[16]

Once Lincoln changed the purpose of the Civil War from preserving the Union that Washington helped forge, to eradicating the institution of slavery which the founders had tolerated, Washington became, for Lincoln if not his image-makers, inexpedient and anachronistic. But the appeal inherent in making evocative comparisons between one president fighting the dissolution of the country that an earlier president had founded remained, for graphic artists, irresistible, and for their audiences, inescapable. It was left now to others to validate the increasingly apparent kinship between the two. Harriet Beecher Stowe, for one, obliged, marveling at mid-war that "since the time of Washington, the

Opposite: Fig. 101. **Printmaker unknown after Sadd and photograph by Mathew B. Brady,** *Union.* **[2nd state of Fig. 100, Lincoln's head substituted for Calhoun's]. Engraving,** *ca.* **1861. (The Lincoln Museum).**

Fig. 103. A. Feusier after Gilbert Stuart (Washington) and photograph by Mathew B. Brady (Lincoln), *Presidents of the United Staes.* Lithograph, published by F. Bouclet, Philadelphia, 1861 (Library of Congress).

Opposite: Fig. 102. Printmaker unknown after Sadd and photograph by Mathew B. Brady, *Union* [3rd state of Fig. 100, Lincoln's beard superimposed]. Engraving, *ca.* 1861 (The Lincoln Museum).

Fig. 104. Middleton, Strobridge & Co. after Gilbert Stuart (Washington) and photograph by Roderick M. Cole (Lincoln), *Peace/ The American Union.* Lithograph, Cincinnati, 1861 (Library of Congress).

state-papers of no President have more controlled the popular mind." And soon after Gettysburg, her brother, Henry Ward Beecher, went even further,

echoing the very words of the Spring-field farewell address in declaring that Lincoln had been "ordained" to purge the Union "of a worse oppression" than

Fig. 105. Johnson & Fry after photograph by Anthony Berger. *A. Lincoln* [facsimile signature], "painted by Alonzo Chappel" [2nd state of print; 1st state based on different photograph]. Engraving, New York, 1863.

confronted the Founders. "Joined together one and inseparable," he predicted uncannily, "we shall hereafter
hear on jubilees the shouts 'Washington
and Lincoln!—the Fathers.'"[17]

Americans would not only hear
such jubilees, but see pictorial equiva-
lents as well. The flood of Lincoln-
Washington images to come would not
only celebrate the two presidents' struggles to create and save the Union, but
in the very decision to portray them
together also highlight attributes of the
Lincoln legend modern Americans take
for granted: modesty, honesty, devotion to duty, devotion to family, and
physical stature. In Washington's case,
such traits had by the Lincoln era been
burned into the national consciousness:
they were the public and private virtues
combining greatness with goodness
which constituted an ideal for Americans to emulate.[18]

Printmakers would make certain
that Lincoln in particular lived up to
the expectations. From the beginning of
his national prominence in 1860, his
portraits had helped affix noticeably
Washingtonian embellishments into the
fabric of his image. Early campaign
prints that showed Lincoln mauling
rails or steering a flatboat *(see Fig. 46)*,
for example, affirmed not only his rise
from poverty and obscurity, but his
physical strength as well, perhaps
reminding voters that the man who
could so effortlessly chop wood was a
worthy successor to a man who according to legend had hurled a coin across
a river. Myth also held that Washington could never tell a lie, and "Honest
Abe's" integrity would be vivified as
well, in prints like the ones *(see Figs.
56 and 58)*, depicting the Greek
philosopher Diogenes discarding his
fabled lantern after finding at last in
Lincoln the long-sought "honest man."

And Lincoln family prints, however
fanciful in their rose-colored portrayals
of so unhappy a domestic circle, proved
worthy successors to the early domestic
images of the ironically childless Washington—reinforcing the image of Lincoln as the second father of his country.

Of course, there were image differences too, but after 1861 they were
pointedly ignored by America's graphic
artists, for Lincoln the happy result of
both philosophy and geography. Southern image-makers, after all, might with
justification have preferred comparing
the aristocratic Washington with their
own aristocratic Southern-born president, Jefferson Davis. Or they might
have seized on Washington's well-
known aversion for the abuse of power,
or his one-time leadership of a revolution, to transform him into a symbol of
the Confederacy instead of the Union—
as indeed they suggested when they
chose an equestrian Washington portrait for their national seal. But seldom
was this link reinforced in graphics (except, indirectly, when early Davis
prints were captioned, "Our First President"). This surprisingly lackluster image competition, from which Lincoln
emerged the undisputed second national paterfamilias, was attributable at
least in part to the withering of the
Southern printmaking industry itself
under the pressures of wartime depriva-
tion. After the War, national images
were made in only one part of the
nation—in the North. There, Abraham
Lincoln was idealized and compared to
Washington, not Jefferson Davis.[19]

The abundant disparities between
Washington and Lincoln were thus
never emphasized in Northern-made
prints after *Harper's Weekly* charged pictorially, only two days before Lincoln's
inauguration, that the president-elect
believed, with Seward, Beecher,

Horace Greeley, and even John Brown, all placed in one caricature, that no communion was possible with, nor presumably for, slaveholders—even a slaveholder like Washington, who here stood convicted before the court of history in a demeaning posture designed to make Lincoln and his cohorts in the print appear blasphemous. But by the time this image was published, Lincoln had so adroitly used Washington's name to sanctify his fight against secession, that such differences were put aside—along with far less subtle incompatibilities, like the obvious fact that Washington had once led an insurrection similar enough to the Confederate struggle to inspire President Davis to remind the South in the year of the Gettysburg Address that he, too, was fighting for "freedom" and "equality."

In addition, as one period observer put it, while Washington "belonged to the colonial aristocracy," Lincoln was "made of . . . homely stuff . . . a man of the people." But even prints *(Fig. 106)* that shrunk the size of Washington's fabled Mount Vernon failed to disguise Washington's great wealth and social status. On the other hand, prints of Lincoln's far humbler house *(Fig. 101)* in Springfield were unable to transform "the simple home of an American statesman," as a journalist of the day described it, into a hearthstone magnificent enough to have bred a successor to Washington. Perhaps that explains why one printmaker decided in 1865—in the words of today's image-making spin doctors—to level the playing field by updating an old image of Henry Clay's huge Kentucky estate, Ashland by simply retitled it, *The Home of Our Martyred President.* However clumsily, the publisher was in a way validating one Lincoln eulogist's prophesy that differences notwithstanding,

"Mount Vernon and Springfield will henceforth be kindred shrines."[20]

There were other differences—also conveniently ignored or overlooked. For example, Washington was also the quintessential military hero *(see Fig. 5)*, and Lincoln very much the civilian. Washington looked as natural in uniform as in mufti, but somehow one cannot imagine Lincoln in Union blue, and even in imaginary scenes *(Fig. 108)* suggesting how he looked conferring with his commanders on the battlefield, Lincoln was always clad in his characteristic black frock coat. Washington epitomized dignity and reserve, what Hawthorne called a "benevolent coldness and apartness." Lincoln, on the other hand, was so famous for his earthy humor that he could invite criticism and attack, such as the calumny leveled against him for allegedly requesting comic songs on a casualty-riddled battlefield. "Washington prayed for assistance from on high when going into battle," one observer pointed out, while "Lincoln . . . asked a companion to sing 'Jump Jim Crow' upon the bloody field of Antietam." Even R. H. Stoddard's flattering 1865 ode to Lincoln took pains to suggest, implying a virtue, that Lincoln was "no Gentleman, like Washington."[21]

But Washington was no emancipator, like Lincoln. As *Harper's Weekly* had obliquely made clear, Lincoln's relationship with black Americans was far different from Washington's—yet printmakers never made an issue of the first president's sole undisguisable personal blemish. Only the most sophisticated period audiences would notice that while several prints showed grateful liberated slaves kneeling to Lincoln *(Fig. 109)*, blacks seen in prints kneeling before Washington *(Fig. 110)* were so posed because they were slaves on

his plantation. Washington owned slaves while Lincoln freed slaves, but this major disparity was never illustrated in prints that portrayed them together, even when their theme was not Union, but liberty.

There was a final difference. From the Revolution onward, Washington was both spoken of and portrayed as an idol *(see Fig. 14)*—"the *Man who unites all hearts,*" whose birthday was already being celebrated as a holiday of "universal joy and festivity" while he lived—and in popular prints, literally a figure on a pedestal: a living monument. Lincoln would achieve monument status, too *(Fig. 111)*, but not until his death. A year earlier, at a moment in his life comparable to that in which Washington was depicted as a heroic statue, Lincoln was a partisan figure gracing a reelection poster, very much of, and limited to, his own time.[22]

All the dissimilarities between them, even if audiences ever wholly contemplated or comprehended them, all the variables in philosophy and breeding that separated them as surely as the generations, were quickly forgotten once the Union was saved. Even as the war was drawing to a close in February 1865, it was apparent to the *New York Times* that "WASHINGTON is completing his second cycle.... He has been with ABRAHAM LINCOLN," they added. "...His spirit leads us in this second war of the Constitution. When Lincoln became its final sacrifice, he was elevated overnight into the realm of martyrdom, a metamorphosis visible quickly in deathbed prints *(see Fig. 84)* that bore an eerie resemblance to those that had depicted the comparatively peaceful but equally lamented death of

Washington *(see Figs. 30, 31)*.[23]

Then, on the Sunday after Lincoln's murder, eulogists ascended pulpits throughout the North on this blackest of Easters to compare Lincoln to Jesus, Moses—and, significantly, to an American god as well. The Rev. Elbert S. Porter told his congregation that Lincoln would go down in history as "the political savior of what Washington . . . founded." In Brooklyn, Beecher predicted that Lincoln's "simple and weighty words will be gathered like those of Washington." So would his portraits. One eulogist would even take note of the fact that a Lincoln picture had been hung directly below Washington's for the occasion of his oration. He shared with his audience his belief that in the "coming days their portaits shall hang side by side." Within weeks, his prophecy would be fulfilled.[24]

Surely it was not lost on ordinary Americans—even those who bore witness to Lincoln's funerals only through the medium of popular prints *(Fig. 112)*, that no such catharsis had gripped the country since the funeral of Washington *(Fig. 113)* had proved the first universal exception to America's deeply rooted fear of hero-worship and "excessive mourning." Still-available images of such Washington tributes looked so uncannily like those of Lincoln's that few print patrons could easily overlook the comparison. The connections were verified even in the acoutrements of mourning. As one hand-lettered sign declared in salute to the remains as they arrived in Jersey City: "GEORGE WASHINGTON, the father/ABRAHAM LINCOLN, the saviour of his country." The "mystic chords of memory" had united them in death.[25]

Opposite: Fig. 106. G. F. Gilman, *Mount Vernon.* **Chromolithograph, 1878 (Library of Congress).**

HOME OF ABRAHAM LINCOLN.

L.PRANG & CO. LITH. BOSTON

Fig. 108. P[eter]. **Kramer after Anthony Berger,** *Lincoln and His Generals.* **Lithograph, printed by A[lphonse]. Brett, published by Jones & Clark, New York, and C. A. Asp, Boston, 1865.**

Meanwhile eulogists and journalists continued hammering away at the theme. Only a few weeks after Lincoln was laid to rest, Charles Sumner amplified the simple sentiments expressed at the Jersey City docks by telling a Boston audience: "The work left undone by Washington was continued by Lincoln," who "raised a reluctant sword to save those great ideas, essential to the life and character of the Republic." In New York, James Gordon Bennett's *New York Herald* said of Lincoln's "solid, brilliant, and stainless" reputation, that "its only peer" existed "in the memory of George Washington." And Wendell Phillips was soon predicting that "History will add . . . [Lincoln's] name to the bright list" of heroes led by Washington—"that galaxy of Americans which makes our history the day star of the nations." Printmakers may well have been inspired to visualize and market such declarations, perhaps even recalling those instructive words from Ecclesiasticus—not only the

Opposite: Fig. 107. **L[ouis]. Prang & Co. after photograph by John Adams Whipple, Springfield, summer 1860,** *Home of Abraham Lincoln.* **Lithograph, Boston, 1860 (The New York Historical Society).**

much-quoted opening phrase, "Let us now praise famous men," but the far less familiar but equally telling addendum, "and our fathers that begat us."[26]

Some historians have likened the impassioned political culture of the 19th century to a civil religion. But in Christian America, secular and religious subjects did not mix in popular prints. Currier & Ives, the most prolific picture publishers of the day, offered along with their military and political titles an abundant selection of saints and saviors, but *un*separating church and state was rare in the graphic arts. Publishers would not risk portraying Lincoln together with either Jesus or Moses, but Washington, the secular God, was another matter. Quite literally, and with astonishing speed for the period, printmakers created in popular art an exclusively American heavenly pantheon, a nondenominational civil afterworld only vaguely religious in nature, and within it visualized Lincoln's apotheosis for the consolation and patronage of his bereaved admirers. Such graphics fulfilled America's need for reassurance that Lincoln had indeed gone, as the preachers were assuring them, to a "better place," and that his violent and sudden death, rather than suggesting a threat to stability, emphasized instead the continuity of the institution of the presidency, founded by Washington, preserved by Lincoln, and unbroken by either rebellion or assassination. However maudlin, such prints *(Fig. 114)* offered reassuring visions of the exaltation which Phillips had described, where it was possible to imagine Lincoln being welcomed into immortality by Washington himself. Difficult as it is to conceive of the results as home decorations, these bathetic pictures appeared in both large formats for the

family parlor, and in *carte-de-visite* size for family photograph albums. And enough examples survive to testify to their immense contemporary popularity.

In these graphics, Washington served as the official gatekeeper of the historical afterworld, extending his arms to welcome an awkwardly posed Lincoln as angels escorted him skyward. An example that portrayed Washington offering a laurel wreath and an embrace proved appealing enough to inspire a crude pirated copy, issued by a printmaker in Ohio. "Heroes and Saints with fadeless stars have crowned him," declared a Lincoln dirge that might easily have been inspired by such prints "— and WASHINGTON'S dear arms are clasped around him." The theme was further echoed in *Liberty and Union,* a "song on the Death of President Abraham Lincoln" to the tune of "Annie Laurie." Silas S. Steele's new lyrics urged:

> Come bind his brows with laurel,
>   Place the olive on his breast,
> And in the free earth lay him,
>   In Honour's Shroud to rest.
> In Honour's Shroud to rest,
>   Let his Counsel still be nigh,
> And the Saviour of our Union
>   Is with WASHINGTON on high.

Neatly illustrating these sentiments, a New York engraver added an angel offering a palm of victory and a laurel wreath symbolizing triumph and eternity *(Fig. 115)*. And a Philadelphia-made example *(Fig. 116)*, scarcely better in artistic realization, could nevertheless boast of capturing the spirit of the apotheosis in a caption: here were "The Founder and the Preserver of the Union," their celestial meeting verifying that the government "brought forth" by Washington had endured under Lincoln.

EMANCIPATION OF THE SLAVES,

Proclamed on the 22ᵈ September 1862, by ABRAHAM LINCOLN, President of the United States of North America.

Published by J. Waeschle, Nº 142, North Third Sᵗ Philadᵃ

Fig. 109. J. Waeschle after photograph by Wenderoth and Taylor, *Emancipation of the Slaves./ Proclaimed on the 22d September 1862 by ABRAHAM LINCOLN, President of the United States of North America.* Lithograph, Philadelphia, *ca.* 1865 (Library of Congress).

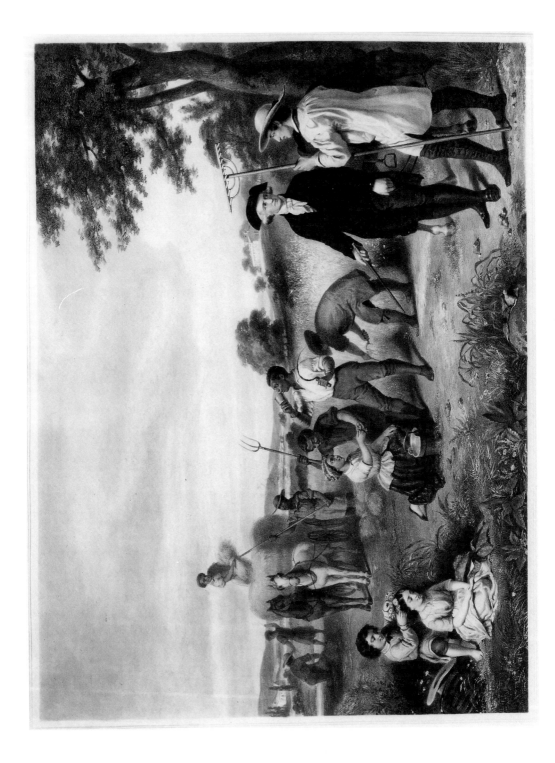

MONUMENT OF ABRAHAM LINCOLN.

Fig. 111. Printmaker unknown, *Monument of Abraham Lincoln.* Lithograph, *ca.* 1865 (The Lincoln Museum).

Opposite: Fig. 110. Regnier after Junius Brutus Stearns, *Life of George Washington/ The Farmer.* Lithograph, printed by Lemercier, Paris, published by M. Knoedler, New York, and Goupil et Cie, Paris, 1853 (Library of Congress).

THE FUNERAL OF PRESIDENT LINCOLN, NEW YORK, APRIL 25TH 1865.
PASSING UNION SQUARE.

Even in those apotheosis scenes in which he did not act as heavenly greeter, Washington was a figure testifying not only to Lincoln's resurrection, but to a new theme emerging in prints, however anomalous, to unite them: freedom. In one example *(Fig. 117)*, it is the figure of Liberty herself who crowns her newest martyr—but while leaning upon a bust of Washington. The allegorical figure carries a capped liberty pole, symbol of the manumission of slaves, and at her feet are broken shackles representing emancipation, together with the Proclamation itself, for those who required their diet of symbolism force fed. Here was fresh evidence that publishers had bridged the gulf between the two presidents on slavery: prints could sidestep the issue and still emphasize the theme of liberty by reminding Americans that the Emancipation was an act "second only in importance to the Declaration of Independence," as artist Francis B. Carpenter described it in a best-selling book, a document that completed the Revolution started under Washington.[28]

The idea of celebrating the work begun by Washington and concluded by Lincoln could be found symbolically lurking in all these ascension prints—particularly in *Reward of the Just* *(Fig. 118)*, a curiosity piece which period viewers likely believed instead as an effort to compare Lincoln with Jesus rising from the grave. Unbeknownst to its audience, however, its design owed its sole creative debt to Washington. The clues to its origins were ample, if obscure. True, many of its ephemeral figures seemed consistent with Lincoln's

martyrdom: allegorical figures representing Faith, Hope, and Charity looking on mournfully; Lincoln rising out of his reopened coffin, to be escorted heavenward by Father Time; and nearby, a liberty figure appropriately hanging her head in woe. But other, less comprehensible symbols appeared as well: an American shield featuring far too few stars for the 1860s; a Roman warrior's *fasces,* an incongruous emblem of power; an American Indian inexplicably prostate with grief; and even the badge of the Society of the Cincinnatus, draped from the open catafalque—hardly Lincolnesque.

The explanation was simple, if invisible: the 1865 print was copied directly from a sixty-year-old original that had depicted the apotheosis of Washington *(Fig. 119)*. All that Philadelphia lithographer D. T. Weist did in pirating the design was to change the name etched onto the sarcophagous, and superimpose the face of Lincoln where Washington's had been, leaving other crucial but irrelevant details unaltered. The result was confusing, but sorting out its origins provided the surest sign yet that Lincoln was literally as well as symbolically beginning to replace Washington as a cultural icon.

Of course, the unbridgeable generation gap dividing the first and sixteenth presidents dictated that Washington's most appropriate place in postassassination Lincoln prints was as inspirational idol, the role assigned him in the old Mendel campaign print. A few engravers and lithographers did so present their relationship after 1865, but they were the exceptions, not the

Opposite: Fig. 112. **Currier & Ives,** *The Funeral of President Lincoln, New York, April 25th 1865./ Passing Union Square.* **Lithograph, New York, 1865 (Kenneth M. Newman, The Old Print Shop, Inc.).**

THE GRAND "WASHINGTON MONUMENT" PROCESSION:

As it appeared on Hamilton Square during the Ceremony of laying the Corner-stone, October 19th 1847.

On Stone from a Drawing taken on the Spot by J.L. Magee.

Entered according to Act of Congress in the Year 1847, by J. Baillie, in the Clerks Office at the District Court of the Southern Dist. of N.Y.

LITH. & PUB. BY J. BAILLIE.

87. 8T. NEAR 3d AVENUE N.Y.

Entered, according to Act of Congress in the year 1865, by J. A. Arthur, in the Clerk's Office of the District Court for the Eastern District of Pennsylvania.
WASHINGTON & LINCOLN. (APOTHEOSIS.)
S. J. Ferris, Pinxt.   Photo. and Pub. by Phil. Pho. Co., 730 Chestnut St.

Fig. 114. Philadelphia Photograph Co. after S[tephen]. J. Ferris, *Washington & Lincoln. (Apotheosis.) Carte-de-visite* photograph of a lithograph, published by J. A. Arthur, Philadelphia, 1865.

Opposite: Fig. 113. J. L. Magee, *The Grand "Washington Monument" Procession./ As it appeared on Hamilton Square during the Ceremony of laying of the Corner-stone, October 19th 1847.* Lithograph, published by J[ames]. Baillie, Philadelphia, 1847.

Fig. 115. John Sartain after a design by W. H. Hermans and a photograph by Mathew Brady Gallery, *Abraham Lincoln. The Martyr./ Victorious.* Engraving, published by W. H. Hermans, Penn Yann, New York, 1865 (The Lincoln Museum).

Fig. 116. Thurston & Herline after Gilbert Stuart (Washington) and Anthony Berger (Lincoln), *The Founder and the Preserver of the Union./ [Apotheosis.]. Carte-de-visite* photograph of a lithograph, Philadelphia, 1865 (The Lincoln Museum).

Fig. 117. Frank Neil, *Liberty Crowning Her Martyr. Carte-de-visite* photograph of a lithograph, Philadelphia, 1865 (The Lincoln Museum).

rule. Many refused to be bound by the logical conventions of chronology. They took liberties only slightly less egregious than D. T. Wiest had for *Reward of the Just.* Other prints submerged their messages in a maze of confusing iconographical complications—such as the Lincoln-Washington pairing that originated as an Andrew Jackson portrait *(Fig. 120)*. Once again, when demand for Lincoln prints after 1865 outpaced artists' creativity, the head of Lincoln replaced the original, to create a somewhat unconvincing "new" likeness *(Fig. 121)* in which not only was the memory of Jackson obliterated, but a Houdon statuette of George Washington was placed for inspirational emphasis at Lincoln's side, its bulk serving to block out the sight of the U.S. Capitol visible in the original, as if to emphasize the unprecedented dominance of the executive branch under Lincoln. The only feature that remained wholly unchanged, except for pose, was the label on the document each president held in his hand. For both it read: "The Union Must and Shall Be Preserved."[29]

Such decorative images-within-images appeared with particular frequency in a genre that had been all but invented for Washington—scenes of the president with his family, which gave assurance, however ill-founded, that great public men enjoy consoling private lives even while grappling with crises of state. Edward Savage and David Edwin's watershed engraving *(see Fig. 9)* of the Washington family circle had proved enormously popular, a family icon for the parlor that in a way provided visual reinforcement of Gouverneur Morris' comforting reminder to 18th century Americans that Washington "had no child—BUT YOU." Ralph Waldo Emerson hung a Washington print in his dining room,

and confided in his diary: "I cannot keep my eyes off of it." So far as we know, however, Lincoln's White House dining room contained no such decoration (although he did display, and apparently liked, the portrait of Jackson in his office). Nonetheless, when Lincoln family prints began flooding the market in 1865, many featured emblematic pictures of Washington looming reassuringly, sometimes merely looming *(Fig. 122)*, over Lincoln's family circle, or dominating the scene in D. T. Wiest's family lithograph, in the form of an absurdly large *(Fig. 123)* statue placed in such proximity to Lincoln that in real life a slight movement of his elbow would have sent it toppling off its pedestal.[30]

By comparison, William Sartain's elegant mezzotint of Lincoln together with his wife and children *(Fig. 124)*—its Washington bust, placed evocatively near a portrait of the Lincolns' dead son, Willie, a further suggestion that these families were somehow linked—offered a more refined (and expensive) alternative for period audiences. Sartain reflected the current affection for Lincoln-Washington connections by issuing it simultaneously with a new print of the first first family.

"Citizens will do well to secure these gems of art," the Schenectady *Gazette* advised in a review praising both pictures, calling them "the most tasteful, appropriate and pleasing ornaments which can embellish an American parlor." A Binghamton, New York, newspaper agreed, urging "every true lover of their deeds" to display "Engravings of both men and their families" on their walls, contending they were "of a quality that will equal as near as possible in exquisite beauty the sacred deeds of the Father and Saviour of our Country." In fact customers could not at first purchase

PUBLISHED BY WILLIAM SMITH, PRINTSELLER N° 705 SOUTH THIRD ST. PHILA.

IN MEMORY OF ABRAHAM LINCOLN.
THE REWARD OF THE JUST.

Fig. 118. **D. T. Wiest after John James Barralet (Washington) and Anthony Berger (Lincoln),** *In Memory of Abraham Lincoln./ The Reward of the Just.* **Lithograph, published by William Smith, Philadelphia,** *ca. 1865* **[2nd state of** *Fig. 119.***] (The Lincoln Museum).**

Fig. 119. John James Barralet after Gilbert Stuart, *Apotheosis of George Washington.* Stipple engraving, published by Simon Chaudron and Barralet, Philadelphia, 1802 (Library of Congress).

Fig. 120. A. H. Ritchie after Dennis Malone Carter, *Andrew Jackson*. Engraving, New York, 1860 (Library of Congress).

Fig. 121. J. C. Buttre after Ritchie and photograph by Anthony Berger, *Abraham Lincoln,/ President of the United States* [2nd state of *Fig. 120*]. Engraving, New York, *ca.* 1865 (Library of Congress).

PRESIDENT LINCOLN AND FAMILY CIRCLE.

one without the other: the catalogue offered them only as a pair—at $7.25 for plain prints, $10 for plain proofs, $15 for india proofs, and $20 for artist's proofs. These were hearty sums for what were essentially pictures of a childless family and a dysfunctional family. But in the popular imagination, the Washingtons and Lincolns had become representational, even inspirational. And when a Lincoln print featured a Washington icon, viewers might even infer that Washington was practically a Lincoln ancestor—his hoary image gracing the family parlor like an old portrait of a grandfather.[31]

Within a generation, Lincoln would graduate into the symbolic category that Washington had held in the Lincoln family prints of the 1860s: that of a parlor icon. When James A. Garfield was assassinated, the only known portrait of *his* family *(Fig. 125)* would show them gathered beneath portraits of both Washington *and* Lincoln, both now what only Washington had been before: household gods.

However appealing, family prints constituted the sole remaining genre which limited the full equalization of the Washington and Lincoln images. In domestic Lincoln settings that included spouse and offspring, Washington could never logically be more than a decoration. But in other designs, artists could find ways to bridge the gulf in time that separated the statesmen, in order to present them, just as most Americans seemed prepared now to remember them, literally side by side.

Lincoln achieved full parity with Washington in prints like P. S. Duval's *Champions of Liberty*—later pirated by

printmaker Saul Levin and reissued as *Champions of Freedom (Fig. 126)*. The image gave full flower to the liberty theme by featuring evocative highlights from each leader's career: Revolutionary soldiers celebrating the independence of 1776 for Washington, colored troops raising the American flag in 1864 for Lincoln. The message was emphasized in the words beneath each portrait: "Under this flag he led us to INDEPENDENCE," the Washington caption declared. "Under this flag he led us to FREEDOM," it said for Lincoln. In the same vein, E. J. Post's print of *The Father/The Preserver of Our Country* presented for each an aptly chosen quote from his final great address—"Avoid all sectional jealousies," the haunting admonition from Washington's farewell speech; and "With malice toward none, with charity for all," the ringing words from Lincoln's second inaugural, offering pardon to those who had failed to heed Washington's warning—the words and images now hovering over allegorical scenes of peace, justice, freedom, and plenty.

"They still live in our hearts," proclaimed another print, *The Martyr and the Father (Fig. 127)*, a sentiment seconded by the anonymous amateur artist who painstakingly copied the image onto a scrimshaw walrus' tusk *(Fig. 128)*, perhaps after carrying the print to sea with him to reproduce. What historian Marcus Cunliffe called the doubled images of Washington and Lincoln were quickly evolving into folklore and folk art alike. Unlike other folk myths, this one seemed almost to demand formality. When, for example, the New York printmakers Kimmel &

Opposite: Fig. 122. **Lyon & Co. after photographs by Anthony Berger and Alexander Gardner (Lincoln) and painting by Gilbert Stuart (Washington),** *President Lincoln and Family Circle.* **Lithograph, New York, 1867 (The Lincoln Museum).**

LINCOLN AND HIS FAMILY.

Forster adapted their lithograph of generals Ulysses S. Grant and William T. Sherman as *The Preservers of Our Union (Fig. 129)*, they made few alterations for their Washington-Lincoln version, *Columbia's noblest Sons (Fig. 130)*, except to make certain that the bare-breasted figure of Columbia crowning each with laurels was now fully draped for the more exalted occasion.

In several of these "twin" pictures, Lincoln and Washington were completely, if unrealistically, liberated from the confinement of these adjoining cameo designs, and placed side-by-side, looking almost like contemporaries except for the different styles of hair and costume. It was, as Cunliffe has described it, "a doubling of compatible unlikes." Placing them thus before a flame of liberty in a print subtitled *The Father and the Saviour of Our Country (Fig. 131)*, Currier & Ives of New York City granted to Washington undeserved superiority of height, as well as the expected dominance of gesture, but otherwise suggested parity by having the men actually shake hands in the most earthly of all gestures of greeting. Rival printmaker J. C. McCurdy's interpretation, *The Father and the Savior of Our Country*, even made Lincoln taller, a final concession that introduced them once and for all as equals before the eyes of the graphic artists—and their audiences. One scholar has suggested that such prints helped reestablish the continuum of the institution of the presidency, interrupted so violently by the Civil War. But in a very real way, Lincoln and the war had broken the so-called "cordon" permanently. Now their prints sug-

gested not continuity—for all the presidents in between, many of them slaveholders evidently harder to forgive than Washington, seemed irretrievably lost in postwar iconography—but the strongest evidence yet that George Washington and Abraham Lincoln had emerged from crisis as peerless and unique symbols of a country made and remade in the crucible of war. "I venture to claim for Abraham Lincoln the place next to George Washington," agreed George S. Boutwell in the 1880s, in words that might have easily been applied to describe the engravings and lithographs of the two which by then were occupying innumerable American parlors. As Boutwell, a former Congressman and cabinet minister, saw it: "Between Washington and Lincoln there were two full generations of men. But of them all, I see not one who can be compared with either." Neither could America's printmakers— or their patrons.[32]

Several of the more bizarre pairings serve to confirm the power of the trend, even as they confuse the issue. They boast occasionally ironic, almost comical provenance, but it is unlikely that many picture buyers of the day were aware of their antecedents. For example, a prewar print of Henry Clay, already transformed in 1860 into a full-length campaign portrait of Lincoln by grafting the reliable Cooper Union photograph onto Clay's body, was now altered further to compete in the Lincoln-Washington arena. To "update" it, one clever printmaker simply copied and inserted a Lansdowne Washington portrait to forge an awkward and unrealistic composite.

Opposite: Fig. 123. **D. [T.] Wiest after photograph by Anthony Berger, *Lincoln and His Family*. Lithograph, published by William Smith, Philadelphia, 1865 (The Lincoln Museum).**

LINCOLN AND HIS FAMILY.

Similarly, a pre-war John C. Calhoun portrait *(Fig. 132)* was adapted into a postwar Lincoln by placing the Berger "five-dollar bill" head *(see Fig. 86)* where Calhoun's head had appeared in the original: the result was a Lincoln *(Fig. 133)* in majestic robes, which if decidedly unlike the plainly dressed original, at least made the inevitable grafting with the Lansdowne Washington *(see Fig. 42)* far more natural looking. *The Father, and the Saviour of Our Country (Fig. 134)*, as it was titled, may be the quintessential pairing: the defender and preserver of the republic as both patriots and patriarchs.

By the end of 1865, such prints had flooded the market. As a result, the creative impetus for new contributions thereafter faded. Multiple copies of existing prints may have continued selling briskly for years, but only a single known Lincoln-Washington print bears a copyright date later than 1865, and that sole exception was an 1867 copy of an image introduced two years earlier. The novelty faded as quickly as it began.

What replaced the vogue in the years that followed echoed—perhaps presaged—the slow but sure transposition in reputation that by the turn of the century placed Lincoln in the preeminent position among American presidents, and left Washington a notch below him. Viewed carefully, period prints convey the same reversal of fortune, for in graphics Lincoln came to dominate Washington, too, a sure sign of the dominance he came to exert over the entire culture.

Early signals could be found in the variants inspired by the lithograph *Our*

Fallen Heroes (Fig. 135), issued in 1865 to honor Lincoln and the Union military martyrs of the late war. In 1867, with Southern markets reopened to northern printmakers, the lithographer adapted the same design for an all-Confederate version featuring Stonewall Jackson and Southern martyrs. That same year, *The Father of our Country and the Heroes of 1776 (Fig. 136)* was copyrighted, with Washington now occupying the central place Lincoln held in the original conception. A Lincoln image had inspired a Washington image instead of the other way around. It would not be the last time.[33]

In earlier days, during Washington's undisputed dominance of the American graphic arts, even Lincoln's single greatest act, the Emancipation Proclamation, could inspire prints that unfairly assigned more prominence to Washington than to the Emancipator himself. Max Rosenthal's *Proclamation of Emancipation,* for example, a decorative piece published back in 1865, featured a portrait of Lincoln, but positioned it beneath the words of the document, and placed it alongside those of other antislavery men, including Horace Greeley, William H. Seward, and Charles Sumner. Crowning the design, meanwhile, were portraits of the founders—central among them, and largest of all, a likeness of Washington.

Now tributes would more than grant Lincoln his retrospective due, as in the primitive but appealing calligraphy prints that formed their Lincoln portraits through the bold outline of the very words of the Proclamation. One such print *(Fig. 137)* went on to inspire a near-identical design *(Fig. 138)*,

Opposite: Fig. 124. **William Sartain after Samuel B[ell]. Waugh and photograph by Anthony Berger,** *Lincoln and His Family.* **Mezzotint engraving, published by Bradley & Co., Philadelphia, 1866 (National Portrait Gallery, Smithsonian Institution).**

ABRAM   MOTHER   IRVIN   HARRY   JAMES   WIFE   MOLLIE

COPYRIGHTED 1882 BY KURZ & ALLISON LITHO, CHICAGO, U.S.A.

J. A. Garfield.

AND FAMILY.

showing Washington's face emerging from the text of the Declaration of Independence. It was no coincidence. Both prints were the work of the same man, W. H. Pratt. But significantly, the Lincoln print had preceded the Washington print to the marketplace, even though the Declaration had preceded the Emancipation by four score and seven years, and even though Declaration prints ornamented with Washington images had been staples of print catalogues for generations.

Their reappearance in 1876 may have owed almost as much to Lincoln's enduring reputation as Great Emancipator—the man who, prints suggested, had completed the work Washington and his generation had begun—as to the approaching centennial of American independence.

Otherwise, the hoopla attending the national hundredth birthday celebration might have inspired tributes only to Washington. Instead it evoked tributes to Lincoln as well—the author of a liberating work as great as the founders'. A typical result was a little-known print by Edward W. Welcke of Brooklyn, New York, presenting the texts of both the Declaration and the Emancipation beneath portraits of Washington and Lincoln, respectively, surrounded by depictions of such historic events as the surrender of Cornwallis and the Battle of Gettysburg. Published by James Miller in the 1876 anniversary year, it was entitled *Centennial.* The birthday honors clearly belonged not only to the father but to his heir.

Further evidence of the trend could be found two years after Gilman R. Russell, a self-proclaimed "professor

of penmanship," reproduced the words of the Emancipation as the background for a celebratory Lincoln portrait *(Fig. 139).* Russell used precisely the same design again for the Declaration of Independence—and for Washington. With the Colonial revival in full flower for the 1876 Centennial, George Washington images would once again compete with, not just complement, those of Lincoln. Only now, the Lincoln image could dominate even a lithographic tribute to the Declaration of Independence, in much the way Washington had overshadowed Lincoln in the preassassination print celebrating Emancipation.

Surely to Americans joyfully celebrating the hundredth anniversary of independence, by 1876 the Union's founder and saviour had become at least full and equal partners in the historical pantheon once the exclusive domain of George Washington. Now it belonged to two men—but most importantly, to these two only. The French printmaker Lemercier could suggest in *Fraternité Universelle (Fig. 141)* that Washington and Lincoln had both achieved fame within a much larger elite of international heroes, martyrs, and symbols, including Benjamin Franklin, Socrates, and Gutenberg. A far more banal message dominated at home, where one print ostensibly celebrating the election of Chester Alan Arthur to the White House *(Fig. 142)* featured a ludicrous gathering of his predecessors, most of whom appeared like spectral apparitions in the blurred background, except for Lincoln and Washington, who remained in focus, front and center, slouching on their chairs as if they had just enjoyed a good smoke.

Opposite: Fig. 125. **Kurz & Allison after Gilbert Stuart and Anthony Berger, *J. A. Garfield/ And Family.* Lithograph, Chicago, 1882.**

Fig. 127. **Printmaker unknown after Gilbert Stuart (Washington) and photograph by Anthony Berger (Lincoln),** *The Martyr and the Father.* **Lithograph,** *ca.* **1865 (The Lincoln Museum).**

What these ubiquitous, if occasionally myopic prints of Washington and Lincoln individually and collectively illuminated as sharply as any documentary evidence, is the conversion of Lincoln's domestic image from heir to the Washington legacy — an image Lincoln first suggested himself — to superior cultural force, if only by an iota.

Invoking Washington had helped the Lincoln of 1861 justify unimaginable sacrifices yet to come, and by waging war in the Washington tradition, Lincoln was rewarded with a place alongside the founder — and eventually above him — in cultural history. It was almost as if one president could no longer comfortably be portrayed without including the other. Perhaps that is why the election of another hero general to the presidency — Ulysses S. Grant — inspired the print, *Our Three Presidents,* which included the wholly civilian Lincoln. Similarly, the assassination of James A. Garfield could compel printmakers Rode & Brand to include Washington in their 1882 memorial lithograph to the nation's newest martyr, entitled *Sixth Commandment, "Thou Shalt Not Kill."* The print was dedicated specifically, if incongruously, "to the memory of the Father of his Country and our two martyred presidents."

[continued on page 226]

Opposite: Fig. 126. **Saul Levin after Gilbert Stuart (Washington) and photograph by Anthony Berger (Lincoln),** *Champions of Freedom.* **Lithograph with tintstone, 1865.**

Fig. 128. Artist unknown after a period print [see *Fig. 127*], *[Lincoln and Washington]*. Scrimshaw carving on a walrus tusk, n.d. [shown with a similar scrimshaw tusk portraying General Sherman]. (Mystic Seaport Museum).

Opposite: Fig. 129. Kimmel & Forster after photograph by Anthony Berger, *The Preservers of Our Union [Grant and Lincoln]*. Lithograph, New York, 1865 (The Lincoln Museum).

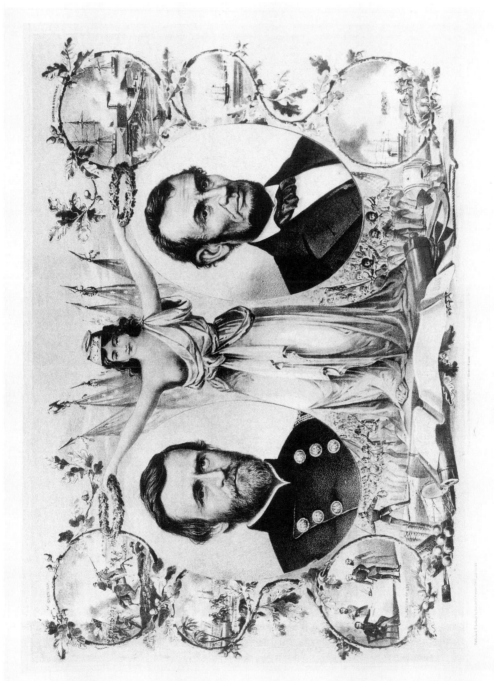

The Preservers of Our Union.

Columbia's noblest Sons

Fig. 131. Currier & Ives after Gilbert Stuart (Washington) and photograph by Anthony Berger (Lincoln), *Washington and Lincoln./ The Father and the Saviour of Our Country.* Lithograph, New York, 1865 (The Lincoln Museum).

Opposite: Fig. 130. Kimmel & Forster after Gilbert Stuart (Washington) and photograph by Anthony Berger (Lincoln), *Columbia's noblest Sons.* Lithograph, copyright Henry and William Vought, published by Manson Lang, New York, 1865 (The Lincoln Museum).

Fig. 132. Johnson & Fry, *J. C. Calhoun*. Engraving, New York, 1864 (Henry Francis du-Pont Winterthur Museum Libraries).

Fig. 133. William Pate after Johnson & Fry and photograph by Anthony Berger, *Abraham Lincoln* [2nd state of *Fig. 132*]. Engraving, 1865 (Library of Congress).

By 1884, Lincoln's friend and biographer, Isaac N. Arnold, would understandably conclude: "There is but one other name in American history which can be mentioned [with Lincoln's] . . . as that of peer—the name of Washington. Lincoln was as pure, as just, as patriotic, as the father of his country." And speaking at Valley Forge in 1904, Theodore Roosevelt would confess he could no longer "see how any American can think of either of them without thinking of the other, too, because they represent the same work."[34]

So the vast array of Lincoln-Washington pairings had long suggested, evocatively illustrating this metamorphosis, and perhaps inspiring it as well. Not until the 1920s would another luminary aspire to join their exclusive fraternity, and even then only temporarily. This time it was neither a general nor a president, but an aviator whose picture, in the words of the Washington *Post,* was found "stuck to the walls of elevators," adorning "the desks of countless stenographers . . . [and] placed in schoolrooms, side by side with Lincoln and Washington." But Charles Lindbergh's exaltation was short-lived. Lindbergh became a national hero, but Washington and Lincoln were America's patron saints, twinned symbols of the Union itself.

In the words to the caption of one J. H. Bufford lithograph, issued along with all the others in 1865, the engraved and lithographed portraits of Washington and Lincoln were—and herein lay perhaps an unintended clue to the commercial profit which their depictions brought to the graphics art trade—"gems of art."[35]

Images like Louis Kurz's primitive but irresistible lithograph *(Fig. 143)*, issued in both large and small formats, made this status clear in many ways: in design (with the presidents suggestively straddling the reunified American continent); in symbolism (with the stacked weaponry at their feet testifying to the return of peace); in ornamentation (each president cluthing historic documents labeled, respectively, "Constitution" and "Emancipation"); and finally in caption ("Under Providence, Washington Made and Lincoln Saved Our Country"). It could have been no more effective an evocation of national sentiment had it been created to illustrate Charles Sumner's 1865 eulogy, in which he imagined "WASHINGTON and LINCOLN associated in the grandeur of their obsequies . . . kindred in service, kindred in patriotism. One sleeps in the East, and the other Sleeps in the West; and thus, in death, as in life, one is the complement of the other." The link was now inexorable, stamped immutably on the national consciousness by Northern printmakers who not only survived the war, but went on to assume total control of the country's visual memory.[36]

Theodore Culyer had declared in another telling 1865 eulogy that "the common people saw the very best that was in themselves when they looked at Lincoln." Similarly, they saw some of the very best that was in Lincoln when they looked at prints that portrayed Lincoln and Washington together. As the subtitle of Kurz's emblematic example confirms, such graphics compellingly invited audiences to "Behold Oh! America, Your Sons. The Greatest Among Men." By pairing Lincoln with Washington, the original national ideal, printmakers provided Americans a comforting vision of both national continuity and national opportunity. One of their own had become a second

[continued on page 236]

Fig. 134. James F. Bodtker after Gilbert Stuart (Lansdowne portrait of Washington), William Pate and photograph by Anthony Berger, *The Father, and the Saviour of Our Country.* [3rd state of *Fig. 132*]. Lithograph, Milwaukee, 1865 (The Lincoln Museum).

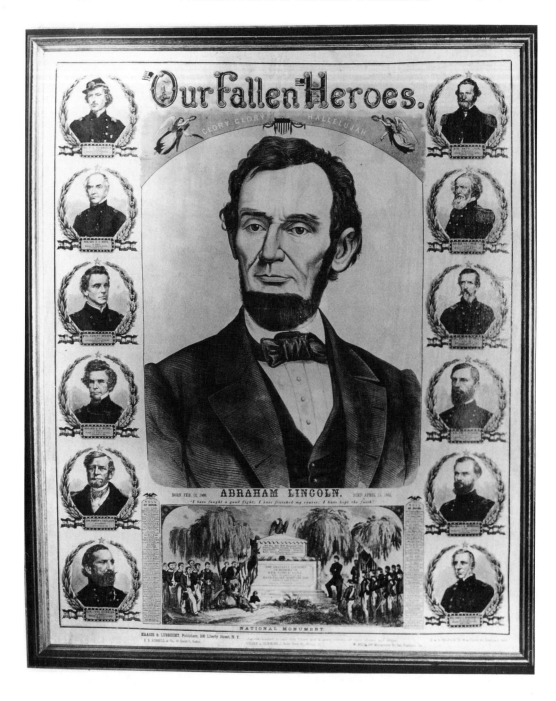

Fig. 135. Haasis & Lubrecht after photograph by Anthony Berger, *Our Fallen Heroes.* Wood engraving, published by Charles Lubrecht, New York, 1865 (The Lincoln Museum).

Fig. 136. Haasis & Lubrecht after Gilbert Stuart, *The Father of our Country/ and the Heroes of 1776.* [3rd state of *Fig. 135*; 2nd state featured Confederate martyrs.] Wood engraving, electrotyped by Smith & McDougal, New York, 1867 (The Old Print Gallery, Washington, D.C.).

Fig. 137. **W. H. Pratt** after photograph by Anthony Berger, *Emancipations Proklamation./ Abraham Lincoln.* **Lithograph and calligraphy, Davenport, Iowa, 1865 (The Lincoln Museum).**

Fig. 138. **W. H. Pratt** after Gilbert Stuart, *Declaration of Independence./ George Washington* [facsimile signature]. Lithograph and calligraphy, published by A. Hageboeck, Davenport, Iowa, 1876 (Library of Congress).

Fig. 139. P. S. Duval & Son after photograph by Anthony Berger, *Emancipation Procla-mation/ Issued January 1st 1863.* Lithograph, designed and published by Gilman R. Russell, Philadelphia, 1865 (The Lincoln Museum).

Fig. 140. Gilman R. Russell after Gilbert Stuart, *Declaration of Independence/ In Congress July 4th 1776./ The Great Centennial Memorial.* Lithograph, Philadelphia, 1876 (The Old Print Gallery, Washington, D.C.).

Fig. 141. C. Schultz, *Fraternité Universelle.* Lithograph, published by Lemercier, Paris, *ca.* 1865 (Library of Congress).

Fig. 142. F. Myers & Co. after Gilbert Stuart (Washington) and photograph by Anthony Berger (Lincoln), *Our Presidents.* Lithograph, 1882 (The Lincoln Museum).

NATIONAL PICTURE.

WASHINGTON MADE   UNDER PROVIDENCE   LINCOLN SAVED

AND

OUR COUNTRY.

LITH. BY CHAS SHOBER CHICAGO

BEHOLD OH! AMERICA, YOUR SONS. The greatest among men.

Fig. 143. Louis Kurz, *Behold Oh! America, Your Sons. The greatest among men.* **Signed:** *L. Kurz.* **Lithograph, copyrighted by E. Shogren, published by Chas. Shober, Chicago, 1865 (Library of Congress).**

Washington; in America, anything was possible. Through deceptively simple, but lovingly treasured pictures like this one, Lincoln permanently became, in the Rev. Henry Bellows' words, "the heir of Washington's place at the hearths and altars of the land." And the hearths themselves were transformed into domestic altars for the icons of the nation's father and saviour. Joint portraits of "Columbia's Noblest Sons," as Kurz's representative print affirmed in its revealing caption, became nothing less than America's "National Picture."[37]

Notes

Chapter I

1. The first major reference work on Lincoln prints was Winfred Porter Truesdell, *The Engraved and Lithographed Portraits of Abraham Lincoln* (Champlain: p.p., 1933). With Mark E. Neely, Jr. and Gabor S. Boritt, this author wrote *The Lincoln Image* (New York: Scribners, 1984), and *Changing the Lincoln Image* (Fort Wayne: Louis A. Warren Lincoln Library and Museum, 1985).

2. Francis F. Browne, *The Every-Day Life of Abraham Lincoln* (Hartford: Park Publishing, 1886), pp. 32–34. See also Edmond S. Meany, *Lincoln Esteemed Washington* (Seattle: Frank McCaffrey, 1933), pp. 9–13.

3. Roy P. Basler, ed., *The Collected Works of Abraham Lincoln* (8 vols., New Brunswick: Rutgers University Press, 1953–55), IV: 235–36.

Chapter II

1. Noble E. Cunningham, Jr., *Popular Images of the Presidency: From Washington to Lincoln* (Columbia: University of Missouri Press, 1991), pp. 19, 287 n. 52.

2. Barry Schwartz, *George Washington: The Making of an American Symbol* (New York: The Free Press, 1987), p. 194.

3. *Ibid.*, p. 195; Cunningham, *Popular Images of the Presidency*, p. 19.

4. Schwartz, *George Washington*, pp. 34–35.

5. *Ibid.*, p. 195.

6. Cunningham, *Popular Images of the Presidency*, pp. 4–5. For an example of Washington caricature, see Ron Tyler, *The Image of America in Caricature and Cartoon* (Fort Worth: Amon Carter Museum, 1975), p. 54.

7. Wendy Wick, *George Washington: An American Icon—The Eighteenth Century Graphic Portraits* (Washington: National Portrait Gallery, 1982), pp. xv, xx.

8. James Thomas Flexner, *George Washington: The Indispensable Man* (Boston: Little Brown, 1969), p. 183. The definitive work on Washington's "Cincinnatus" image is Garry Wills, *Cincinnatus: George Washington and the Enlightenment—Images of Power in Early America* (New York: Doubleday, 1984).

9. Cunningham, *Popular Images of the Presidency*, p. 130; Michael Kammen, *Mystic Chords of Memory: The Transformation of Tradition in American Culture* (New York: Alfred A. Knopf, 1991), p. 130.

10. Gustavus A. Eissen, *Portraits of Washington* (3 vols., New York: Robert Hamilton, 1932),

I: 312. Eissen attributed the famous quote to novelist John Neal, but it has also been credited to Mark Twain (see, for example, *Book-of-the-Month Club News,* February 13, 1943).

11. Harry T. Peters, *America on Stone: The Other Printmakers to the American People* (New York: Arno Press, 1976), pp. 11, 17, 22; David Tatham, "John Henry Bufford: American Lithographer," in *Proceedings of the American Antiquarian Society* 86, part 1 (Worcester: American Antiquarian Society, 1976), pp. 47–74.

12. Margaret Brown Klapthor and Howard Alexander Morrison, *George Washington: A Figure Upon the Stage* (Washington: National Museum of American Art, 1982), p. 13. For history of the construction of the monument, see Harold Holzer, "'There Is About It the Mantle of Pure Radiance': The Washington Monument," *American History Illustrated* December 1984; for status of Mount Vernon during the Civil War era, see Mark E. Neely, Jr, and Harold Holzer, *The Lincoln Family Album* (New York: Doubleday, 1990), pp. 17–18.

13. Charles Henry Hart, "Life Portraits of George Washington," *McClure's Magazine* 8, no. 4 (February 1897), p. 291.

14. Linda Crocker Simmons, "The Emerging Nation, 1790 to 1830," in David S. Bundy, ed., *Painting in the South: 1564–1980* (Richmond: Virginia Museum of Fine Arts, 1983), pp. 48, 69.

15. Schwartz, *George Washington,* pp. 35–36.

16. Flexner, *George Washington*, pp. 40–41; Schwartz, *George Washington,* p. 19.

17. Wick, *George Washington: An American Icon,* p. 82.

18. *Ibid.,* p. 15; Joan Dolmetsch, "Prints in Colonial America: Supply and Demand in the mid-Eighteenth Century," in John D. Morse, ed., *Prints in and out of America to 1850* (Charlottesville: Winterthur Museum and University Press of Virginia, 1970), pp. 53–74; Wick, *George Washington: An American Icon,* pp. 18–19; Sinclair Hitchings, "London's Images of Colonial America," in Joan D. Dolmetsch, ed., *Eighteenth-Century Prints in Colonial America* (Charlottesville: Colonial Williamsburg Foundation, 1979), pp. 25–27.

19. Wick, *George Washington: An American Icon,* pp. 10-11, 16, 85; Edgar P. Richardson, Brooke Hindle, and Lillian B. Miller, *Charles Wilson Peale and His World* (New York: Harry N. Abrams, 1982), p. 57; Charles Henry Hart, *Catalogue of the Engraved Portraits of Washington* (New York: Grolier Club, 1904), pp. 3–4.

20. Richardson, Hindle, and Miller, *Charles Wilson Peale,* p. 77; Charles Sellers, *Portraits and Miniatures by Charles Wilson Peale* (Philadelphia: American Philosophical Society, 1968), pp. 224–25; Charles Sellers, *Charles Wilson Peale* (New York: Scribners, 1969), p. 166; Wick, *George Washington: An American Icon,* p. 85; Wendy J. Shadwell, "The Portrait Engravings of Charles Wilson Peale," in Jean D. Dolmetsch, ed., *Eighteenth-Century Prints in Colonial America: To Educate and Decorate* (Williamsburg: Colonial Williamsburg Foundation, 1979), pp. 140–41.

21. Shadwell, "The Portrait Engravings of Charles Wilson Peale," pp. 130, 139–40.

22. William S. Baker, *The Engraved Portraits of Washington* (Philadelphia: Lindsay & Baker, 1880), p. 17.

23. *Ibid.,* pp. 16–19, 87, 88, 108.

24. *Ibid.,* pp. 41, 106-7.

25. *Ibid.,* p. 43; Flexner, *George Washington,* pp. 39, 60; Schwartz, *George Washington,* p. 123.

26. Wick, *George Washington: An American Icon,* pp. 43, 124.

27. *Ibid.,* pp. 44, 124.

28. Peters, *America on Stone,* p. 115.

29. *Washington and His Family, ca.* 1866, advertising sheet in the Lincoln Museum, Fort Wayne.

30. *Ibid.*

31. *Ibid.*

32. Wick, *George Washington: An American Icon,* pp. 50–51; Rita S. Gottesman, *The Arts and Crafts in New York, 1726-1804* (3 vols., New York: New York Historical Society, 1954–65), III: 50–51.

33. Flexner, *George Washington,* pp. 339–40. The "Athenaeum" portrait was so-named because the canvas went to the Boston Athenaeum. See Henry T. Tuckerman, *Book of the Artists: American Artist Life. . .* (New York: James T. Carr, 1967 reprint of 1867 ed.), pp. 118–19.

34. Tuckerman, *Book of the Artists,* p. 117.

35. *Ibid.,* pp. 112, 115, 118; Schwartz, *George Washington,* p. 159.

36. Karal Ann Marling, *George Washington Slept Here: Colonial Revivals and American Culture, 1876–1976* (Cambridge: Harvard University Press, 1988), pp. 10–11: Wick, *George Washington: An American Icon,* p. 131; Cunningham, *Popular Images of the Presidency,* pp. 19–20.

37. Gottesman, *The Arts and Crafts in New York,* III: 50–51.

38. Klapthor and Morrison, *George Washington: A Figure Upon the Stage,* pp. 18–19; E. McSherry Fowble, *Two Centuries of Prints in America: A Selective Catalogue of the Winterthur Museum Collection* (Charlottesville: University Press of Virginia, 1987), p. 25.

39. Wick, *George Washington: An American Icon,* p. 131.

40. *Ibid.*

41. Schwartz, *George Washington,* p. 93; Cunningham, *Popular Images of the Presidency,* pp. 4–5; John P. Kaminski and Jill Adair McCaughan, *A Great and Good Man: George Washington in the Eyes of His Contemporaries* (Madison: Madison House, 1989), p. 126.

42. Cunningham, *Popular Images of the Presidency,* pp. 10, 43, 106.

43. *Ibid.,* p. 6.

44. Gottesman, *The Arts and Crafts in New York,* III: 51.

45. Phoebe Lloyd Jacobs, "John James Barralet and the Apotheosis of George Washington," *Winterthur Portfolio* 12 (1977), pp. 115–37.

46. *Ibid.,* pp. 133–34. For emblems of Masonry in Washington prints, see Barbara Franco, "Masonic Imagery," in James F. O'Gorman, ed., *Aspects of American Printmaking, 1800–1950* (Syracuse: Syracuse University Press, 1988), pp. 14–16.

47. Cunningham, *Popular Images of the Presidency,* pp. 17–18; words accompanying *[George Washington's] Inaugural Address Delivered on Being Sworn into Office April 30th, 1789,* engraving, n.d., copy in the Boston Public Library; John Adams quoted in Jacobs, "John James Barralet," p. 132.

48. Stanley Idzerda, Anne C. Loveland, and Marc H. Miller, *Lafayette, Hero of Two Worlds: The Art and Pageantry of His Farewell Tour of America, 1824–1825* (Hanover: The Queens Museum, 1989), p. 67; Sylvia Neely, *Lafayette and the Liberal Ideal, 1814–1824 . . .* (Carbondale: Southern Illinois University Press, 1991), pp. 80–81; Frederic A. Conningham, *Currier & Ives Prints: An Illustrated Check List* (New York: Crown, 1970), pp. 283–86; Joshua C. Taylor, *America as Art* (New York: Harper & Row, p. 30).

49. Schwarz, *George Washington,* pp. 42, 125; *America in Print 1796–1941* (catalogue) (New York: Hirschl & Adler Galleries, 1987), p. 18.

50. Joseph C. Sindelar, ed., *Washington's Day Entertainments* (Chicago: Teacher's Supply Bureau, 1910), pp. 14–15.

51. Cunningham, *Popular Images of the Presidency,* pp. 37, 39, 48, 120–26; Bernard E. Reilly, *American Political Prints, 1766–1876: A Catalog of the Collections in the Library of Congress* (Boston: G. K. Hall, 1991), pp. 15, 141, 417–19; for an example from the Grant presidency, see Mark E. Neely, Jr., "Grant's Image a Hundred Years Later," *Lincoln Lore* 1758 (August 1984): 1.

52. Cunningham, *Popular Images of the Presidency,* p. 49.

53. George C. Groce and David H. Wallace, *The New York Historical Society's Dictionary of Artists in America, 1564–1860* (New Haven: Yale University Press, 1957), p. 600; *The Old Print Gallery Showcase* 19, no. 1 (April 1992), p. 24.

54. Flexner, *George Washington,* p. 39.

55. *Ibid.,* pp. 400–1; D. J. Enright, *The Oxford Book of Death* (New York: Oxford University Press, 1983), pp. xii, 6, 43–44; Philippe Aries, *The Hour of Our Death* (New York: Vintage Books, 1982), p. 409; Nigel Lewellan, *The Art of Death: Visual Culture in the English Death Pictorial . . .* (London: Reakton Books, 1991), p. 95; Mark E. Neely, Jr., "Lincoln's Death," *Lincoln Lore* 1742 (April 1984): 1–2.

56. *The Old Print Gallery Showcase* 17, no. 2 (May 1990), p. 27; Paul F. Boller, Jr., *George Washington and Religion* (Dallas: Southern Methodist University Press, 1963), pp. 7, 8, 33. One of Washington's wartime bodyguards reportedly observed the general "repeatedly . . . on his knees" in prayer, but relatives testified that Washington avoided kneeling in church.

57. Marling, *George Washington Slept Here,* pp. 136, 155.

58. Reference for the history of the Leutze effort is Natalie Spassky et al., *American Paintings in the Metropolitan Museum of Art,* Volume II (New York: Metropolitan Museum of Art, 1985), pp. 13–24 (includes the comments by Henry James and Mark Twain, and the story of the painting's adaptation by Goupil).

59. Groce and Wallace, *Dictionary of Artists,* p. 284; Marzio, *The Democratic Art,* p. 27.

60. Garry Wills, *Cincinnatus...,* p. 246.

61. Izerda, Loveland, and Miller, *Lafayette: Hero of Two Worlds,* pp. 23–24.

62. Reilly, *American Political Prints,* p. 495; Mark E. Neely, Jr., Harold Holzer, and Gabor S. Boritt, *The Confederate Image: Prints of the Lost Cause* (Chapel Hill: University of North Carolina Press, 1987), pp. 11–21.

63. William C. Darrah, *Cartes-de-Visite in Nineteenth Century Photography* (Gettysburg: William C. Darrah, 1981), p. 4.

64. Richardson, Hindle, and Miller, *Charles Wilson Peale and His World,* pp. 57, 70.

65. *National Portrait Gallery Permanent Collection: Illustrated Checklist* (rev. ed., Washington: Smithsonian Institution, 1982), p. 237; Wick, *George Washington: An American Icon,* pp. 60–61; Cunningham, *Popular Images of the Presidency,* p. 135; Eisen, *Portraits of Washington,* p. 103; Richard McLanthan, *Gilbert Stuart* (New York: Harry N. Abrams, 1986), p. 96. Peale planned his own engraving "executed upon a large scale by an eminent artist," see p. 97.

66. Eisen, *Portraits of Washington,* pp. 57, 312.

67. *Ibid.,* p. 892.

68. *Ibid.,* pp. 300, 312.

69. Wills, *Cincinnatus,* pp. 171–72, 228.

70. Fowble, *Two Centuries of Prints in America,* p. 313.

71. Marling, *George Washington Slept Here,* pp. 99, 338.

72. "Address of Herbert Hoover," *George Washington Bicentennial Celebration* 2:13.

73. Mason Locke Weems, *The Life of George Washington,* ed. Marcus Cunliffe (Cambridge: Harvard University Press, 1962), pp. xviii–xix.

74. Baker, *The Engraved Portraits of Washington,* p. 16.

75. Cunningham, *Popular Images of the Presidency,* pp. 17–18.

76. Kaminski & McCaughan, *A Great and Good Man,* p. 155.

77. Charles Dickens, *American Notes: A Journey* (New York: Fromm Publishing, 1985 reprint of 1842 ed.), pp. 88, 183; Henry T. Tuckerman, *The Character and Portraits of Washington* (New York: G. P. Putnam, 1859), p. 34.

Chapter III

1. Stefan Lorant, *Lincoln: A Picture Story of His Life* (New York: W. W. Norton, 1969), p. 208.

2. Wayne C. Williams, *A Rail Splitter for President* (Denver: University of Denver Press, 1951), pp. 144–45.

3. Lorant, *Lincoln,* p. 104; Herbert Mitgang, ed., *Abraham Lincoln: A Press Portrait* (Chicago: Quadrangle Books, 1971), pp. 137, 179.

4. Roy P. Basler, *et al.,* eds., *The Collected Works of Abraham Lincoln* (hereafter referred to as *Coll. Works*) (8 vols., New Brunswick, N.J.: Rutgers University Press, 1953–55), IV: 89; Wendell Garrett, "Editorial," *Magazine Antiques* 107, No. 2 (February 1975): 279.

5. Charles Hamilton and Lloyd Ostendorf, *Lincoln in Photographs: An Album of Every Known Pose* (Norman: University of Oklahoma Press, 1963), p. 217; *Coll. Works* IV: 89.

6. Hamilton and Ostendorf, *Lincoln in Photographs,* pp. 359–92; Rufus Rockwell Wilson, *Lincoln in Portraiture* (New York: Press of the Pioneers, 1935), pp. 87–114, 119–132, 141–44, 161–70, 185–92, 221–28, 237–42, 247–56, 269–88; Leonard Wells Volk, "The Life Mask and How It Was Made," *Century Illustrated Monthly Magazine* (December 1881): 223; Lloyd Ostendorf, "A Relic from His Last Birthday: The Mills Life Mask of Lincoln," *Lincoln Herald* 75, No. 3 (Fall 1973): 79–88; Harold Holzer, "How the Printmakers Saw Lincoln: Not so Honest Portraits of 'Honest Abe,'" *Winterthur Portfolio* 14, No. 2 (Summer 1979), pp. 144–51.

7. For the best cumulative checklist, see Winfred Porter Truesdell, *The Engraved and Lithographed Portraits of Abraham Lincoln, Vol. II* (Champlain, N.Y.: p.p., 1933). There was no Volume I.

8. Advertisement on verso of print, *Lincoln,* published for the "Lincoln Art Series" by J. P. McCaskey, Lancaster, Pa., 1889.

9. R. Gerald McMurtry, *Beardless Portraits of Abraham Lincoln Painted from Life* (Fort Wayne: Public Library of Fort Wayne and Allen Co., 1962), pp. 12–13.

10. Hamilton and Ostendorf, *Lincoln in Photographs,* pp. 139, 354.

11. *Ibid.,* pp. 359–92.

12. Lloyd Ostendorf, *The Photographs of Mary Todd Lincoln* (Springfield: Illinois State Historical Society, 1969), pp. 1–64.

13. For example, Alban J. Conant's painting was commissioned by a Republican club, never engraved, and hence remained little-known in Lincoln's own time. In contrast, an 1860 Currier & Ives catalogue listed 956 prints priced from 8¢ to $3.75. See Wilson, *Lincoln in Portraiture,* pp. 119–28; John Lowell Pratt, ed., *Currier & Ives Chronicles of America* (Maplewood, N.J.: Hammond Press, 1968), p. 14. For status of art in New York, see James Thomas Flexner, *History of American Painting: That Wilder Image* (New York: Dover, 1962), p. xi.

14. Truesdell counted 550 different prints.

15. An illustration in *Harper's Weekly,* May 12, 1860, featured Seward, with Lincoln relegated to the bottom row of candidates alongside John C. Frémont, the party's 1856 standard bearer.

16. The last photograph of Lincoln beardless was made August 13, 1860, the first bearded on November 25, 1860. See Hamilton and Ostendorf, *Lincoln in Photographs,* pp. 369–72; the best recent study of the politics of the campaign is William E. Gienapp, "Who Voted for Lincoln?" in John L. Thomas, ed., *Abraham Lincoln and the American Political Tradition* Amherst: University of Massachusetts Press, 1986), pp. 50–88.

17. Louis A. Warren, "The Shower of Lincoln Prints at the Wigwam," *Lincoln Lore* 1044 (April 11, 1949); R. Gerald McMurtry, "Lincoln's Wigwam Print," *Lincoln Lore* 1444 (June 1958): 3; R. Gerald McMurtry, "Lincoln and the Vice Presidency," *Lincoln Lore* 1567 (September 1968): 3.

18. Hamilton and Ostendorf, *Lincoln in Photographs,* pp. 6–7.

19. Mark E. Neely, Jr., and Harold Holzer, *The Lincoln Family Album* (New York: Doubleday, 1990), p. 42; see also *Coll. Works* IV: 114.

20. *Coll. Works* IV: 89.

21. Earl Schenck Miers, ed., *Lincoln Day by Day: A Chronology* (3 vols., Washington: Lincoln Sesquicentennial Commission, 1960), II: 280–96; Reinhard H. Luthin, *The First Lincoln Campaign* (Cambridge: Harvard University Press, 1944), p. 48; R. Gerald McMurtry, "Some Early Lithographs of Abraham lincoln," *Lincoln Lore* 1574 (April 1969): 1–4.

22. Thomas Hicks in Allen Thorndike Rice, ed., *Reminiscences of Lincoln by Distinguished Men of His Time* (New York: North American Publishing Co., 1888), pp. 593–602.

23. McMurtry, *Beardless Portraits,* p. 28.

24. *Ibid.,* pp. 20, 24, 35; Harold Holzer, Gabor S. Boritt, and Mark E. Neely, Jr., *The Lincoln Image: Abraham Lincoln and the Popular Print* (New York: Scribners, 1984), pp. 57–66.

25. Harold Holzer, "Some Contemporary Paintings of Abraham Lincoln," *Magazine Antiques* 107, no. 2 (February 1975): 314–22.

26. Hamilton and Ostendorf, *Lincoln in Photographs...* (rev. ed., Dayton: Morningside Press, 1985), p. 30.

27. Harold Holzer, "How the Printmakers Saw Lincoln," p. 151.

28. Hamilton and Ostendorf, *Lincoln in Photographs* (rev. ed.), p. 36; Francis B. Carpenter, *Six Months at the White House with Abraham Lincoln* (New York: Hurd & Houghton, 1866), p. 47.

29. *Portraits and Sketches of the Lives of All the Candidates for the Presidency and Vice Presidency for 1860...* (New York: J. C. Buttre, 1860), advertising sheets after p. 32.

30. *Ibid.*

31. *Ibid.*

32. The best studies are Rufus Rockwell Wilson, *Lincoln in Caricature* (New York: Horizon Press, 1953); and Albert Shaw, *Abraham Lincoln: His Path to the Presidency* (2 vols., New York: Review of Reviews, 1929). See also Bernard F. Reilly, Jr., *American Political Prints, 1766-1876: A Catalogue of the Collections in the Library of Congress* (Boston: G. K. Hall, 1991), pp. 435–53.

33. *Coll. Works* IV: 129–30; R. Gerald McMurtry, "Mr. Lincoln's Whiskers," *Lincoln Lore* 1557 (November 1967): 1.

34. Harold Holzer, "The Bearding of the President, 1860: How the Printmakers Put on Hairs," *Lincoln Herald* 78, no. 3 (Fall 1976), pp. 95-102.

35. Victor Searcher, *Lincoln's Journey to Greatness* (Philadelphia: John C. Winston Co., 1960). The inside back cover features a map of Lincoln's route to Washington for his inauguration. It covered 1904 railroad miles and 23 cities.

36. Letter of "True Republicans" to Abraham Lincoln, October 12, 1860, in Abraham Lincoln Papers, Library of Congress (microfilm).

37. George P. A. Healy, *Reminiscences of a Portrait Painter* (Chicago: A. C. McClurg, 1894), p. 70.

38. "True Republicans" to Lincoln, October 12, 1860; Holzer, Boritt, and Neely, *The Lincoln Image,* pp. 71-72.

39. *Coll. Works* IV: 130.

40. Hamilton and Ostendorf, *Lincoln in Photographs* (rev. ed.), pp. 67, 71.

41. Harold G. and Oswald Garrison Villard, eds., *Lincoln on the Eve of '61: A Journalist's Story by Henry Villard* (New York: Alfred A. Knopf, 1941), pp. 92-93.

42. *Coll. Works* III: 29; Holzer, Boritt, and Neely, *The Lincoln Image,* pp. 68-69; Milton Kaplan, "Heads of State," *Winterthur Portfolio* 6 (1979), pp. 139-41.

43. *Coll. Works* IV: 219.

44. Mark E. Neely, Jr., Harold Holzer, and Gabor S. Boritt, *The Confederate Image: Prints of the Lost Cause* (Chapel Hill: University of North Carolina Press, 1987), pp. 44-54; Hamilton and Ostendorf, *Lincoln in Photographs* (rev. ed.), pp. 76-77.

45. For prints of Ellsworth, see Winfred Porter Truesdell, *Catalog Raisonne of the Portraits of Col. Elmer E. Ellsworth* (Champlain: The Print Connoisseur, 1927).

46. *Coll. Works* V: 388-89.

47. Tyler Dennett, ed., *Lincoln and the Civil War in the Diaries and Letters of John Hay* (New York: Dodd, Mead & Co., 1939), p. 272; Carpenter, *Six Months at the White House,* p. 353; Francis B. Carpenter, "Anecdotes and Reminiscences," in Henry G. Raymond, *Life, Public Services, and State Papers of Abraham Lincoln* (New York: Derby & Miller, 1865), pp. 763-64.

48. P. J. Staudenraus, *Mr. Lincoln's Washington: Selections from the Writings of Noah Brooks, Civil War Correspondent* (New York: Thos. Yoseloff, 1967), p. 361.

49. *Ibid.,* pp. 361-63.

50. *Ibid.,* p. 363.

51. *Ibid.,* p. 57; Chicago *Times,* September 24, 1862.

52. *New York Herald,* September 27, 1862.

53. LaWanda Cox, *Lincoln and Black Freedom: A Study in Presidential Leadership* (Columbia: University of South Carolina Press, 1981), p. 13.

54. Charles Eberstadt, *Lincoln's Emancipation Proclamation* (New York: Duschnes Crawford, 1950), p. 23.

55. Wilson, *Lincoln in Portraiture,* pp. 189-91; Holzer, Boritt, and Neely, *The Lincoln Image,* pp. 102-10.

56. Eberstadt, *Lincoln's Emancipation Proclamation,* pp. 44-45; Harold Holzer, Gabor S. Boritt, and Mark E. Neely, Jr., *Changing the Lincoln Image* (Fort Wayne: Louis A. Warren Lincoln Library and Museum, 1985), pp. 72-73.

57. Advertising material published in Fred. B. Perkins, *The Picture and the Men . . .* (New York: A. J. Johnson, 1867), after p. 190.

58. *Ibid.*

59. *Ibid.*

60. Harold Holzer, Gabor S. Boritt, and Mark E. Neely, Jr., "Francis B. Carpenter (1830-1900): Painter of Abraham Lincoln and His Circle," *American Art Journal* 16, no. 2 (Spring 1984), p. 76.

61. *Ibid.,* p. 77; *New York Times,* June 9, 1866.

62. George E. Perine to Abraham Lincoln, May 6, 1864, Abraham Lincoln Papers, Library of Congress (microfilm).

63. A photo taken inside Ford's Theater soon after the assassination showed that a part of the bunting had come undone. See Dorothy Meserve Kunhardt and Philip B. Kunhardt, Jr., *Twenty Days* (New York: Harper & Row, 1965), p. 23.

64. *Ibid.,* pp. 66, 78–79, 122.

65. Notation in the Francis B. Carpenter diary, private collection.

66. *Ritchie's Picture Death of Lincoln* (advertising brochure) (New York: A. H. Ritchie, 1868), p. 5.

67. *Ibid.,* pp. 6–9.

68. Harold Holzer, "Living Monuments: The Image of the Lincoln Family," *Papers from the Fourth Annual Lincoln Colloquium,* ed. George L. Painter with Mary Ellen McElligott (Springfield: Lincoln Home Natl. Historic Site, 1990), pp. 33–44.

69. Rev. G. W. Bethune quoted in Nicholas B. Wainwright, *Philadelphia in the Romantic Age of Lithography* (Philadelphia: Historical Society of Pennsylvania, 1958), p. 45.

70. *Art Interchange* quoted in Peter Marzio, *The Democratic Art: Pictures from a 19th Century America* (Boston: David R. Godine, 1979), p. 128; Flexner, *That Wilder Image,* p. 186.

71. Justin G. Turner and Linda Levitt Turner, *Mary Todd Lincoln: Her Life and Letters* (New York: Alfred A. Knopf, 1972), p. 268.

72. John S. Goff, *Robert Todd Lincoln: A Man in His Own Right* (Norman: University of Oklahoma Press, 1969), pp. 26, 46–48; Rufus Rockwell Wilson, ed., *Intimate Memories of Lincoln* (Elmira: Primavera Press, 1945), p. 499; Turner and Turner, *Mary Todd Lincoln,* pp. 188–89; John Hay, "Tad Lincoln," *Illinois State Journal,* July 21, 1871; Tad Lincoln quoted in Carpenter, *Six Months at the White House,* p. 293.

73. James A. Garfield quoted in Wendy Wick Reaves, *Private Lives of Public Figures: The 19th Century Family Print,* labels for a National Portrait Gallery exhibition, September 1985 (xerox).

74. Hamilton and Ostendorf, *Lincoln in Photographs* (rev. ed.), pp. 182–83; Carpenter, *Six Months at the White House,* pp. 30–31, 92.

75. Noah Brooks quoted in Hamilton and Ostendorf, *Lincoln in Photographs* (rev. ed.), p. 183; *Harper's Weekly,* May 6, 1865, p. 1.

76. Turner and Turner, *Mary Todd Lincoln,* p. 302; Flexner, *That Wilder Image,* p. 186.

77. Wendy Wick Reaves quoted in "Private Lives of Public Figures," National Portrait Gallery press release, August 7, 1985.

78. *Lincoln and His Family* (Rochester: R. H. Curran, n.d.), advertising brochure in the Lincoln Museum, Fort Wayne.

79. Holzer, Boritt, and Neely, "Francis B. Carpenter," pp. 79–83.

80. Van Deren Coke, *The Painter and the Photograph: From Delacroix to Warhol* (Albuquerque: University of New Mexico Press, 1964), p. 28.

81. *Lincoln and His Family* (advertising brochure).

82. Turner and Turner, *Mary Todd Lincoln,* pp. 269, 315–16.

83. See Gabor S. Boritt, Mary E. Neely, Jr., and Harold Holzer, "The European Image of Abraham Lincoln," *Winterthur Portfolio* 21, nos. 2–3 (Autumn 1986), pp. 153–84.

84. Phillips Brooks, "The Character, Life, and Death of Abraham Lincoln," quoted in Waldo W. Braden, ed., *Building the Myth: Selected Speeches Memorializing Abraham Lincoln* (Urbana: University of Illinois Press, 1990), p. 50.

85. Perkins, *The Picture and the Men,* after p. 190.

86. Nicolay quoted by Carl Sandburg, "The Face of Lincoln," in Frederick Hill Meserve, *The Photographs of Abraham Lincoln* (New York: Harcourt Brace, 1944), p. 61.

87. Henry C. Deming, *Eulogy of Abraham Lincoln* (Hartford: A. N. Clark & Co., 1865), p. 13.

Chapter IV

1. Jacob L. Tudor to Abraham Lincoln, June 23, 1861, Abraham Lincoln Papers, Library of Congress (microfilm).

2. Roy P. Basler, et al., eds., *The Collected Works of Abraham Lincoln* (cited hereafter as *Coll. Works*) (8 vols., New Brunswick: Rutgers University Press, 1953–55), IV: 439.

3. Harold Holzer, Gabor S. Boritt, and Mark E. Neely, Jr., *The Lincoln Image: Abraham Lincoln and the Popular Print* (New York: Scribners, 1984), pp. 3, 7–9.

4. *Coll. Works,* III: 511; VII: 512; see also Charles E. Schutz, *Political Humor from Aristophanes to Sam Ervin* (Rutherford: Fairleigh Dickinson University Press, 1977), p. 144.

5. *Coll. Works,* III: 29.

6. *Ibid.,* I: 115, 279; Barry Schwartz, *George Washington: The Making of an American Symbol* (New York: The Free Press, 1987), p. 194.

7. *Coll. Works,* I: 333, 439; III: 18–19, 527; IV: 6; Ezra Stiles quoted in Schwartz, *George Washington,* p. 41.

8. *Coll. Works,* III: 536–37; Bernard F. Reilly, Jr., *American Political Prints, 1766–1876: A Catalog of the Collections in the Library of Congress* (Boston: G. K. Hall, 1991), pp. 12, 84–85, 208–10, 275.

9. Mark E. Neely, Jr., *The Abraham Lincoln Encyclopedia* (New York: McGraw-Hill, 1982), p. 73.

10. Charles Hamilton and Lloyd Ostendorf, *Lincoln in Photographs: An Album of Every Known Pose* (rev. ed., Dayton: Morningside Books, 1990), p. 30; Pekin (Illinois) Tazewell County *Republican,* July 13, 1860; *Coll. Works,* IV: 89; Roy P. Basler, ed., *The Collected Works of Abraham Lincoln: Supplement* (Westport: Greenwood Press, 1974), p. 55; Holzer, Boritt, and Neely, *The Lincoln Image,* p. 32; Noble E. Cunningham, Jr., *Popular Images of the Presidency: From Washington to Lincoln* (Columbia: University of Missouri Press, 1991), p. 17.

11. Harold Holzer, Gabor S. Boritt, and Mark E. Neely, Jr., *Changing the Lincoln Image* (Fort Wayne: Louis A. Warren Lincoln Library and Museum, 1985), pp. 34–40.

12. *Coll. Works,* IV: 160, 190; Schwartz, *George Washington,* p. 17.

13. *Coll. Works,* IV: 199,203, 236, 244, 341; Andrew A. Freeman, *Abraham Lincoln Goes to New York* (New York: Coward-McCann, 1960), pp. 108–9; Victor Searcher, *Lincoln's Journey to Greatness*. . . (Philadelphia: John C. Winston, 1960), p. 198.

14. Holzer, Boritt, and Neely, *The Lincoln Image,* pp. 68–69.

15. *Catalogue of Elegant, National and Patriotic Steel Engravings Published by William Pate* (ca. 1861).

16. *Coll. Works,* V: 136; James M. McPherson, *Abraham Lincoln and the Second American Revolution* (New York: Oxford University Press, 1990), pp. 3–22.

17. Herbert Mitgang, ed., *Abraham Lincoln: A Press Portrait* (Chicago: Quadrangle Books, 1971), p. 376; *New York Times,* November 27, 1863.

18. George Forgie, *Patricide in the House Divided: A Psychobiographical Interpretation of Lincoln and His Age* (New York: W. W. Norton, 1979), p. 37; Schwartz, *George Washington,* pp. 119–30.

19. Mark E. Neely, Jr., Harold Holzer, and Gabor S. Boritt, *The Confederate Image: Prints of the Lost Cause* (Chapel Hill: University of North Carolina Press, 1987), pp. 2–21.

20. R. M. Whiting, ed., *Our Martyr President Abraham Lincoln: Lincoln Memorial Addresses* (New York: Abingdon Press, [1915]), p. 136; *Frank Leslie's Illustrated Newspaper,* March 9, 1861; Schwartz, *George Washington,* p. 197.

21. Kenneth A. Bernard, *Lincoln and the Music of the Civil War* (Caldwell, Idaho: Caxton Printers, 1966), p. 259; Marcus Cunliffe, *The Doubled Images of Lincoln and Washington* (Fortenbaugh Memorial Lecture; pamphlet) (Gettysburg: Gettysburg College, 1988), pp. 17, 24.

22. Schwartz, George Washington, pp. 77–79.

23. *New York Times,* February 23, 1865.

24. Whiting, *Our Martyred President,* pp. 22, 154; Schwartz, *George Washington,* p. 154.

25. Schwartz, *George Washington,* p. 99; David T. Valentine, ed., *Obsequies of Abraham Lincoln in the City of New York*. . . (New York: Edmund Jones & Co., 1866), p. 114.

26. Charles Sumner, *The Promises of the Declaration of Independence: Eulogy on Abraham Lincoln*. . . (Boston: J. E. Farwell & Co., 1865), p. 6; Waldo W. Braden, *Building the Myth: Selected Speeches Memorializing Abraham Lincoln* (Urbana, IL: Univ. of Illinois Press, 1990), pp. 1–2; Mitgang, *Abraham Lincoln: A Press Portrait,* p. 468.

27. Schwartz, *George Washington,* p. 196; *Liberty and Union* (songsheet) (Philadelphia: J. Mafnus, 1865).

28. Francis B. Carpenter, *Six Months at the White House with Abraham Lincoln: The Story of a Picture* (New York: Hurd & Houghton, 1866), p. 25.

29. Cunningham, *Popular Images of the Presidency,* p. 187.

30. Wendy Wick, *George Washington: An American Icon—The Eighteenth Century Graphic Portraits*

(Washington: Smithsonian Institution, 1982), pp. 122–23; Edward Waldo Emerson and Waldo Emerson Forbes, eds., *Journals of Ralph Waldo Emerson* (10 vols., Boston: Houghton Miflin, 1909–14), VIII, p. 300. Holzer, Boritt, and Neely, *The Lincoln Image,* pp. 168–87; Forgie, *Patricide in the House Divided,* p. 38.

31. *Lincoln and His Family* (advertising brochure) (Rochester, New York: R. H. Curran, n.d.); Holzer, Boritt, and Neely, *The Lincoln Image,* p. 172.

32. Cunliffe, *The Doubled Images of Lincoln and Washington,* p. 24; Cunningham, *Popular Images of the Presidency,* pp. 6, 128, 217, 266.

33. The Old Print Gallery *Showcase* 17, No. 2 (May 1990), p. 1; Allen Thorndike Rice, *Reminiscences of Abraham Lincoln by Distinguished Men of His Time* (New York: North American Review, 1888), pp. 108, 616–17.

34. Cunliffe, *The Doubled Images of Lincoln and Washington,* p. 8; Isaac N. Arnold, *The Life of Abraham Lincoln* (Chicago: A. C. McClurg, 1906), p. 454.

35. Karal Ann Marling, *George Washington Slept Here: Colonial Revivals and American Culture, 1876–1986* (Cambridge: Harvard Univ. Press, 1988), p. 258.

36. Sumner, *Eulogy,* p. 6.

37. Whiting, *Our Martyred President,* pp. 33, 136.

Index

Page references in italics refer to illustrations

Adams, John 5, 6, 32, 36, *49,* 175, *235*
Adams, John Quincy 42, *49, 234*
Anderson, Robert 117, 181, *182,* 183, *184*
Apotheosis prints: of Lincoln *205*; of Washington 33, 35–36; of Washington and Lincoln 199, *201–205, 207*
Arnold, Chester Alan 217, *235*
Arnold, Isaac N. 226
Arthur, Joseph A. 51; print by *49*
Asp, C. A.: print by *193*
"Athenaeum" painting of Washington 1, 25, 27–28, 30, *31,* 33, 74, 178; *see also* Stuart, Gilbert
Atlantic Monthly 128

Baillie, James 63, 69; prints by *62, 77, 200*
Baker, J. E.: print by *xii*
Baker & Godwin 90, 93; prints by *94, 96*
Barker, William S. 76
Barralet, John James 36; prints by or after *206, 207*
Bartsch, Gustave: print after *169*
Beaumont, Gustave de 6
Bedell, Grace 101, 103, 105, 109, 115
Beecher, Henry Ward 186, 188
Bell, John 99, 101, *118, 122,* 178, *180,* 181
Bellows, Henry 236
Bennett, James Gordon 193
Berg & Porsch 165
Berger, Anthony 1, 214; photographs by *153, 157, 162;* prints after *132, 156, 158, 161, 163, 169, 187, 193, 203, 206, 209, 210, 212, 214, 216, 218, 219, 221, 222, 223, 225, 227, 228, 230, 232, 235*
Bettoni, N.: print by *47*
Biddle, Clement 24
Bingham, George Caleb 61

Bingham, John H. *see* Bingham & Dodd
Bingham & Dodd: print by *34*
Bivinley & Co.: print by *146*
Blada, V. *see* Volck, Adalbert
Blair, Montgomery 119, *136*
Bodtker, James: print by *227*
Bols (engraver) 25
Booth, John Wilkes 135
Bornemann, C. 165; print by *166*
Boston *Columbian Centennial* 42
Boston *Post* 155
Bouclet, F.: print by *185*
Boutwell, George S. 213
Bradley & Co.: print by *214*
Brady, Mathew B. 5, 99, 101, 109, 149, 156, 164, 178; photographs by *112, 172;* prints after *111, 114, 116, 123, 182, 184, 185, 202; see also* Berger, Anthony
Brainard, C. H. 91, 93; print by *98*
Braintree (home of Adams) 5
Breckenridge, John C. 98, 99–101, *118, 120, 122*
Brett, A.: print by *193*
Bromley & Co. 134
Brooks, Noah 119, 121, 131
Brown, F. H. 87; prints by *84, 89*
Brown, John 189
Brown, John Henry 91; print after *97*
Brown, M. E. D. 24–25; print by *26*
Brown University 140
Browne, Francis F. 4
Brunton, Richard 18
Buchanan, James *180,* 181, *235*
Bufford, J. H. 115, 226; prints by *xii, 98, 127*
Bumstead (publisher): print by *19*
Buono & Borrani 165; print by *167*
Butler, Benjamin 181–*182, 183*–184
Butler, Preston: print after *97*

Butterfield, D. W.: print by *ii [see iv]*
Buttre, J. C. 95, 98, 131, 143, 155; advertisement for *113*; prints by *78, 114, 143, 159, 209*
Buxton, Charles 30

Calhoun, John C. 107, 109, 179, *180*, 215, 224
calligraphy prints *230, 231*
Camillo (publisher) 165
Campbell, Alexander 12; print by *14*
Campbell, M. H. 35
Canty, Samuel 67; print by *70*
Carpenter, Francis B. 117, 119, 121, 128, 131, 137, 140, 149, 155, 199; prints after *132, 136*
Carr, Benjamin 33
Carter, Dennis Malone: prints after *208*
cartes-de-visite (small photographs) 81; of Abraham Lincoln 87, 139; of George Washington 67, 69, *71*; of Washington and Lincoln *201, 203–204*
Chappel, Alonzo: prints after *187*
Charleston *Mercury* 79
Chase, Salmon P. 117, *136*
Chaudron, Simon: print by 207
Cheesman, Thomas 25, 69; print by *29*
Church, J., Jr.: print by *104*
Cincinnatus *see* Washington, portraits as Cincinnatus
Civil War 8, 67, 109, 117, 164–165, 181–188
Clay, Henry 107, 109, 175, *180*, 181, *182, 184*, 189, 213
Cobb, Howell *180*, 181
Cogniet (artist) 41; print after *43*
Cole, Roderick M., photograph by *2*; print after *186*
Colonial revival 39; *see also* Washington-Lincoln, 1876 centennial
Cooper Union: Lincoln speaks at 177; photograph of Lincoln 95, 99, 101, *112*, 164, 177, 181, 213
Cornwallis, Lord Charles 217
cost of prints *see* prints, cost
Couder, Louis Charles: print after *47*
Crane, Charles 139, *153*
Cruise, Tom 145
Culyer, Theodore *226*
Cunliffe, Marcus 211, 213
Cunningham, Noble E., Jr. 8
Currier, Nathaniel 39, 53, 66; prints by 41, *55, 68*; *see also* Currier & Ives
Currier & Ives 39, 40, 61, 95, 99–101, 115, 194, 213; prints by *111, 118, 198, 223*
Custis, George Washington Parke 23, 72
Custis, John Parke (Jackie) 22, 23, *26*
Custis, Martha Parke (Patsy) 22, 23, 26

Dana, Charles, A. 91
Davis, Jefferson 67, 91, 134, 142, 161, 164, 188–189
Davis & Booth *44*
Day, B. H.: print by *70*
Deming, Henry 171
Derby & Miller: print by *136*
Dickens, Charles 76
Dodd, William Henry *see* Bingham & Dodd
Doggetts (printsellers) 42
Doney, Thomas 90; prints by *92, 126*
Douglas, Stephen A. 87, 90, 99, 101, *118, 120, 122*, 177, 183
Durand, Asher 39; print by *42*
Duval, P. S. (& Son) 37, 211; prints by *40, 232*

Eberstadt, Charles 121
Edwin, David 25, 33, 36, 67, 205; prints by *23, 35*; *see also* Savage, Edward
Ehrgott, Forbriger & Co. 93; print by *104*
Elliot & White: print by *127*
Ellsworth, Elmer E. 117
Emancipation Proclamation *see* Lincoln, Great Emancipator image
Emerson, Ralph Waldo 28, 174
Endicott, William 40; print by *7*
Everett, Edward 181, *182, 184*

Fabius (Roman general) 9
Fabronius, Dominique 75; prints by *98, 102, 138*
Farrell, E.: print by *66*
Fassett, Samuel 93; photo by *100*; prints after *102, 104, 176*, 177
Federal Almanack 19, 21
Federal Gazette 32–33
The Federalist 74
Fenderich, Charles 41, print by *45*
Ferris, J. L. G. 28
Ferris, S. J.: print after *201*
Feusir, A. 181; print by *185*
Fillmore, Millard 90, 96, *235*
Flexner, James Thomas 27, 151
Ford's Theatre 135
Foss, Sam Walter 39
Franklin, Benjamin 217, *234*
Fredericks (photographer): print after *141*
Frothingham, James: print after *106*
Fulton, Robert 5

Gardner, Alexander 115, 165; photograph
    by *124*; prints after *127, 166, 167,
    210*
Garfield, James A. 149, 211, 219, *234*
George III, King of England 12, 30
German, C[hristopher]. S. 109
Gettysburg Address 189
Gilman, G. F.: print by *190*
Gimbrede, Thomas 42
Girardet, Paul 59; print by *60*
Goethe, Johann von 53
Goupil & Co. 51, 59; prints by *50, 53,
    60*
Grant, Ulysses S. 165, *168*; and Lincoln im-
    age 213, 219, *221*; with other presidents
    235
Greeley, Horace 91, 99, 189, 215; in carica-
    ture *116*, 117
Grozelier, Leopold 91
Gurley, Phineas T. 239
Gutenberg, Johannes 217, *234*

Haasis & Lubrecht: prints by *228, 229*
Hageboeck, A.: print by *231*
Hale, John P. 61
Hall, Mrs. Basil 72
Hall, George R. 63; print by *64*
Hall, H. B.: print by 110
Halpin, Frederick 128; print by *132*
Hamlin, Hannibal 87, *98*, 105, *122*, 178
Hancock, John 13, 183
Harper's Weekly 149; and anti-Lincoln cari-
    cature 188–189
Harrison, William Henry 5, *46*, 51,
    235
Hartwich, F.: print by *169*
Hawthorne, Nathaniel 28, 189
Hay, John 147, *153*; at Brown University
    Library 140
Healy, G. P. A. 93
Heath, James 69, 72; print after *75*
Hermans, W. H.: print by *202*
Herndon, William H. 128
Herring, James *43*
Hesler, Alexander 85–87, 95, 107; photo-
    graph by *86, 108*; prints after *84*, 89, *92,
    94*, 99, 110
Hicks, Thomas 91
Hitchings, Sinclair 12
Hollis, L.: print after 160
Hoover, Herbert 74
Houdon, Jean Antoine 39, 205; prints after
    42, 209
Houston *Telegraph* 79
Hyde, J. N.: print by *98*

Independence Hall 125
Irving, Washington 65

Jackson, Andrew 42–43, 51, 175, 205, *208,
    235; see also* Washington, George, Jack-
    sonian imagery
Jackson, Thomas J. "Stonewall" 215
Jacobs, Phoebe Lloyd 36
James, Henry 61
Jarvis, John Wesley 21
Jason, and Washington image 9
Jefferson, Thomas 5, *49*, 69, 175, 183, *235*
Johnson, Andrew *137*, 139, *235*
Johnson, Eastman 59
Johnson, J. R. 35
Johnson & Fry 183; prints by *187, 224*;
    prints after *225*
Johnston, Thomas 91; print after *98*
Jones & Clark, print by *193*
The Journal of Congress 72

Kansas-Nebraska Act 177
Kellogg, E. B. & E. C. 10, 57
Kennedy, John F., Jr. 145
Kennedy, S. 35
Kimmel & Forster 211, 213; prints by *156,
    221, 222*
King, William R. *180*, 181
Knoedler, M. 51; prints by *50, 52, 60, 196*
Kramer, P[eter].: print by *193*
Kurz, Louis 226, 236; print by *236*

Lafayette, Marquis de 39, *41, 49*, 51, 65, *66*
Landis, John 56; print by *55*
Lang, Manson: print by *222*
"Lansdowne" painting of Washington 69,
    72, 74, *75*, 213, 215, *227, 233; see also*
    Stuart, Gilbert
Laugier, Jean Nicolais 40–41; print by *43*
Lavater, Johann Kaspar 18
Lear, Tobias 53
Lee, Billy 24
Lee, Charles 23
Lee, "Light Horse" Harry 6
Lemercier (printer) 51, 217; prints by *50,
    52, 166, 196, 234*
Leutze, Emanuel G. 57–61, 63; paintings
    and prints after *58, 60*
Levin, Saul 211; print by *218*
Lincoln, Abraham: apotheosis prints 194,
    199; appearance 79–82, 170; biographical
    sketch of 174; caricatures of 99, 115, *116,*

Lincoln, Abraham (*cont.*) *118, 122,* 125–126, 128, *129, 130,* 135, 170, 188–189; comparison to Washington 186, 188, 213, 219; family prints of 145, 147, 149, 151, 155, 158–159, *161, 162, 163;* foreign prints of 161, 164–165, 170; Great Emancipator image 87, 117, 119, 121, 125, 126, 128, 131, *133, 135, 136, 146, 160,* 171, *194,* 199, 215, 217, *230, 232;* grows beard 87, 101, 103, 105, 107, 109, 115, *126,* 181, *182;* head transposed on other bodies in prints *94, 96, 180, 182, 184, 208, 209;* "Honest Abe" or "Diogenes" image 93, 95, 110, *170,* 188; invokes name of Washington xi, 173, 175, 177, 178–179; legendary strength of 188; log cabin-to-White House image *88,* 90, 170; market for prints, sluggish 117, 133, 179; martyr image (assassination and deathbed prints) 87, 133, 135, 137, 139, 143, *148, 150, 152,* 159, 161, 164–165, 170–171, 191, 197, *200,* 215, *228;* opinion of portraits 177–178; as peacemaker 159; as presidential candidate (1860) 2, 83, *84,* 85, 90–91, 93, *94,* 95, *98–101, 100,* 103, *110–111,* 114, *123,* 177; presidential candidate (1864) 133–135, *142, 144, 146,* 191; "railsplitter" image 99, 105; sittings for painters and photographers 80, *83,* 91, 93, *97, 100, 105, 108, 112, 124,* 125, 128, *132, 136, 140;* and with Washington emblem *210,* 211, *212, 214; see also* Washington-Lincoln image
Lincoln, Mary: and assassination prints 137, 139, *148, 150;* and Lincoln family prints 147, 155, 158–159, *161,* 205, *210, 212, 214;* opinion of husband's portraits 82, 90, 93, 128, 176
Lincoln, Robert T. 128, 137, 147, *152, 153, 161, 210, 212, 214*
Lincoln, Thomas (Tad) 137, 147, 149, 151, 155, *161, 162, 163, 210, 212, 214*
Lincoln, William Wallace (Willie) 143, 147, 155, *161,* 205, *212, 214*
Lindbergh, Charles 226
Lloyd, H. H. 101, 178; prints by *123, 148*
Lovett, J. D.: print by *89*
Lubrecht, Charles *see* Haasis & Lubrecht
Luzerne, Chevalier de 69
Lyon & Co., print by *210*

McClellan, George B. *78,* 133–135, *142, 144,* 183
McClurg, Trevor 75
McCurdy, J. C. 213
M'Elwee's Looking Glass Store 23
McPherson, James M. 183

Madison, James 5, *49, 235*
Magee, J. L. 137; print by *200*
Mangum, W. P. *180,* 181
Marchant, Edward Dalton 125
Marshall, John 53, 65
Marshall, William Edgar 128, 131; print by *134*
Martin & Judson 125
Massee, G. W.: print by *161*
Matteson, Tompkins Harrison, print after *180*
Maurer, Louis: prints by *116, 118*
Meigs, Montgomery 139, *152, 153*
Mendel, Edward 93, 125, 177–178; prints by *102, 176,* 199
Middleton, Strobridge & Co. 181; print by *186*
Miller, James 217
Miller, Lillian 9
Montgomery, Richard 33, *34*
Monticello (home of Jefferson) 5
Moore, Thomas: print by *49*
Morris, Gouverneur 205
Mount Vernon (home of Washington) 9–10, 16, 18, 21, 25, 30, 36, *41,* 42, 65, *66, 68,* 189, *190*
Mudd, Samuel 135
Myers, F.: print by *235*

Nagel, L.: print by *169*
Nahl, C.: print by *169*
Napoleon III 165
National Gazette 8
Neil, Frank: *carte-de-visite* print by *204*
New Jersey State Senate (Lincoln address before) xi
New York *Commercial Advertiser* 25, 28, 30, 69
New York *Evening Mirror* 61
New York *Herald* 193
New York *Mercantile Advertiser* 33
New York Times 61, 73, 121, 131, 191
Nicolay, John G. 91, 170
Nixon, Richard M. 61
Norman, John 18; print by *17*

Otis, Bass 10

Pate, William 63, 65, 181; prints by or after *64, 92, 180, 225*
Peale, Charles Wilson 11, 13, 16, 18, 21, 32, 36, 39; paintings and prints by or after *15, 16, 19*
Peale, Rembrandt 33, 36, 69, 72, 76; paintings and prints by or after *37, 38, 40*

Pennsylvania *Gazette* 18, 24
Pennsylvania *Packet* 13
Perine, George E. 131, 133–134; print by *141*
Philadelphia *Almanack* 18
Philadelphia *Gazette* 36
Philadelphia Photograph Co.: print by *201*
Phillips, Wendell 193–194
Pierce, Franklin 145
Polk, James Knox 177, *235*
Porter, The Rev. Elbert S. 191
Post, E. J. 211
Pound, D. J. 101
Prang, Louis: print by *192*
Pratt, W. H. 217; calligraphy prints by *230, 231*
prints: cost of 13, 18, 25, 33, 69, 95, 98, *113*, 128, 139, 155, 211; as decoration 143, 145
Providence *Journal* 25

Read, John M. 91
Reagan, Ron, Jr. 145
Reagan, Ronald 106
Reaves, Wendy Wick 12, 151
Regnier (lithographer) 51, 53; prints by *50, 52, 196*
Revere, Paul 12
Ripa, Cesare 36
Ritchie, Alexander Hay 72, 128, 131, 137, 139–140, 143; prints by *136, 152, 153, 208;* print after *209*
Rivers, Larry 61
Robertson, Walter 36
Robin, A.: print by *161*
Robinson, H. R. 51; print by *48*
Rochester *Evening News* 25
Rode & Brant 219
Roosevelt, Theodore 145, 226
Rosenthal, Max 215
Rush, Benjamin 12
Russell, Benjamin B.: prints by *158, 160*
Russell, Gilman R. 217; prints by *232, 233*

Sadd, Henry S.: prints by and after *180, 182, 184*
Sarony & Major 41; print by *46*
Sartain, John 125; print by *202*
Sartain, Samuel 91; print by *97*
Sartain, William 24–25, 151, 156, 158, 206; print by *214*
Savage, Edward 21–25, 67, 72, 145, 155, 205; paintings and prints by and after *20, 22, 73; see also* Washington, family portraits

Schaus, W. H. & Co. 91
Schenectady *Gazette* 205
Schultz, C.: print by *234*
Schussele, Christian 25
Schwartz, Barry 8, 33
Scott, Winfield 115, *180, 182,* 183, *184*
Seehagen, Oswald, print by *169*
Seward, William H. 99, *116,* 117, 119, *136, 159,* 181, *182, 184,* 188, 215
Shaudron's (printsellers) 36
Shepherd, C. 12–13
Sherman, William T. 213, *220*
Shober, Cha[rle]s.: print by *236*
Siebert, M. W. 134
slavery 5, 135; *see also* Lincoln, Great Emancipator image
Smith, L. Franklin 125
Smith, William: prints by *206, 212*
Smith & McDougal: print by *229*
Socrates 217, *234*
Sorel, Edward 61
Southworth & Hawes 63
Spassky, Natalie 59
Stanton, Edwin M. *136,* 137, 139, *152, 153*
Stearns, Junius Brutus 51; prints after *50, 52, 196*
Steele, Silas S. 194
Stephens, Alexander H. 143, *159,* 178
Stoddard, R. H. 189
Stone, Robert King 139, *152, 153*
Stowe, Harriet Beecher 183, 186
Stuart, Gilbert 1–2, 9–10, 24–25, 27–28, 30–31, 39–41, 63, 69, 72, 74, 178; prints by or after *2, 31, 32, 43, 44, 45, 46, 53, 75, 77, 185, 186, 203, 207, 210, 216, 218, 219, 222, 223, 227, 229, 231, 233, 235*
Sumner, Charles 121, *152, 153,* 193, 215, 226
Svinin, Pavel Petrovich 6, 30

Thackeray, William Makepeace 28
Thayer, S. O.: print by *158*
Thomas, Charles & Co. 93, *106*
Thurston & Herline: print by *203*
Ticknor & Fields 128, 131; print by *134*
Tiebout, Cornelius 30, 33, 51; print by *32*
Tocqueville, Alexis de 8
Topham, S. 41; print by *44*
Trenchard, John 18
Trochsler, A.: print by *138*
Trumbull, John 11, 25, 39; print after *29*
Tuckerman, Henry T. 27–28, 40–41
Tudor, Jacob L.: Abraham Lincoln 173; George Washington 173; letter to Lincoln 173
Twain, Mark 61

Van Buren, Martin *48, 49,* 51, *235*
Vanderlyn, John 61
Volck, Adalbert J. 115, 117, 125–126; prints
    by *129, 130; see also* Lincoln, caricatures of
Vought, Henry & William, print by *222*

Waeschle, J.: print by *195*
Walter, A. B.: print by *163*
Warren, Joseph 33, *34, 49,* 51
Washington, George: appearance 11, 69, 72;
    bicentennial of birth 74; Cincinnatus,
    portraits as 9, 18, 39, 53, 63, *64,* 65; on
    currency and stamps 1, 39–40; deathbed,
    funeral, and tomb prints 33, *34, 35,* 39,
    41, 52, 53, *54,* 55, 191; in European
    prints 12, 51, 53, *234;* family portraits 21,
    22, 23–25, *26,* 39, *50,* 53, 67, 69, *70, 71,*
    73, 145, 155, 205; farewell address 183,
    211; as father of his country and national
    emblem 37–38, 51, *77,* 181, 215; as heroic
    figure on a pedestal 30, *32,* 178, 191, *212;*
    in history prints 51, 53; honesty 188;
    Jacksonian imagery 42, 43, 51; military
    hero, portraits as 13, *14, 15, 16, 17,* 18, 25,
    29, 32, 37, 38, 40, 42, *43, 47,* 57, *58, 60,*
    61, 62, 63, *64,* 65, 191, 211; as national
    saint (religious emblem) *55,* 56–57, 63,
    175, 177; president, portraits as *20,* 21,
    27, 31–32, 42, 69, 72; presidential cam-
    paign, mention of (1860) 98–99; sittings
    for painters 10–11, 18, 27–28, 39; and
    slavery 177. 189, 191; *see also* Lincoln,
    Abraham; Washington, Lincoln image
Washington, Martha 21, *22,* 23–24, *26,* 53,
    66, 73
Washington, Mary *71*
Washington-Lincoln image: apotheosis prints
199, *201, 202, 203, 204, 206, 207;*
    calligraphic prints of 215, 217, *230, 231,*
    232, 233; differences 188–189; 1876
    centennial 217, *233;* founder and saviour
    images 215, *227, 236;* heads transposed on
    other bodies 205, *208, 209,* 213, 215, *224,*
    225, 227; limited appeal of during seces-
    sion crisis 179, 181, 183, 189; after Lincoln
    assassination 191, 193, 205; Lincoln at-
    tains image dominance 217, 219; origins
    115, 171, 174; presidential campaign, men-
    tion of (1860) 178, 181; as secular gods
    194; similarities 188; twinned images 211,
    213, *218, 219, 220, 222, 223, 227, 234,*
    235, 236; in wartime 191
Washington Monument 10, 74
The Washington Post 226
Washington's birthday xi; and Lincoln 177,
    179, 183, 191
The Watchman & Reflector 115
Waugh, Samuel B. 151; print after *214*
Webster, Daniel 93, 95, *106,* 107, 109, *180,*
    181, *182, 184*
Weems, Mason Locke 76, 179
Welcke, Edward 217
Welles, Gideon 119, *136*
West, Benjamin 33
Whipple, John Adams: print after 192
Whitefield, E.: print after *88*
Whitman, Walt 8, 174, 179
Wiest, D. T. 205; prints by *206, 212*
Will, John Martin: print by *24*
Wills, Garry 72
Wood, Fernando 179
Wood, Grant 61
Woodcock & Harvey 93; prints by *106, 110*
Wool, John 181, *182*
Wright, George Frederick 93